Kay's

K. Cope
Uni Hall
Penylan

Dear Siôn, I hope you get hours of
pleasure from this highly exciting book!

Understanding
Arguments

Dear Kay,
Bet you're glad
you got rid of this
(Shit -woops!) gorgeous
book .

Understanding Arguments

Donald Evans
and
Humphrey Palmer

'Nabod o'n iawn
DaRLittydd Siôn, 1991.

Drake Educational Associates
University of Wales Press
1986

© Donald Evans and Humphrey Palmer, 1986

First edition 1983
Second edition 1986

British Library Cataloguing in Publication Data

Evans, Donald, 1927—
   Understanding arguments.—2nd ed.
   1. Debates and debating
   I. Title II. Palmer, Humphrey
   168   PN4181

   ISBN 0-7083-0914-3

Drake Educational Associates
St Fagans Road, Fairwater, Cardiff CF5 3AE.

University of Wales Press
6 Gwennyth Street, Cathays, Cardiff CF2 4YD.

Printed by Billing & Sons Ltd., Worcester

This short course in proper reasoning is for young people of all
ages who find themselves beset by arguments: persuasions open and
hidden, put forward in books or on buses, blown up onto hoardings
or piped right into the home by an illuminated box. Such arguments
may need to be critically weighed and cautiously assessed, if the
argu-ee is not to be taken for a ride. For such analysis, some
introduction to logic is required.

The skills here deployed and exercised are fundamental in any subject-
matter involving inference, so this topic is a truly General Study,
and relates to all the others in the curriculum. Logic is also the
plain man's form of self-defence, in a world much given to smear and
bamboozle, to unproof and authoritative irrelevance.

This book covers all the topics set down for the 0-level Logic
examination of the Welsh Joint Education Committee.

PARK PLACE PAPERS

This book was published in 1983 by the Department of Extra
Mural Studies of University College, Cardiff, as No. 15 in the
Park Place Papers. The Welsh version Ymresymu i'r Newyddian
is still available in that series (Nos. 4, 6 and 14) from

Department of Extra Mural Studies
38 Park Place
Cardiff CF1 3BB

The Department will be pleased to provide details of the other
volumes in the series (mostly on local history).

CONTENTS

Note: Either system of deduction (Chapters 2 to 7 OR Chapters 8 to 21) may, if preferred, be postponed to a later stage. Fallacies are best tackled beside their corresponding forms of valid argument, but are here gathered together at the end for easy reference.

The authors both teach philosophy in the University of Wales.

Dr. Donald Evans studied philosophy at the University College of Swansea.
He has variously lectured in Africa and in the United States of America,
has written a programmed textbook in logic and published articles in various
learned journals; and is associate editor of Philosophical Investigations.
Dr. Humphrey Palmer studied classics and philosophy at Oxford. He has
written on methods of biblical research, on qualification and argument in
theology, and on so-called 'transcendental' arguments. He spent some time
teaching in India, when logic was still a subject at the pre-University
stage.

The project ...

A unit has been set up to study and promote the teaching of logic in
secondary schools:
>   Logic in Schools,
>   Department of Philosophy,
>   University College, Cardiff
with support and encouragement from
>   South Glamorgan Education Department
>   Welsh Joint Education Committee
>   The Welsh Office
>   Cardiff High Schools' Headmasters
>   University College, Cardiff, Departments of Education
>   and Extra-Mural Studies
and from many teachers, pupils and other individuals.

Besides producing this text and games, the Project makes 'Guides' available
to teachers, and holds a small collection of books on logic, for loan to
them. It has undertaken the teaching of an initial, central class, to
set the subject going in an area; and has provided induction courses
for teachers.

For information or assistance please write to us at the address given
above.

PREFACE

Everyone argues, and most of them think sometimes that someone is using a bad argument. This course shows you how to decide which arguments are sound, and to see what makes the bad ones bad. It is, in fact, impossible to avoid the rules of logic when we think straight about anything. A study of such rules will therefore be of benefit in deliberating about all sorts of issues in all sorts of areas.

With such benefits in mind the Logic in Schools project was launched in the City of Cardiff several years ago. First came a lively logic-class of local sixth-formers and adults, held by our Extra-Mural Department and supported by the South Glamorgan Education Department. Encouraged by this, we wrote up the course in two booklets, which were published by the Extra-Mural Department in English and in Welsh, and have been used in several schools. These we have now combined into a single volume, with substantial fresh material, to cover the extended syllabus for the O-level Logic paper offered by the Welsh Joint Education Committee.

This course introduces the basic principles of logic in such a way as to avoid 'symbol-fright'. Symbols are man-made devices for doing certain jobs more easily, and will not upset anyone used to handling them. The game of Logicon (Chapters 2ff.) and the Matchpenny Diagram (Chapters 8ff.) have been specially designed to secure such familiarity, quite painlessly; and form an essential part of this course.

This course has been used in teaching General Studies in the Sixth Form, undergraduates at University, and adults in Extra-Mural classes. It has also been used in introducing Logic in the Middle School.

We are much indebted to the Extra-Mural Department for their continuing support, in the publication and translation of this book; and to Mrs. Suzanne Ball, from whose definitive typescript this book is produced.

        Donald Evans   Humphrey Palmer

Chapter One: Introduction to Arguments

Outline:

    I   Defining Arguments

    II Classifying Arguments

    III Evaluating Arguments

I   Defining Arguments

In this course we shall not be studying something which is entirely new to you. You can already argue. That means you can already handle many of the rules of argument even though you may not be able to identify or describe them, just as you can walk though you have little idea of all the physiological processes walking involves. There is nothing to fear then. We shall simply be concerned to bring out into the open those rules we have already mastered in practice.

Why should we bother with such an enterprise? Well, we all use arguments of one sort or another every day of our lives. Whilst it is true that one does not have to study logic in order to argue well it would be surprising if those who had paid some attention to the processes of argument were not better performers than they would otherwise have been. Further if a study of logic produces an awareness of and a respect for clarity, relevance and consistency, as it ought to do, then most of our activities would benefit from it.

What precisely are we studying?

We are to study the methods and principles of reasoning. Thus we do not use the word argument in the sense of row or quarrel. Some rows and quarrels involve reasoning but others do not. A reasoning consists in affirming a proposition (the conclusion) on the basis of one or more other propositions (the premises). Such a process is called inferring. It is in this sense that we take the word argument.

1)   Invent a piece of reasoning. _____
/

_____

If you have correctly completed the exercise your argument probably contains a word or words like: therefore, hence, for, because, must, ought, should, we may infer that, since. These are all signals that some sort of argument may be going on.

Where such words denote the presence of an argument they denote logical relations between propositions or ideas. These have to be distinguished from psychological relations.

The logician is not interested in what causes someone to link one idea to another. It could be a connection based on memories, wishes, desires, imagination, free association or whatever. Such connections may be purely personal.

Logical relations however are inter-personal in the sense that they occur wherever someone reasons.

2)   For example: Which idea, if any, do the following ideas suggest
to you?   All men are mortal   Complete your answer

               Socrates was a man   before reading on

_____

If you wrote: Socrates was mortal then you responded in the same way
that anybody would respond if he or she was thinking clearly. There is
a logical relation between these ideas in that an acceptance of the truth
of the first two statements commits one to an acceptance of the third.
Failure to accept the third betrays a failure to understand one or other
or the three propositions.

3)   Describe the kind of process logic is concerned with.

II   Classifying Arguments

There are many different kinds of argument. They fall into two
main categories.

A   Deductive Arguments   B   Inductive Arguments

It is not difficult to make this distinction.

In both categories conclusions are drawn/on the basis of premisses. The
relation between premisses and conclusion is not the same in each group
however.

A.   In deductive arguments the conclusion is thought to follow
necessarily from the premisses. In other words it is impossible for
the premisses to be true and the conclusion false at the same time

e.g. Either it is raining or the sun is shining.

It is not raining. Therefore the sun is shining.

To conclude that the sun is not shining would involve the arguer
in a contradiction. Of course people do sometimes contradict themselves;
logic cannot stop that happening. When we say that an arguer must draw

the conclusion that the sun is shining we mean that he is logically forced to do so not psychologically compelled. In other words if he fails to draw this conclusion we say that he is not thinking logically.

B.   In inductive arguments the premises do not necessitate the conclusion. They provide supportive evidence in good arguments but never conclusive evidence. That is, however good an inductive argument may be it is never contradictory to deny the conclusion while accepting the premisses.

The premisses of an inductive argument render the conclusion more or less probably true. Think of the following example:

When the density of population of a colony of rats passes a certain point the inhabitants begin to attack each other. We should expect anti-social phenomena therefore in high-rise apartment blocks.

Now it is possible that no such correlation occurs. It would not be a contradiction to assert that there was no such similarity. Even if there is such a correlation much more work would have to be done before it was demonstrated that the density of population was the cause of the violence. We shall look more closely at such arguments later. Nevertheless the evidence of the rat behaviour is interesting and clearly lends support to the claim that density of population affects social behaviour adversely as it passes certain limits.

4)   Invent a deductive argument and an inductive argument.

In each of the classes of argument we have mentioned there are sub-classes. Think of the analogy of a shoe shop. You may know which general style of shoe you wish to purchase. In each style however there are different sizes. And for each size there are different fittings.

Similarly there are many arguments of the deductive kind which fall into different groups. We shall be studying one of these groups to begin with, and the system of analysis we shall develop first is therefore limited in its scope. Later we shall extend it to cater for other types of argument.

The group we shall study first makes up the subject matter of what has been called the propositional logic.

The second group makes up the subject matter of what has been called predicate logic.

Do not worry too much about this distinction at this point. A couple of examples will illustrate it.

(a)   If rain comes the crops will prosper. The crops will not prosper therefore rain will not come.

(b)   All those who study logic are wise. Everybody present is studying logic. So everyone present is wise.

Argument (a) can be shown to be good by treating the two propositions making it up as simple. Namely:

Rain comes. The crops will prosper.

The goodness or otherwise of the argument depends solely upon the way in which the truth or falsity of these propositions are related in the argument. No analysis of these constituent parts is required. (The same is true of the argument about the rain on page 13.)

Argument (b) however cannot be treated in this way. It can only be shown to be good by analysing the structure of the constituents in terms of which properties (or predicates) belong to which class of things. (See Socrates argument p12.)

5)   (i) Invent an argument which depends on class considerations

      (ii) Invent an argument which depends solely upon relations between propositions such as if...then, and, either...or.

We shall not concern ourselves with any further kinds of deductive arguments.

We have mentioned two classes of deductive arguments which we shall concern ourselves with. Let us also note two kinds of inductive arguments. These are not as distinct from each other as may first appear any more than the two classes of deductive argument are totally distinct.

The first group are arguments from analogy.
The second group are causal arguments.

Here is an example of each:

(c)   Heath, Wilson and Callaghan have been prime ministers of England during the last decade. Heath and Wilson were Oxbridge graduates. Therefore Callaghan is an Oxbridge graduate.

(d)   More heavy smokers die of lung cancer on average than non-smokers. The correlation between the number of cigarettes smoked and the chances of contracting the disease shows that smoking causes lung cancer.

6)   Do you think that the above arguments are good? If so why? If not why not?

Much of our everyday reasoning follows the above patterns. Indeed without such procedures we would find life quite impossible. We shall learn how to assess some arguments of these sorts later in this book.

III   Evaluating Arguments

The ultimate goal of our studies is to distinguish between good and bad arguments. Classifying the arguments is but a first step in this direction for each group of arguments obeys its own set of principles.

We can make two kinds of distinction.

i   Valid/Invalid.

ii   Sound/Unsound.

The first distinction applies only to deductive arguments. The second distinction applies to inductive arguments.

Let us look briefly at distinction i.

Remember that a valid argument claims that the truth of its conclusion follows necessarily from the truth of its premisses. If it is possible therefore for the conclusion to be false when the premisses are true the claim made by the argument is untrue.

In some cases it is easy to pick out validity or invalidity. Usually however it is not possible to tell at a glance whether or not an argument is valid. So we need to devise procedures for going about this task.

The first step in testing a deductive argument is to identify its form. The form of an argument is its shape, the arrangement of its parts. Consider the following analogy. We can easily distinguish between containers and what they contain. A tin of salmon and a tin of processed peas may be of identical size and shape though their fillings are quite distinct. Similarly various liquids will assume the common shape of a bottle into which they are poured. Consequently we can discuss the <u>form</u> irrespective of the filling or <u>content</u>.

So it is with arguments. Like containers they come in various shapes and sizes. It is their form (in the case of deductive arguments) which decides whether or not they are good arguments and not their content.

Compare the following arguments:

(a)   All pigs are pink.   (b)   All men are mortal.

       <u>Napoleon is a pig</u>.   <u>Socrates is a man</u>.

       Napoleon is pink.   Socrates is mortal.

It is not difficult to see that the two arguments share a common form. Yet they are about very different subjects. I know of nothing which ties the content of the two together except perhaps the famous dictum used to refute hedonism to the effect that it is better to be Socrates dissatisfied than to be a pig satisfied!

Yet clearly if one of these arguments is good the other must be equally good. This is because they share the same <u>formal</u> properties.

The most difficult invalid arguments to identify are those whose form is so like the form of valid arguments that they deceive. Such arguments are called <u>fallacies</u>, or to be more precise in the case of deductive arguments <u>formal fallacies</u>.

The most notorious examples are the fallacies of material implication. There are two of these:

    i   Affirming the consequent.

    ii   Denying the antecedent.

A material implication is a proposition of the kind:

If such and such is so then so and so is the case. Given the truth of this proposition it does follow that the truth of such and such demands the truth of so and so. It also follows that the falsity of so and so demands the falsity of such and such.

In other words affirming the antecedent entitles one to affirm the consequent and denying the consequent entitles one to deny the antecedent.

The fallacies referred to reverse each of these procedures however and deceive because of their likeness to the valid moves.

7)   Invent two arguments of the same form.
      Decide whether they are valid or invalid and try to give reasons.

      Let us now look briefly at the distinction ii

              viz. Sound/Unsound.

Like deductive arguments some inductive arguments are good and some are bad. (Note: in some logic textbooks the terms sound and unsound are used for a different purpose.) Whereas an invalid argument is of no use in providing guidance some poor inductive arguments may not be totally valueless. Some have premises which afford more probability to their conclusions than others. Some of the others however may afford some probability to their conclusions.

You are already able to evaluate arguments of this kind with some ease. What do you think of the following argument for example?

Each Friday for the past two months my car has failed to start in the early morning. On all other days it has started perfectly well.

I conclude that it will not start next Friday morning simply because it will be Friday again.

8)   Is my argument persuasive? If so why? If not why not?

Write down your answers before reading on.

If you found it at all persuasive it was either because you are super-stitious about Friday the 13th or because you were to some extent aware of similarities between this argument and other good arguments you have used or come across from time to time.

If you did not find it persuasive it was probably because you could not link the events in question in any meaningful way; i.e. its being Friday has no bearing on the starting of motor cars, it is not a relevant consideration.

Maybe your reaction was a mixture of both the above. That illustrates the way in which fallacies are deceptive.

There is a family of fallacies which have nothing to do with the form of arguments which we might well note.

They are called   informal fallacies. They are probably those which most commonly occur in public bars after rugby matches, in political election campaigns and wherever people want passionately to persuade others to their way of thinking about things.

Again they are called fallacies because they are persuasive. They are persuasive for psychological rather than logical reasons however (unlike formal fallacies).

One of the most familiar and effictive is the <u>ad hominem</u> fallacy (i.e. the fallacy of arguing against the arguer rather than his argument.)

The idea behind the fallacy is to discredit the presenter of the argument and by so doing dispose hearers to doubt the argument itself, though in so doing one has not brought one reason against the conclusion drawn by the arguer.

e.g. One only has to remember that it was the hippies of the sixties who first advocated that people should make love not war to see that it is not a sensible way to run the affairs of nations. We all know what a bunch of lazy, run-down parasites they were don't we?

9)   Invent an unsound argument. Give reasons for its unsoundness.

If you have time, try the following exercises:

i   How would you describe the study of logic?

ii   Classify the following arguments as either deductive or inductive:

(a) The tides vary as they do because of the behaviour of the moon, there is a correlation between their movements.

(b) If the spring moon means high tides and it is now the time of the spring moon then there are now high tides.

(c) Either there are high tides or there is no spring moon. There are no high tides therefore there is no spring moon.

(d) As a magnet can disturb material which lies in its field so the moon exerts an influence over the tides.

iii   Try to evaluate each of the arguments in question ii and give reasons for your answers.

iv   Do any of the arguments in question ii share the same form?

v   In each of the following, underline the conclusion, and put a V (for valid) in the margin if you think it follows from the supporting statements (the premisses).

(a) He must be an officer for he is carrying a pistol as all officers do.

(b) Every officer carries a pistol, so you can be sure he has one, for he is an officer.

(c) All military men are proud of their country, so all soldiers are military men, for of course all soldiers are proud of their country.

(d) All soldiers are proud of their country, so all military men must be so too, for all soldiers are military men.

(e) All military men are proud of their country, and all soldiers are military men; it therefore follows that all soldiers are proud of their country.

TRUE OR FALSE:

Relations between
Statements

Chapter Two: <u>Symbols, Simples and Complexes</u>

Outline:

    I   Simple and Complex Propositions

    II   Symbolising Propositions

        (a) Logical Connectors

        (b) Logical Punctuation

———————————

1.   In this Chapter we shall begin to examine one subclass of deductive argument mentioned in Chapter 1, viz. propositional arguments.

What is a proposition?

When a logician uses this word he means something precise. Logicians sometimes bring out this meaning by contrasting a <u>proposition</u> with a <u>sentence</u>.

Different sentences may express the same proposition. For example: ⟨Il pleut⟩ says the same thing as ⟨It is raining⟩. They are clearly different sentences. One is French the other English. One contains two words the other three. What they have in common however is what they say. This entails that if the first is true then the second is true also; or that if the first is false the second is false also.

We shall treat propositions in this way. That is, we shall assume that they are capable of being either <u>true</u> or <u>false</u> and that they can have no other values. We shall give the name truth-values to true and false and denote them by means of the capital letters T and F respectively.

What is a simple proposition?

A simple proposition is one which contains no component propositions. That is, it is not made up of any elements which can stand alone as true or false.

Our example <It is raining> is such a proposition whereas the proposition <It is raining and it is Friday> is clearly not simple.

1) Name the simple propositional elements in the above proposition

_____

If you answered the question correctly you were left with one surplus word, viz. and. This word connects the two simple propositions placed either side of it to form another proposition. The resultant proposition is a complex proposition.

All complex propositions contain more than one simple proposition and at least one connector. (There is one exception to this rule we shall mention later viz. negations.)

How many kinds of connections are there?

We shall use four (besides negation). They are:

and, either...or, if...then, if and only if.

You may think that there must be other possible connections. You would be right to think this. For example there is the connection <neither...nor>. However we can build this connection out of those already listed. <Neither...nor> is the same as <It is not the case that either...or>.

It is interesting to note that all the connections can be built out of repeated use of this one connection, viz. neither...nor... This is important in the history of logic though there is no need for you to worry about it. Maybe a little later you will see how such building is possible.

2)   Construct complex propositions each containing one of the above connections _____

The connections we have listed are given various names in logic textbooks. The terms and, either...or etc. are variously called logical connectors, logical constants, logical operators. We shall call them logical operators for a reason which will become obvious in our next lesson.

Understanding Complex Propositions
_ _ _ _ _ _ _ _ _ _ _ _ _ _ _ _ _

There are no formal rules for identifying the precise meaning of a complex proposition. However two observations should help you to accomplish this task.

i   Numerous forms of operators

The operators we have listed are not always expressed in the same way in our day to day conversation. For example, the and relation can be variously expressed by using words like both, each, too, also, or even by using a comma.

Consider the following propositions about Mary and her little lamb:

(a) Mary and her lamb visited the zoo.

(b) Both of them visited the zoo.

(c) The zoo was visited by each of them.

(d) Mary visited the zoo, the lamb did too.

(e) Mary, her lamb and others visited the zoo.

All of the propositions say the same thing except for the last one which says all the others say and more. They all link the two component propositions <Mary visited the zoo>, <Her lamb visited the zoo> in the same way.

Part of the task of analysing propositions and arguments is to penetrate disguises of this sort. You are already capable of performing this task with some skill for you are able to understand many complex propositions which you come across in your daily affairs. You may be surprised however at the subtle differences which the position of a word can make in a proposition and the resulting effect it can have upon the goodness or otherwise of any argument in which that proposition occurs.

3) Invent two propositions which contain disguised operators

ii <u>Numerous operators in one proposition</u>

Propositions may be more or less complex. There is no end to the possible complexities one may incorporate into a proposition by using more and more operators and component propositions.

For example proposition (a) in the list of propositions about Mary and her little lamb may be further complexed by using the either...or operator and one further component proposition.

Either Mary and her lamb visited the zoo or Mary stayed home.

In our example no ambiguity is introduced by multiplying the number of operators. Sometimes however the sense of such complexes is by no means obvious.

Consider the following examples:

(a)   Either John is not feeling well or he is uninterested in the lecture.

(b)   It is not the case either that John is feeling well or that he is uninterested in the lecture.

The same operators are used in both propositions as well as the same component propositions. The senses of the complexes are different however.

(a)   is an either...or proposition (i.e. a disjunction) between a negative proposition and an affirmative proposition

(b)   is a negation of a disjunction of two affirmative propositions.

In other words, in our example (b) denies that John is feeling well and denies that he is uninterested. Whereas (a) does not actually deny that John is feeling well but says it is one of only two possible alternatives.

In cases of this sort it is crucial to pick out the main operator in order to get the sense clear. In (a) it is disjunction, whilst in (b) it is negation. This is a question of comprehension of the proposition. As I said a while ago, there are no formal rules for understanding. However close regard to the role of the operators in such propositions is an indispensable part of the procedure of understanding. Believe it or not you have implicitly known this as you have read and listened in the past. It may now become a more explicit procedure.

4) Pick out the main operator in the following propositions:

(a) John gave up chemistry in his third year as did Susan.

(b) Neither John nor Susan dropped chemistry in their third year.

(c) John gave up chemistry in his third year but Susan didn't.

(d) It is not the case that John dropped chemistry in his third year but Susan did.

(e) If Susan dropped chemistry in her third year then John certainly did not.

(f) If Susan dropped chemistry in her third year either she or John dropped it.

(g) Either John and Susan both dropped chemistry in their third year or neither did.

(h) It is not the case that John dropped chemistry in his third year nor Susan neither.

(i) If John dropped chemistry in his third year then and only then did Susan do the same.

(j) Chemistry was not dropped by Susan in her third year but it was by John in his.

II Symbolising Propositions

There is no need to be afraid of symbols. You use them every day of your life. Just think of the role that road signs play in the lives of motorists and pedestrians.

5) List some of the advantages of using symbols

One of the foremost advantages which probably occurred to you was the speed with which one may grasp quite a complicated message when symbols are used. This is of great importance in the case of road signs. You will be equally glad of them in logic. Treat symbols as friends and not as enemies.

Not only is time and effort saved in understanding expressions when they are symbolised, one is also saved from the dangers of misunderstanding the expressions. The clarity of symbols resolves ambiguities.

Symbols achieve this by bringing into bold relief the shapes or forms of propositions and arguments.

What are the symbols?

Firstly we need to learn which symbols we should use to stand for the component propositions (simples) which make up complexes and arguments.

The lower case letters p, q, r and s are used for this task. Thus the complex <Mary and her lamb visited the zoo> would require two of these signs (called propositional variables) in its symbolisation.

Mary visited the zoo = p
Her lamb visited the zoo = q
The complex becomes <p and q>.

This is also the symbolisation of the complex proposition <Callaghan and Trudeau were prime ministers>. Remember that the logician is only interested in the form of propositions and arguments and not their content.

Do we have symbols for the operators?

Yes we do. They will be new signs which you have never used before.

i	Conjunction.	The <u>and</u> relation. Symbol · as in p · q
ii	Disjunction.	The <u>either...or</u> relation. Symbol v as in p v q
iii	Implication.	The <u>if...then</u> relation. Symbol ⊃ as in p ⊃ q
iv	Equivalence.	The <u>if and only if</u> relation. Symbol ≡ as in p ≡ q
v	Negation.	The <u>not...</u> relation. Symbol ∼ as in ∼ p

Precisely what these relations come to we shall leave until our next lesson. For the moment we shall simply substitute them for the common sense relations of <u>and</u>, <u>either...or</u>, <u>if...then</u>, <u>if and only if</u> and finally <u>not</u>.

6) Using the symbol p to mean <John dropped chemistry in his third year> and the symbol q to mean <Susan dropped chemistry in her third year> symbolise propositions a,c,e in exercise 4 _____

You will already have noticed from your solutions to question 6 that the form of a proposition becomes crystal clear when it is symbolised. This will become even more obvious as you attempt to analyse more complicated examples.

Before we can hope to cope with more difficult cases however we need to pay some attention to the business of <u>logical punctuation</u>.

It will be helpful at this point to list the rules for constructing what are called <u>well formed formulae</u>. These are often referred to as WFF's.

What is a WFF?

You are familiar with most of the rules of syntax for constructing good English sentences. Not all strings of English words constitute sentences do they? For example

<Tuesday Thursday sometimes generous clever above>.

There is no verb present, amongst other things. Only when the rules are observed do we produce an intelligible expression. Even then it may not be a sentence with one clear meaning. For example:

The hunting of lions takes place at sunset.

Can you detect the ambiguity?

What is unclear is whether the lions are the hunters or the hunted. In written English mere introduction of punctuation marks could not resolve such an ambiguity (though in other cases ambiguities can be so resolved).

In. logic we need to be clear always about the precise meaning of propositions. Consequently we need rules of formation of meaningful expressions which ensure that no ambiguities remain. The following list constitutes those rules which together guarantee both meaningful and unambiguous expressions.

1.   p,q,r,s are symbols <u>variables</u> which can stand for any proposition.

2.   ⊃,·,v,≡, are binary constants (i.e. they link two simple or complex terms standing immediately next to them).

3.   ~ qualifies the term it immediately precedes.

4.   Any variable can stand alone as a WFF.

5.   Any negation of a WFF is itself a WFF.

6.   Any two WFF's joined by a binary constant is a WFF.

7.   All logical constants have equal strength.

8.   Brackets are to be used as explained in the following paragraphs.

The use of parentheses is crucial in eliminating ambiguity.
Remember the example (d) in exercise 4, page 29.

There are two possible ways of reading the proposition.
In the one reading we have a denial of a conjunction.   In the other
we simply have a denial of one proposition conjoined with the second
proposition.   They would be symbolised as follows:

    i $\sim(p \cdot q)$ ii $\sim p \cdot q$

You may argue that the sense of the <u>but</u> tips the balance in
favour of the latter account as it suggests a contrast between John's
case and Susan's case. I think that is fair enough. If the word used
had been <u>and</u> however the ambiguity would have been more vicious.

The example serves to show that well formed formulae have one
precise meaning only.

7)   Invent three WFF's each of which include one set of brackets
and at least three logical operators.

Multiple bracketing
- - - - - - - - - -

You will often need more than one set of brackets in order to
eliminate all ambiguity from an expression. Look at the following example:

If it is Friday and it is the thirteenth then it is an unlucky
day and people will either take extra care or have nasty accidents.

Until you become skilled at analysing such involved propositions it will help you to first ring all the constituent propositions:

If $\boxed{\text{it is Friday}}$ and $\boxed{\text{it is the thirteenth}}$ then $\boxed{\text{it is an unlucky day}}$ and either $\boxed{\text{people will take extra care}}$ or $\boxed{\text{people will have nasty accidents}}$.

If we use the symbols A,B,C,D,E to stand for these constituents then the string becomes:

If A and B then C and D or E.

Using our constant symbols we get:

A · B ⊃ C · D v E

This is not yet a well formed formula. We obviously need some brackets.

It is fairly clear that A and B are conjoined antecedents. Thus we link them with brackets and they become one complex term (A · B).

Yet still there is much ambiguity remaining.

We have to decide whether they only entail C or whether they entail both C and the disjunction of D and E.

It is fairly clear that the latter is the sense of the proposition isn't it? Thus we need to link D and E together to form a disjunction. (D v E).

This gives us: (A · B) ⊃ C · (D v E)

But this is still ambiguous allowing for both the possible meanings we identified a moment ago.

What we finally need to do is link C and D and E together as parts of the consequent of the total if...then expression.

We do this by placing brackets (preferably a different shape) around the three terms thus:

[C · (D v E)]

Now they form one complex term. This is linked by the implication constant to another complex term so satisfying rule 2 and making the expression a WFF.

(A · B) ⊃ [C · (D v E)]

8)   Using the variables p and q as in question 6 symbolise propositions b,f,g,h,i,j of question 4.

It would be a good idea to attempt this exercise before we meet again.

You are now ready to play the first game with your Logicon kit. It is called WFF. The rules are at the end of the book.

It will help you to become familiar with the symbols and rules which you have studied during Chapter 2.

Examples

I.   Pick out the main operator in each of the following propositions.

     i.   Neither boys nor girls find homework enjoyable.

     ii. Boys find homework enjoyable whereas girls do not.

     iii. It is true that if girls find homework enjoyable then
          boys do too.

     iv. Either girls do not find homework enjoyable or boys do.

     v.   Whenever boys find homework enjoyable then girls do too
          and vice versa.

     vi. Either boys or girls find homework enjoyable or neither do.

     vii. That boys and girls find homework enjoyable is not the case.

II. Using the symbol p for the proposition Boys find homework
     enjoyable, and the symbol q for the proposition Girls find
     homework enjoyable, symbolise propositions i-vii in
     Exercise I.

III. Invent three well-formed formulae which each include at least
     one set and one sub-set of brackets and at least three operators.

Chapter Three : <u>It All Depends</u> ....

Outline:

   I   Truth-functional Dependence

   II   Truth Tables

      (a) Definitions of Logical Operators

      (b) Truth-value Calculations

You have already learned to construct WFF's. These are symbolic representations of the form of the things we say and write. You well know that there are, indeed that there need to be, various kinds of connections between the various things we say. Logic is concerned with such connections and they become clear when they are presented as relations holding between WFF's.

Once again this chapter you will not be learning something which is entirely new to you. You will, for the most part, be making explicit the relations which you have used in your thinking for years.

————————

I   <u>Truth-functional Dependence</u>

In our last chapter we decided to treat propositions as being either true or false. That is, they are thought by us to have only two possible truth values, viz. T and F.

Now the truth values of propositions can be related to each other in various ways. For example if the proposition <Today is Friday> is true then <It is not the case that today is Friday> must be false.

This relation is plain to see. Others may be more difficult to trace though they are familiar to you.

1)   Given that <Today is Friday> is true invent

   (i)   a false complex proposition using the conjunction
          operator _____

   (ii)   a true complex proposition using the disjunction
          sign _____

Now, of course, many propositions have truth values which are totally unrelated to the truth values of many others.

   e.g. <Today if Friday> <Susan is pretty> <Water is wet>

Wherever relations between truth values of propositions occur some logical operator is present together with at least one common component proposition. (We will ignore some important exceptions throughout our course.)

Look at our previous example:

<It is Friday> p <It is not Friday> ~p

Here you see clearly one common component and an operator.

2)   Symbolise your answers to exercise 1 and identify the common components and the operators used in the related propositions _____

_____

The kind of dependence we have outlined is called truth-functional dependence. Do not be afraid of this technical term. It simply means that the truth value of one proposition can be calculated from the truth values of others. It is said to be a _function_ of them.

_____

We have so far worked with our common sense notions of either...or, if...then, etc. Before you consider the precise meaning given to them in logic complete the following exercise using your common sense.

3)   Given that p is true and q is false, calculate the truth values of the following:

i.   p · q   ii. ~~q   iii. p v q   iv. p v ~ q   v. p ⊃ q
vi.   ~ p ⊃ q   vii. p ≡ ~ q

You might have found it difficult to make up your mind about iv. and vi. because there is no one precise way in which we use the expressions either...or etc. in ordinary language.

In the case of vi. the fact that the antecedent was false might have caused you to suppose that the whole expression was false. This temptation is reinforced when you consider propositions like:

If the Duke of Wellington was your aunt then I'll eat my hat.

In the case of iv. we come up against a more common difficulty. Often when we use the either...or relation we mean <at least one and at most one...> as in:

Either it is Friday or it is not Friday.

Sometimes we use the relation less strictly however, as in:

<Either Mr. Callaghan was Prime Minister or he was leader
of the Parliamentary Labour Party>.

It cannot be said that this is not a well-formed proposition.
Neither can it be said that it is false. Yet both the disjuncts are
true. If we press the strict use of either...or then we would be
forced to say that the proposition is false. This would be rather
clumsy to say the least for: <It is false that either...or...>
suggests that neither disjunct is true.

In formal logic we shall see that a precise and unambiguous
meaning is given to these operators.

II   Truth Tables

A truth table is a device for setting out clearly the relations
between the truth values of propositions.

The simplest truth table of all is the one setting out the relation
between p and ~ p discussed earlier (p. 38).

How many possible truth values does p have?

It has two, viz. T and F.

We can set out all these possibilities in a column under the
heading p thus:

$$\frac{p}{\begin{array}{c} T \\ F \end{array}}$$

Now we set alongside it a column representing the possible truth values
of ~ p thus:

p	~ p
T	
F	

4)   Complete the truth table of ~ p.

The final column which you have provided is the definition of the sign ~. It is not a deduction. The completed truth table shows that ~ p is true when p is false and false when p is true. This is what negation comes to in formal logic.

What happens when more than one component occurs?
We first have to set out all the possible combinations of the truth values of the components.

When p and q are the only components it is easy. For example they could both be true.

5)   Write down all the other possible combinations of the truth values of p and q. _____

We can set out all the possibilities in column form thus:

p	q
T	T
F	T
T	F
F	F

There is a rapid way to calculate how many lines you will need to draw up a complete truth table for any complex proposition.

Where n is the number of component propositions in the complex then the number of lines needed will be 2^n.

In the case of a complex containing just two components the number of lines needed is 2^2, which is 4.   When p,q and r occur in a complex then the number of lines needed is 2^3, which is 8 and so on.

There is a simple mechanical method of setting out all these possibilities.

Step 1   Insert alternative values (T and F) in the lines of the first column.

Step 2   In the second column double the numbers of T's and F's as you alternate (i.e. 2 T's alternate with 2 F's etc.)

Step 3   In the third column representing a component proposition alternate by doubling up the second column (i.e. 4 T's alternate with 4 F's) and so on, always making sure that in the last column representing a component proposition you have an equal number of T's and F's.

The early columns must be extended according to their patterns to the same length as the final column of component propositions. Thus the truth possibilities of a complex proposition containing two components will begin:

p	q
T	T
F	T
T	F
F	F

and one containing three components:

p	q	r
T	T	T
F	T	T
T	F	T
F	F	T
T	T	F
F	T	F
T	F	F
F	F	F

(a)   Defining Logical Operators

Before we can use truth tables to calculate the truth value of complex propositions we need to discover the precise meanings of the logical operators used in such propositions.

We have already defined the negation operator in exercise 4 (p. 41).

Conjunction is quite straightforward

p	q	p · q
T	T	T
F	T	F
T	F	F
F	F	F

Disjunction corresponds to the less strict
account we discussed on p. 40

p	q	p v q
T	T	T
F	T	T
T	F	T
F	F	F

Implication The if...then relation simply rules out one possible
combination of truth values as allowing the complex
to be true, i.e. where the antecedent is true and the
conclusion is false.

p	q	p ⊃ q
T	T	T
F	T	T
T	F	F
F	F	T

Equivalence is the if and only if relation

p	q	p ≡ q
T	T	T
F	T	F
T	F	F
F	F	T

_____

6)   Using the above definitions decide whether the following
propositions are true or false given that p is false and q is true.

(a)   q ⊃ p

(b)   p ⊃ q

(c)   ~ p v ~ q

(d)   p v ~ q

(e)   p ≡ ~ q

(f)   p · q

e.g. (a) This suggests that T ⊃ F is
true. If you look at the table
defining implication the line
suggesting that T ⊃ F is line 3.
In that line the complex is F.
Thus (a) is F.

(b)   Truth Value Calculations

You have already performed this task in connection with simple
examples in Exercise 6.

Where the proposition to be examined is much more complex we have to build it up in the truth table.

e.g.   (p v q) ⊃ (∼ q ⊃ p)

We begin by setting out all the component propositions and their truth possibilities thus:

1	2
p	q
T	T
F	T
T	F
F	F

It is easy to draw up the column for p v q for we have used this as our definition of the v relation on p.43 relating columns 1 and 2

1	2	3
p	q	p v q
		T
		T
		T
		F

Until you are familiar with all the operators do not jump any steps. Thus before attempting to map out the column for ∼ q ⊃ p draw up the column for ∼ q from column 2.

1	2	3	4
p	q	p v q	∼ q
			F
as above			F
			T
			T

Now we are ready to map out the column under ∼ q ⊃ p thus: Using columns 4 and 1.

1	2	3	4	5
p	q	p v q	∼ q	∼ q ⊃ p
				T
as above				T
				T
				F

Now we are ready to complete the column under the heading of the whole complex proposition using columns 3 and 5, thus:

p	q	p v q	~ q	~ q ⊃ p	(p v q) ⊃ (~ q ⊃ p)
		T		T	T
		T		T	T
		T		T	T
		F		F	T

This is a very interesting case in that the complex proposition is one which is true for all possible states of affairs. That is, it is true for every conceivable combination of the truth values of its component propositions. A proposition which is always true in this way we call a tautology. We shall have much more to say about these propositions later on.

If one was asked to determine the truth value of this complex proposition given the conditions holding in exercise 6, viz. that p is false and q true, then one would read off the value of the complex in line 2. Of course it is true there.

7)(a) Draw up the truth table of the proposition:

(p v q) ⊃ p   _____

(b) Given that p is false and q is true read off the truth value of the complex proposition _____

You can imagine how long the procedure would be to draw up the full truth table of a complex proposition containing five components or more. We can however calculate the truth value of such complex propositions by means of a shorthand method.

This method embodies the idea of the truth table but saves us the trouble of drawing up the whole table.

Consider the following problem:

Given that p and q are true and that r, s and t are false, calculate the truth value of the proposition:

$$(p \ v \ q) \supset [(r \cdot s) \ v \sim t]$$

We begin our calculation as follows:

Step 1   Write the truth value under each component thus:

$$(p \ v \ q) \supset [(r \cdot s) \ v \sim t]$$
  T   T   F F   F

Step 2   Write the truth value under the negation signs thus:

$$(p \ v \ q) \supset [(r \cdot s) \ v \sim t]$$
  T   T   F F   F
                            T

Step 3   Write the truth value of the operators within the inside brackets thus:

$$(p \ v \ q) \supset [(r \cdot s) \ v \sim t]$$
  T   T   F F   F
               F   T

Step 4   Write the truth values under the main operators in the outer brackets thus:

$$(p \ v \ q) \supset [(r \cdot s) \ v \sim t]$$
  T   T   F F   F
               F   T
        T   T

Step 5   Calculate the truth value under the main operator. As Step 4 left us with T $\supset$ T the final value is T.

If you always follow this procedure, viz.

Step 1   Assign given truth values to components.

Step 2   Calculate negations of simple terms (i.e. not negations outside brackets qualifying complex terms).

Step 3   Calculate the truth values of subsidiary brackets.

Step 4   Calculate the truth values of main brackets.

Step 5   Calculate the value under the main operator.

then the complexity of propositions should not worry you. This is a much shorter route than drawing up the whole truth table. There is also less risk of making a slip.

———————

You are now ready to play the second game with your Logicon kit. viz. True/False. The rules are at the end of the book.

The more you play this game the clearer the idea of truth functional dependence will become to you.

_____

Try the following exercise before you go on.

8)   Calculate either by means of a full truth table or by the shorter method of assigning truth values the truth value of the following propositions given that: p and q are true and that r and s are false.

(a)   [(p ⊃ r) v (q ⊃ s)] ≡ s

(b)   [(p v r) · (q v s)] ≡ p

_____

Examples

I. Draw up the truth table of each of the following propositions.

    i.   [(p · q) v r] ⊃ (q v r)

    ii.   [(p v q) · r] ⊃ (q · r)

    iii. [(p · q) · r] ⊃ (q v r)

II. Given that p is true, q is false and r is true read off the truth values of the propositions in exercise I from the truth tables you have constructed.

III. By means of assigning truth values determine the truth values of the following propositions given that:

        p and q and r are true

        s and t are false

    i.   [p ⊃ t) · (r v s)] ⊃ (p ⊃ s)

    ii.   [(s v q) ⊃ p] · [(~ q · s) ⊃ t]

    iii. {[(t ≡ p) ⊃ r] · q} ≡ s

    iv. [(q v r v s v t) · p] ⊃ [~ (q · r · s · t) ⊃ p]

Chapter Four: Tautologies Never Lie

Outline:

I   Definition of Tautology

II   Tautologies and Valid Arguments

III Valid Argument Forms

I   Definition of Tautology

You have already come across the word tautology in this course
(see p.45). At that point we observed that tautologies were expressions
possessing a unique quality. That is, for all possible values of the
component propositions the tautology can have only one value, namely T
(true).

Look at the following simple example.

$$(p \cdot r) \supset (p \vee r)$$

The truth table is not difficult to construct:

p	r	p · r	p ∨ r	(p · r) ⊃ (p ∨ r)
T	T	T	T	T
F	T	F	T	T
T	F	F	T	T
F	F	F	F	T

You will readily notice that the final column is populated
entirely by T's. In other words there is no line where the antecedent
(p · r) is true and the conclusion (p ∨ r) is false at the same time.
Consequently we can say that whatever the truth values of p and r may

be it is impossible for the complex proposition (p · r) ⊃ (p v r) to be false. The proposition can never lie.

Contradictions, on the other hand, are propositions which can never tell the truth. In other words they are false for all the possible combinations of the truth values of their component propositions. The simplest example of a contradiction is a statement of the form:

p · ~p   The truth table shows the contradictory nature of the statement form by having only F's in the final column:

p	p	p·~p
T	F	F
F	T	F

Contingent propositions are those which are neither tautologies nor contradictions.

These are the propositions which describe the world - those we use every day to convey information. We cannot tell whether or not they are true without looking at the world itself. We can know that tautologies are true and that contradictions are false by just understanding them. With contingent propositions we first have to understand them and then, as a separate activity, discover whether they are true or false.

For example, the proposition <It is raining> is a contingent proposition. It claims that something is the case which may well not be the case. That is, sometimes it is raining (then the proposition is true) and sometimes it is not (then the proposition is false). Whether it is in fact doing so is something we have to discover by looking through the window, etc. No amount of study of the proposition itself could give us the required information.

The final column of the truth table of such propositions contain a mixture of T's and F's. For example:

p v r

Its truth table is:

p	r	p v r
T	T	T
F	T	T
T	F	T
F	F	F

The presence of just one F in the final column is sufficient to mark off the propositional form as contingent.

1)   By drawing up truth tables decide whether the following propositional forms are tautologous, contradictory, or contingent.

i   (p v r) ⊃ p

ii   (p v r) ⊃ ~ p

iii   p ⊃ (p v r)

iv   (p · r) · (~p v ~r)

II   Tautologies and Valid Arguments

Why are tautologies important?

If we understand their nature we know a great deal about valid arguments. You will remember that in Chapter 1 we defined deductive arguments as those which claim that their conclusions follow necessarily from their premisses (see p.13). This meant that in a good or valid deductive argument it was impossible for the conclusions to be false when the premisses were true.

We can express the matter by saying that the claim made by a valid argument, viz., that <u>if</u> the premises are true <u>then</u> the conclusion <u>must</u> be true is equivalent to the claim -- <If premisses true then conclusion true> is a tautology.

This provides us with a ready means for testing the validity of arguments. If we express the whole argument in the form of a conditional statement: <If (premisses) then (conclusion)> and draw up the truth table for that statement we shall be able to decide whether it is a tautology, contradiction or contingent proposition. If it turns out to be a tautology then we know that it represents a valid argument (a necessary truth).

Consider the following example:

Mr. Callaghan is Prime Minister and yet he is not a member of the European Parliament. It follows therefore that it is not the case either that he is a member of the European Parliament or that he is not Prime Minister.

This argument can easily be represented in the form of a conditional statement as follows:

If Mr. Callaghan is both Prime Minister and not a member of the European Parliament then it is not the case either that he is a member of the European Parliament or that he is not Prime Minister.

This can be symbolised as follows:

$$(p \cdot \sim q) \supset \sim(q \vee \sim p)$$

Its truth table is:

p	q	~q	p · ~q	q v ~p	~(q v ~p)	[(p · ~q) ⊃ ~(q v ~p)]
T	T	F	F	T	F	T
F	T	F	F	T	F	T
T	F	T	T	F	T	T
F	F	T	F	T	F	T

As the conditional statement form <Premisses ⊃ Conclusion> is a tautology the argument is valid.

.Let us review the steps we have taken in testing the above argument.

Step One   Rewrite the argument in the statement form of
If Premisses then Conclusion.

Step Two   Symbolise the statement form.

Step Three Draw up the truth table of the statement form.

Step Four   Decide whether the statement form is tautologous.

———————————

Before you attempt to evaluate arguments in this way play Game Three in your Logicon pack - Must and Can't. Playing this game will teach you a great deal about the nature of tautology and prepare you for the business of argument evaluation.   The rules are at the end of the book.

———————————

2)   Write down any properties of tautologies you discover whilst playing the game, e.g. Any negation of a contradiction produces a tautology.

———————————

Now that you are more familiar with the notion of tautology you should be able to evaluate the following arguments by means of the procedure outlined above.

3)   Evaluate the following arguments by means of full truth tables.

i   Since the study of logic is fun and students of logic are fun
         seekers it follows that if students of logic are fun seekers
         then the study of logic is fun.

ii   Because it is true that if students of logic are fun seekers
         then the study of logic is fun we can conclude that the study
         of logic is fun and that students of logic are fun seekers.

III   Valid Argument Forms

        We have learned earlier in this lesson that a valid argument form
is one which is tautologous when presented as a conditional of the kind
If Premisses then Conclusion.

        Some of these forms are very common and especially useful in
demonstrating the validity of arguments. Becoming familiar with them
will save us a lot of time and effort later.

        We shall learn nine of these forms many of which will be
immediately recognised by you. Each of them have names.

        Valid Form 1   Modus Ponens

                    $p \supset q$

                    $p \quad \therefore \quad q$

        Where a hypothetical proposition ($p \supset q$) is true and we assert
that its antecedent (p) is true then we are committed to asserting that
its consequent (q) is true.

        This is easily demonstrated by means of the truth table:

p	q	$p \supset q$	$[(p \supset q) \cdot p] \supset q$
T	T	T	T
F	T	T	T
T	F	F	T
F	F	T	T

        The propositional form is tautologous therefore the argument form
is valid.

Valid Form 2   Modus Tollens

> p ⊃ q
>
> ~q / ∴   ~p

In this argument form given the truth of the hypothetical then if the consequent can be truthfully denied the antecedent can also be truthfully denied.

4)   Draw up the truth table for this argument form.

Now that you have become familiar with these two valid argument forms it would be helpful to review what was said about formal fallacies in our first lesson (pp.18-19).You will see how like the valid forms the fallacious forms are. It is precisely this similarity which deceives us into thinking that the fallacious arguments are good.

Valid Form 3   Hypothetical Syllogism

> p ⊃ q
>
> q ⊃ r / ∴ p ⊃ r

You will notice that there are three component propositions contained in this argument. Consequently the truth table which represents the hypothetical proposition into which we may convert the argument form will consist of eight lines rather than four as follows:

p	q	r	p ⊃ q	q ⊃ r	p ⊃ r	[(p ⊃ q) · (q ⊃ r)] ⊃ (p ⊃ r)
T	T	T	T	T	T	T
F	T	T	T	T	T	T
T	F	T	F	T	T	T
F	F	T	T	T	T	T
T	T	F	T	F	F	T
F	T	F	T	F	T	T
T	F	F	F	T	F	T
F	F	F	T	T	T	T

It will help you to remember this valid argument form if you notice that it is entirely made up of conditionals or <u>hypotheticals,</u> hence its title.

If you insert a particular argument into this form you will readily see that it is valid. For example:

If it is Friday then Thursday has gone and if it is Thursday then Wednesday has gone. Therefore if it is Friday Wednesday has gone.

<u>Valid Form 4</u>   <u>Disjunctive Syllogism</u>

p v q

~ p / ∴ q

Given that a disjunction is true then if one of the disjuncts is not true the other must be true.

The truth table for this valid form is easy to draw up. Construct it if you are in any doubt about the validity of the form.

<u>Valid Form 5</u>   <u>Constructive Dilemma</u>

(p ⊃ q) · (r ⊃ s)

p v r   / ∴ q v s

Given that two hypothetical statements are true together then if one or other of the antecedents is true it follows that one or other of the consequents is true.

You may usefully compare this valid form with the first valid form we considered, viz., Modus Ponens (p.54).

Truth tables can of course be drawn up for all these valid forms in which the final column will be inhabited solely by T's.

Wherever you are in any doubt about the validity of one of the forms as we review them then it would be wise to draw up the corresponding table to put your mind at rest.

<u>Valid Form 6</u>   <u>Destructive Dilemma</u>

$(p \supset q) \cdot (r \supset s)$

$\sim q \ v \sim s \ / \therefore \ \sim p \ v \sim r$

Given that two hypothetical propositions are true then if one or other of the consequents is not true it follows that one or other of the antecedents is not true.

You may usefully compare this valid form with Modus Tollens (p.55).

You may already have noticed a marked similarity between both the valid forms which are called Dilemmas. They each contain the premiss that two hypothetical propositions are true.

The second premisses distinguish them. In the Constructive case one or other of the antecedents is said to be true, i.e. something positive or constructive is said. In the Destructive case one or other of the consequents is said to be false (hence the title Destructive Dilemma).

<u>Valid Form 7</u>   <u>Simplification</u>

$p \cdot q \ / \therefore \ p$

For example: If it is Friday and it is raining then it follows
              that it is raining

Valid Form 8   Conjunction

$$p$$
$$q \; / \; \therefore \; p \cdot q$$

This form embodies the use of the comma in a long-hand argument instead of the word and.

Valid Form 9   Addition

$$p \; / \quad p \vee q$$

N.B. ADDITION IN FORMAL LOGIC INVOLVES THE USE OF THE <u>EITHER...OR</u> OPERATOR NOT THE <u>AND</u> OPERATOR

It is important that you become familiar with each of these argument forms. Try to commit them to memory for they will become friends to you as you embark on the enterprise of demonstrating the validity of arguments.

All arguments constructed in accordance with one of these 'valid forms' will be valid arguments; so we can regard these valid forms as so many 'Rules of Inference', telling us how to go about the job of arguing (see Chapter 7).

Examples

I.   By means of truth tables classify the following expressions as tautologies, contradictions or contingent propositions.

    i. $(p \supset \sim\sim q) \supset (q \vee \sim p)$

    ii. $[(p \cdot q) \equiv r] \vee [r \supset \sim (p \cdot q)]$

    iii. $\sim(\sim p \vee \sim q) \supset \sim (p \cdot q)$

    iv. $[p \supset (q \supset p)] \vee r$

    v. $\{[p \cdot (q \vee r)] \cdot (q \supset p)\} \supset q$

II.   Evaluate the following arguments by means of truth tables.

    i.   Mr. Callaghan cannot be Prime Minister because it is not both true either that he is Prime Minister or that he is leader of the Parliamentary Labour Party and that he is popular with the electorate.

    ii. Given that July is the sunniest month of the year it follows either that we have a pleasant holiday or that we did not book early enough if it is also true that if we book early enough and July is the sunniest month then we have a pleasant holiday.

Chapter Five: A Rose by any other Name is just as Sweet

Outline:

I   Definition of Logical Equivalence

We have already come across the idea of equivalence in Chapter 3 (see p.43).

The truth table defining the operator ≡ shows that two propositions are materially equivalent when they are either true together or when they are false together. In other words, when the truth values of two propositions are the same they are said to be materially equivalent.

Thus the propositions <Robert the Bruce was a Scot>

                      and <Apples grow on trees>
are materially equivalent because they both happen to be true.

However, our two examples show clearly that there is no connection of sense between propositions which simply happen to have the same truth value. That is, the meanings of the propositions in question are unrelated. Knowing that the first was true would not tell us whether or not the second was true. Connectedly understanding the second would not help us in any way to understand the first.

Logical Equivalence is another matter. Propositions which are logically equivalent to each other do exhibit a connection of sense.

Their truth values do not simply happen to coincide. Rather they necessarily coincide.

This can be expressed by saying that their equivalence is a tautology.

It will be helpful to contrast these two kinds of equivalence in a truth table.

Consider the equivalences: $p \equiv q$ and $(p \supset q) \equiv (\sim p \vee q)$. We can compare them in one truth table:

p	q	$p \supset q$	$\sim p \vee q$	$p \equiv q$	$(p \supset q) \equiv (\sim p \vee q)$
T	T	T	T	T	T
F	T	T	T	F	T
T	F	F	F	F	T
F	F	T	T	T	T

The final column shows that the equivalence of the propositions $p \supset q$ and $\sim p \vee q$ is a tautology. In other words whatever state of affairs makes one of them true always makes the other true, and whatever state of affairs makes one of them false always makes the other false.

1. By drawing up a truth table decide which of the following are logical equivalences.

i $\sim\sim(p \vee r) \equiv (p \vee r)$

ii $(p \vee r) \equiv (r \vee p)$

iii $(p \vee r) \equiv (r \cdot p)$

iv $(p \vee r) \equiv (p \supset r)$

II   Rules of Replacement

What are logical equivalences important?

They are important because, like the valid argument forms we outlined in
our last chapter, they provide us with very useful tools for demonstrating
the validity of arguments. These tools are called Rules of Replacement.

What sort of operation is replacement?

Imagine that you are purchasing goods in a grocery store whose cost totals
to exactly one pound. It makes no difference, so far as your debt to the
store is concerned, whether you hand the cashier a One Pound Note or two
Fifty Pence Pieces does it?   They have exactly the same monetary value.
Of course it may be more convenient for one reason or another to pay with
the note rather than with the coins. It would most certainly be inconvenient to pay by means of two hundred half pence pieces even though from
the financial point of view you would be doing exactly the same thing,
namely paying a debt of One Pound.

One may similarly substitute one proposition in an argument for
another which always has the same truth value. The argument's quality
is not affected by such replacement.

For example:

If the argument: ~ p v q

                    p   / ∴ q is valid then so is the
argument: p ⊃ q

                p   / ∴ q   a good argument

This is because we have seen that the propositions ~ p v q and
p ⊃ q are logically equivalent.

You may well ask why we should ever bother to juggle propositions in this way. The reason is similar to that for paying your grocery bill in one way rather than another. That is, it is sometimes more convenient to handle an argument in one form than it is to handle it in another. Look at our two examples on p. 62.

If we were asked to decide which of them, if any, was valid, we would find it easier to make up our minds about the second. This is because it is identical with a valid argument form which we have learned, viz. Modus Ponens. By replacing propositions in this way we will often be able to demonstrate the validity of arguments which would otherwise defeat us.

There are ten logical equivalences which we shall adopt as standard Rules of Replacement. You will need to become as familiar with these as with the valid argument forms. Many of them will be very obvious.

Wherever the equivalence is not self-evident we can satisfy ourselves about it by drawing up the requisite truth table.

Rule of Replacement 1   DeMorgan's Theorems

(a) $\sim (p \cdot q) \equiv (\sim p \vee \sim q)$

(b) $\sim (p \vee q) \equiv (\sim p \cdot \sim q)$

Look at the truth table of (a).

p	q	$\sim (p \cdot q)$	$\sim p \vee \sim q$	$\sim (p \cdot q) \equiv (\sim p \vee \sim q)$
T	T	F	F	T
F	T	T	T	T
T	F	T	T	T
F	F	T	T	T

If you look carefully at the formations of the operators either side of the two equivalences forming this rule you will soon see a pattern. Pointing this out will help you to apply the rule.

In each case you will note that three operators are used: negation, conjunction and disjunction.

Working from left to right in each case we have:

(a)   a negation of a conjunction

(b)   a negation of a disjunction

The right hand side of the equivalences are produced in each case by (i) moving the negation sign inside the brackets before each of the component propositions, (ii) changing the connector from either conjunction to disjunction or from disjunction to conjunction.

Of course the operation can move in either direction. When it moves from right to left the negation sign moves away from the component propositions outside the brackets. The connectors change as in the left to right operation.

Rule of Replacement 2   Commutation

     (a) $(p \vee q) \equiv (q \vee p)$

     (b) $(p \cdot q) \equiv (q \cdot p)$

This is a much simpler rule. If you think of what commuters do, i.e. change positions, then you will find this rule easy to remember.

Change of position of component propositions is possible without affecting truth value around either conjunction operators or around disjunction operators.

2)   Draw up the truth table for (a).

Rule of Replacement 3   Association

(a) [(p v q) v r] ≡ [p v (q v r)]

(b) [(p · q) · r] ≡ [p · (q · r)]

If you remember that Associations are various groupings of people then this rule will be readily called to mind. Again such regroupings are only possible where the operators involved in the regrouping are either all disjunctions or are all conjunctions.

Rule of Replacement 4   Distribution

(a) [p v (q · r)] ≡ [(p v q) · (p v r)]

(b) [p · (q v r)] ≡ [(p · q) v (p · r)]

Moving from left to right we can see that the proposition outside the small brackets is in a sense shared between the propositions inside the brackets,i.e. distributed amongst them.

Note again the similar patterns in the two equivalences. The signs connecting the single proposition to the complex proposition on the left hand side become the signs inside the brackets on the right. The sign inside the brackets on the left hand side becomes the sign between the brackets on the right. Once again only conjunctions and disjunctions occur.

Of course, as with all other rules of replacement the operation works in both directions.

(If you know any algebra you will see that there are similarities between these equivalences and multiplying through brackets in algebraic formulae.)

Rule of Replacement 5   Double Negation

$p \equiv \sim\sim p$

Two negatives make a positive in formal logic.

Rule of Replacement 6   Transposition

$(p \supset q) \equiv (\sim q \supset \sim p)$

You may usefully compare this rule to the valid argument form
Modus Tollens (see p. 55).

The difference is that in Modus Tollens the consequent is
actually denied whereas in Transposition we are told that _if_ it were
denied then the antecedent could also be denied.

Rule of Replacement 7   Material Implication

$(p \supset q) \equiv (\sim p \vee q)$

This is the logical equivalence which we used earlier (see
p.61) as an example.

A little thought shows that the two sides of the equation balance
for if p is true then q is true. Now either p or $\sim$ p must be true.
So either $\sim$ p or q must be true.

Rule of Replacement 8   Material Equivalence

(a) $(p \equiv q) \equiv [(p \supset q) \cdot (q \supset p)]$
(b) $(p \equiv q) \equiv [(p \cdot q) \vee (\sim p \cdot \sim q)]$

These accounts of material equivalences may look forbidding.
In fact they are quite straightforward. On page 60 we described two
propositions which are materially equivalent as simply happening to have

the same truth value. If they are either true together or false together then clearly each implies the other for True ⊃ True is true and False ⊃ False is true. This is what (a) says.

Similarly they are either jointly true or jointly false. This is what (b) says.

Rule of Replacement 9   Exportation

$$[(p \cdot q) \supset r] \equiv [p \supset (q \supset r)]$$

Remember that if you are in doubt about any of these equivalences you can confirm them by drawing up a truth table.

Rule of Replacement 10   Tautology

(a) $p \equiv (p \lor p)$

(b) $p \equiv (p \cdot p)$

III   i Use of Rules of Inference

The Rules of Inference consist of the nine valid argument forms listed in Chapter 4.

Remember that they are patterns of argument. Many different propositions may be inserted into those patterns.

For example, consider the pattern of Modus Ponens:

$p \supset q$ Precisely this pattern is present in the argument:

$p \ / \therefore q$ $(p \cdot r) \supset (q \lor s)$

$p \cdot r \ \ / \therefore q \lor s$

That is, in each case we have an hypothetical proposition asserted together with an assertion of its antecedent. This entitles us to assert its consequent. If you remember that in a well formed formula a bracketed expression forms a proposition in its own right the matter becomes clear. If we numbered the propositions whose relations make the arguments valid we get the same picture in both cases, viz.

$$1 \supset 2$$
$$1 \; / \therefore \; 2$$

3)   Pick out the rules of inference used in the following arguments.

i $(p \supset r) \supset (s \vee t)$
        $\sim (s \vee t) \; / \therefore \; \sim (p \supset r)$

ii $(q \cdot r) \vee [p \supset (r \cdot s)]$
        $\sim (q \cdot r) \; / \therefore \; [p \supset (r \cdot s)]$

iii $[p \supset (r \cdot s)] \cdot [(p \cdot q) \supset (r \vee s)]$
        $\sim (r \cdot s) \vee \sim (r \vee s) \; / \therefore \; \sim p \vee \sim (p \cdot q)$

III   ii Use of Rules of Replacement

We need to make a similar point about the use of Rules of Replacement to the point we have just made about the use of Rules of Inference.

Once again we are concerned with patterns of propositions which are capable of an infinite number of different fillings.

For example consider the Rule of Commutation.

The following replacements follow the same pattern:

(a) $(p \lor q) \supset (r \cdot s)$ / $\therefore$ $(q \lor p) \supset (r \cdot s)$

(b) $[(p \cdot q) \lor r] \supset t$ / $\therefore$ $[r \lor (p \cdot q)] \supset t$

This will become clear if you follow the procedure we followed on p.59. Each substitution has the form:

$(1 \lor 2) \supset 3$ / $\therefore$ $(2 \lor 1) \supset 3$

4)   Pick out the Rules of Replacement used in the following:

i $[(p \cdot q) \lor (r \lor s)] \cdot t$ / $\therefore$ $([(p \cdot q) \lor r] \lor s) \cdot t$

ii $(p \cdot q) \supset r$ / $\therefore$ $\sim (p \cdot q) \lor r$

iii $[(p \supset q) \cdot r] \supset s$ / $\therefore$ $(p \supset q) \supset (r \supset s)$

Examples

I.   Use truth tables to determine which of the following expressions are logical equivalences.

    i.   (p · ~r) ≡ ~(~ p v r)

    ii.   (~ p ⊃ q) ≡ (q v p)

    iii. (p · q) ≡ (~~ p v ~~ q)

    iv. (p ≡ q) ≡ (p · q)

    v.   [p ⊃ (q v r)] ≡ [r v (q v ~ p)]

II.   Pick out the Rules of Inference employed in the following arguments:

    i.   s ⊃ (r v t)
         (r v t) ⊃ (u · v) / ∴ s ⊃ (u · v)

    ii.   [(p v s) ⊃ (r · t)] · [(t ≡ r) ⊃ p]
         ~ (r · t) v ~ p   / ∴ [~(p v s) v ~ (t ≡ r)]

    iii. s ≡ [p v (r · t)]
         p   / ∴ p v s

    iv. (p ⊃ r) v (s · t)
         ~ (s · t)   / ∴ (p ⊃ r)

III. Pick out the Rules of Replacement used in the following arguments.

    i.   {(p ⊃ r) v [(q v r) ⊃ s]} / ∴ {[(r v q) ⊃ s] v (p ⊃ r)}

    ii.   ~ [s v (p ⊃ r)] · t / ∴ [~s · ~(p ⊃ r)] · t

    iii. [(s · q) ⊃ (p ⊃ r)] v (p ≡ r)
                          / ∴ {s ⊃ [q ⊃ (p ⊃ r)]} v (p ≡ r)

    iv. [(p · r) · (q ⊃ s)] ⊃ t / ∴ {p · [r · (q ⊃ s)]} ⊃ t

    v.   p ⊃ [q ⊃ (r · s)]   / ∴ p ⊃ [~ (r · s) ⊃ ~q]

Chapter Six: <u>Separating the Sheep from the Goats</u>

Outline:

    I   The Shorter Truth Table Method

    II Application of the method to valid arguments

    III Application of the method in complex cases

I   The Shorter Truth Table Method

We have already seen that though arguments which claim that their conclusions follow necessarily from their premisses are called deductive arguments, some of them are invalid. That is, their claim is unjustified.

We now have to answer the question; How can we distinguish the good arguments from the bad?

We have sufficient rules of argument to demonstrate the validity of any good deductive argument in the family we have been concerned with. However, it would not be wise to jump straight into an attempt to prove the validity of an argument before knowing whether or not it was valid. Failure to prove its validity would not mean that the argument was invalid. The failure may lie as much in our poor reasoning as in the fabric of the argument.

Is there any way of finding out whether or not an argument is valid? Yes. It is called the Shorter Truth Table Method.

What is the principle involved in this method?

You will remember that an invalid argument is one whose <u>premisses</u> may sometimes be <u>true</u> when its <u>conclusion</u> is <u>false</u>.

If therefore we can pick out any line in the truth table of the argument when presented in the form of an hypothetical proposition (see p. 41 ff) in which the premiss columns are true together whilst the conclusion column is false, we shall know that the argument is invalid. One such line is sufficient to reveal an argument's invalidity for it ensures that the hypothetical proposition is not a tautology.

How can we pick out such a line?

One way would be to draw up the complete truth table. You have already discovered how laborious and time-consuming this procedure can be. Many arguments will contain more than three component propositions making the procedure even longer than any you have had to tackle in this book.

Is there any short cut available to us?

Yes, fortunately there is.

Consider the following example:

$$p \supset q$$
$$r \supset s$$
$$\sim (p \lor r) \quad / \therefore \quad \sim (q \cdot s)$$

To deal with this argument by means of the Shorter Truth Table Method we need to take the following steps:

Step One   Draw up the heads of the truth table for the argument as
follows:

Component Propositions	Premiss 1	Premiss 2	Premiss 3	Conclusion
p q r s	p ⊃ q	r ⊃ s	~ (p v r)	~ (q · s)

To avoid confusion it is best only to include the component
simple propositions, the premisses and the conclusion in the table.

Step Two   Insert the truth value T in all the premiss columns and
the value F in the conclusion column.

p q r s	p ⊃ q	r ⊃ s	~ (p v r)	~ (q · s)
	T	T	T	F

If we are able to find a set of values of p,q,r and s which will
allow these truth values to stand then we will have discovered one
situation where the hypothetical <Premisses ⊃ Conclusion> is false.
Thus the argument will be invalid because this hypothetical is not
a tautology.

Step Three Decide which of the inserted truth values yields most
information about the truth values of the component simples. Proceed
to insert such values in the component proposition columns until a
complete set of values is obtained.

Number each move made. For example we shall use the information
provided by the inserted value in the Premiss 3 column first. Thus we
put the figure 1 alongside it and alongside the truth values we discover
from it in columns p and r thus:

p	q	r	s	p ⊃ q	r ⊃ s	~ (p v r)	~ (q · s)
F₁	T₂	F₁	T₂			T₁	F₂

At move 2 both q and s are true.

<u>Step Four</u>   Now that we have a full set of values all that remains to be done is to see whether the outstanding inserted truth values can stand given the values of the component propositions.

p is false so p ⊃ q is true

r is false so r ⊃ s is true

Thus we have a situation where the premisses are true and the conclusion is false. This shows that the argument is invalid.

1.   Following the above method show that the following arguments are invalid.

i   p v q / ∴ ~p ⊃ ~ q

ii   p ⊃ q

~ q · r

r ⊃ ~ s / ∴ p v s

iii   p v r

~ p ⊃ ~ s / ∴ r ⊃ ~ s

II   Application of the Method to Valid Arguments

You may well be asking what happens when the argument is valid. How do we know when there is no line in a truth table where the premisses are true and the conclusion false?

Consider the following example:

$$\sim p \vee \sim r$$

$$\sim p \supset s$$

$$\sim s \qquad / \therefore \sim r$$

If we follow the steps outlined in the previous section of this lesson the following results occur:

<u>Stages</u> One, Two and Three

p	r	s	$\sim p \vee \sim r$	$\sim p \supset s$	$\sim s$	$\sim r$
T_3 F_4	T_1 F_4	F_2	T_4	T_3	T_2	F_1

The first two values used speak for themselves. If $\sim r$ is false then clearly r is true. Similarly, if $\sim s$ is true then s is false.

We next use the premiss $\sim p \supset s$ because it yields us definite information about the truth value of the remaining component proposition p. The other premiss leaves the truth value of p an open question. Now if $\sim p \supset s$ is true and s is false then $\sim p$ must be false. This means that p must be true.

Thus we have a full set of values for the component propositions. All that remains to be done is to take Step 4. It is here that the contrast with invalid arguments occurs.

In order for the remaining premiss to retain the inserted truth value T it is necessary for either $\sim p$ or $\sim r$ to be true. This means that we must ascribe the value F to either p or r. But we have already determined that they should each have the value T in order to ensure that the other premisses of the argument be true and the conclusion false.

In other words it is only possible to deny that the conclusion of this argument follows necessarily from its premises by assigning contradictory truth values to one or more of the component propositions. Thus the argument is valid.

In the following exercise you are not told whether the arguments to be examined are valid or invalid. By employing the above contrast you are asked to assess the quality of the arguments.

2.   Determine the validity or invalidity of the following arguments by means of the Shorter Truth Table method.

   i   p v ~ s

         ~ s / ∴ ~ p

   ii   p ≡ ~ s

         ~ p · r / ∴ s

   iii   p ⊃ (r · s)

         s ⊃ ~ t

         t · r / ∴ ~ p

   iv   p · (r v s)

         ~ s v q

         s   / q ≡ p

III   Application of the Method in Complex Cases

Whenever the Shorter Truth Table method is applied to arguments the same principle operates, viz., to try to pick out one line in the truth table of the hypothetical proposition representing the argument where the premisses are true whilst the conclusion is false.

However, applying the method is a little more complicated in some cases than in others.

In each of the examples which you tackled in Exercises 1 and 2 you had no need to select options at any stage in the procedure. Each stage provided definite information about the truth value of one or more of the component propositions. You will not always be so fortunate as this. The aim of this section of the chapter is to show you how to cope with cases where such options do occur.

We will first work through a complex case involving an invalid argument and then through a complex case involving a valid argument.

(a)   Complex Case Involving an Invalid Argument

Consider the following argument: $s \supset (p \cdot t)$

$$\sim p \lor t$$

$$t \lor s \quad / \therefore p \equiv s$$

The complexity arises in applying the method at the third stage of dealing with this argument. If you look carefully at the column headings you will see that not one of the inserted truth values of the premisses or conclusion yields any definite information about the truth values of the component propositions p, s and t.

p	s	t	Premiss I $s \supset (p \cdot t)$	II $\sim p \lor t$	III $t \lor s$	Conclusion $p \equiv s$
			T	T	T	F

Now there are three possibilities which would make Premiss II true. Similarly with Premiss III. There are many more possible situations which would make Premiss I true. Only two situations would make the conclusion false. Thus it yields most information about the truth values of the component propositions, viz.

either p is true and s is false

or p is false and s is true

Thus we make our first choice here. Let us opt for the situation where p is false and s is true. We mark the table accordingly and proceed with the method thus:

p	s	t	s $\supset$ (p $\cdot$ t)	$\sim$ p v t	t v s	p $\equiv$ s
F_1 T_2^1	T_1	T_2	T_2	T	T	F_1 First choice

Having opted for the values of p and s we are told something definite about the value of t by premiss I, viz. that t is true. However, if premiss I is true then, given the values of p and s we have opted for it follows that p is also true. This is contradictory. Therefore the line

p s t

F T T in the truth table cannot allow the premisses
to be true whilst the conclusion is false.

Does it follow that the argument is valid then?

No, because we have not yet exhausted all the possibilites. To do this we must retrace our steps to the point where we made our last choice of options and select a different option. Let us now opt for the situation where p is true and s is false and work out the consequences for lines containing that combination.

p	s	t	s ⊃ (p · t)	~ p v t	t v s	p ≡ s
T_1	F_1	T_2	T	T	T_2	F_1

Premiss III now yields us definite information about the truth value of t, viz. that it is true.

Now we have a complete, and so far non-contradictory set of values for the component propositions. All we have to do is see whether the further inserted truth values of the remaining premisses can stand given these values.

Well, premiss I remains true for its antecedent is false. Premiss II similarly remains true for one of the disjuncts is true.

Thus we have found a line where the premisses can be true together whilst the conclusion is false. Thus the argument is shown to be <u>invalid</u>.

Sometimes subsidiary choices have to be made. These should be marked Choice 1a, Choice 1b etc. and if no suitable choice is found then you must return to the point where the latest choice was made and exhaust all possibilities at that point before returning to the point of earlier choices and exhausting those. (Such a procedure would have arisen if in our last example we had first used Premiss I.)

3.   Show that the following arguments are invalid by means of the Shorter Truth Table Method

    i   p ⊃ (s ⊃ t)

        ~ s v t / ∴ (s ⊃ t) · p

    ii   q ⊃ (r · s)

        p v ~ s / ∴ (q v r) · ~ p

(b)   Complex Case Involving a Valid Argument

Consider the following argument: $p \supset q$

$\sim q \vee \sim (\sim r \vee \sim s)$

$/ \therefore p \supset (r \cdot s)$

Let us set out the whole calculation and then examine each stage separately:

p	q	r	s	$p \supset q$	$\sim q \vee \sim (\sim r \vee \sim s)$	$p \supset (r \cdot s)$
T_1	T_2 F_3	T_1	F_1	T_2	T_3	F_1 Choice 1
T_1	T_2 F_3	F_1	T_1	T_2	T_3	F_1 Choice 2
T_1	T_2 F_3	F_1	F_1	T_2	T_3	F_1 Choice 3

None of the inserted truth values in the premiss and conclusion columns yields definite information about some of the truth values of the component propositions.

The conclusion's being false is the most promising source of information. Its antecedent must be true and its conclusion false. However, this leaves us with a number of options for a conjunction can be false in three ways. Choices 1, 2 and 3 work through these options. The first two choices fail to yield a line where the premisses are true and the conclusion false.

The third choice also fails to produce such a line. However, this choice exhausts all the possibilities. Thus we know that no such line exists in the complete truth table and that, consequently, the argument is valid.

N.B.   <u>Only when all choices, if any have been made in the examination,</u>
<u>have been exhausted can we know that the argument in question</u>
<u>is valid</u>

4.   Determine the validity or invalidity of the following arguments
by means of the Shorter Truth Table Method

   i   p v ~ q
      s ⊃ (q · r) / ∴ s · p

   ii   (p · ~ q) v r
      (q · r) ⊃ s
      ~ r   / ∴ q ⊃ p

   iii   ~ p ⊃ (q v r)
      ~ q · ~r / ∴ p · ~ r

Examples

I. By means of the shorter truth table method show that the
following arguments are invalid.

    i.   p ⊃ q   ii.   p ≡ q
        ~ r ⊃ ~ q / ∴ p ⊃ ~ r   q ⊃ (r v s) / ∴ ~ r ⊃ ~ p

    iii. ~ p v r   iv. ~ r · s
         r ⊃ (s · ~ t) / ∴ p ⊃ t   p · (q v r) / ∴ ~ q v t

II. Determine the validity or invalidity of the following arguments
by means of the shorter truth table method.

    i.   p ⊃ q   ii.   p (r · s)
        (r v s) ⊃ p / ∴ r ⊃ q   ~ s v t / ∴ ~ t   p

    iii. p · ~ (r ⊃ s)   iv. r v (p · q)
        ~ s   / ∴ r   ~ (r v s) / ∴ p v q

III. Show by means of the shorter truth table method that the
following arguments are invalid.

    i.   p v (r ⊃ s)   ii.   s ⊃ (p v q)
        q v (r ⊃ ~ s) / ∴ p v q   ~ q · r / ∴ p · r

    iii. s ⊃ p   iv. (p v q) ⊃ ~ r
        ~ r v (s · p) / ∴ p · (r ⊃ s)   s ⊃ ~ q / ∴ ~ p ⊃ (r · s)

IV. Determine the validity or invalidity of the following arguments
by means of the shorter truth table method.

    i.   r ⊃ p   ii.   p ⊃ (r v s)
        ~ (p v q) / ∴ ~ [(p · q) v r]   p ⊃ ~ t / ∴ ~ (s ⊃ t)

    iii. (p · q) v r   iv. (s ⊃ q) · ~ t
        r ⊃ (t · s) / ∴ p · ~ t   ~ (~ s v r) v t
                               / ∴ s · (q v r)

Chapter Seven: <u>Prove It!</u>

Outline:

———————

In Chapter 6 we learned to determine whether or not an argument was valid or invalid. Of course once we have shown that there is no line in the truth table of an hypothetical proposition (representing the relation between the premisses and the conclusion of an argument) where the premisses are true together whilst the conclusion is false we have also demonstrated that the argument in question is valid.

Demonstration or proof can take a more familiar form however. By means of the Rules of Inference and the Rules of Replacement learned in Chapters 4 and 5 we can move by deductive steps from the premisses to the conclusion. If the premisses are true then each successive step from them must be true where the moves are deductive. Thus ultimately we will, by arriving at the conclusion of the argument, show that if the premisses are true then the conclusion must be true. In other words we will have shown that the argument is valid.

———————

I   Employing the Rules of Inference

You will remember that there are nine Rules of Inference (see pp. 43-46).

We will learn to use them in groups beginning with the three simplest rules, viz., Rules 7, 8 and 9.

Then we shall include Rules 1, 2, 3 and 4.

Finally, we shall expand our examples to include use of the remainder of the Rules, viz., Rules 5 and 6.

Use of Rules 7, 8 and 9

These rules are simplification, conjunction and addition (see pp. 46 and 47).

Consider the following example: p · q

r   / ∴ p · (r v s)

The formal proof would take the following form:

1.   p · q
2.   r   / ∴ p · (r v s)
3.   p Simplification 1.
4.   r v s Addition 2.
5.   p · (r v s) Conjunction 3 and 4.

Note that each line is deduced by means of one rule only from one or more previous lines. At each step the rule justifying the move is stated together with the lines employed in that move.

You should be able to manage the following exercises without much difficulty.

1)   Provide justification for each line in the following proof.

    1. p
    2. s   / ∴ (p v r) · (s v q)
    3. p v r _____
    4. s v q _____
    5. (p v r) · (s v q) _____

2)   Provide a proof of the validity of the following argument.

    p · q
    r v s   / ∴ [p · (r v s)] v t

    _____

Now that you have tried your hand at using the three simplest rules you will have more confidence to tackle the second group of Rules.

These are Modus Ponens, Modus Tollens, Hypothetical Syllogism and Disjunctive Syllogism (see pp. 54-55).

Bear in mind the point made about the application of Rules of Replacement (p. 68) which applies equally to the use of Rules of Inference. The Rules represent patterns of argument and either simple or complex propositions can be slotted into these patterns. Read pp. 67-69 again before moving on.

Consider the following example:

1	$(p \lor q) \supset r$	You are already able to
2	$p \cdot q$	provide justification
3	$(r \supset s) \cdot (s \supset t) \quad / \therefore t$	for lines 4 and 5.
4	p _____	Notice that line 6 uses
5	p ∨ q _____	an hypothetical (line 1)
6	r Modus Ponens 1 and 5	and its antecedent
7	r ⊃ t Hypothetical Syllogism 3	(line 5). These are
8	t _____	linked by means of Rule 1,
		Modus Ponens. Modus

Tollens is employed in a similar way. If we need the denial of the antecedent of a given hypothetical in a proof and we can deduce the denial of its consequent then the Rule 2 enables us to deduce the denial of the antecedent.

Line 7 speaks for itself. Wherever you have two hypotheticals where what is the consequent in one is the antecedent in the other you know that Rule 3 can be applied if it is needed.

You should now be able to provide a justification for line 8 of our example.

_____

Try the following examples. In exercise 4 you are provided with some parts of the proof which will help you to devise the remainder of the proof. In exercise 5 you must try to devise a complete demonstration.

3)   Provide justifications for each line of the following proof.

    1. p ⊃ q

    2. p · q

    3. (q v r) ⊃ ~ s

    4. t ⊃ s   / ∴ ~ t

    5. p_____

    6. q_____

    7. q v r _____

    8. ~ s _____

    9. ~ t _____

4)   Complete the following proof.

    1. p ⊃ ~ s

    2. t ⊃ p

    3. t

    4. s v (p ⊃ r) / ∴ r

    5. _____ Hypothetical Syllogism 1 and 2

    6. _____

    7. p ⊃ r Disjunctive Syllogism 4 and 6

    8. _____

    9. _____

5)   Provide a proof of the validity of the following argument.

    p ⊃ r

    s v q

    r ⊃ ~ s

    p   / ∴ q

_____

Finally we can extend our attention to proofs which employ the final two Rules of Inference, viz., the Dilemmas. (See pp. 56-57). It would be good to read these two pages again before you proceed. You will see how useful are these rules in the following example.

1. p ⊃ q   You will be able to

2. p · (q v r)   provide justification

3. r ⊃ s   / ∴ q v s   for lines 4 - 6 with

4. p_____   little difficulty.

5. p v r_____

6. (p ⊃ q) · (r ⊃ s)____

7. q v s Constructive Dillema 6 and 5

There is no substitute for practice in learning to recognise situations where the various rules of inference are usefully employed. The more examples you tackle the more readily you will see your way through proofs.

6)   Complete the proof (a) and provide a demonstration of validity of argument (b).

(a)   1. p ⊃ q   (b) p ⊃ q

        2. r ⊃ s   ~ t · s

        3. s v p   s ⊃ t / ∴ p v ~ s

        4. ~ s · t / ∴ q v s

        5. _____

        6. p_____

        7. _____ Addition

        8. _____

        9. _____ Constructive Dilemma 8 and 7

_____

II   Employing the Rules of Replacement

There is no more difficulty in employing the Rules of Replacement than there is in employing the Rules of Inference. We will first consider the employment of Rules 1 - 5 in isolation from all other Rules of Inference and Replacement. Then we shall consider the use of Rules of Replacement 6 - 10 together with the first five. Finally we shall consider the use of all the Rules of Inference and Replacement together.

Use of Rules of Replacement 1 - 5 (see pp.63-67)

In learning these rules you learned to detect various signals of the possible applications of the rules. It would be advisable at this point to remind yourself of the hints attached to rules 1 - 5.

Consider the following demonstration which uses only Rules of Replacement 1 - 5.

1.   ~ (~ p v ~ q) v (r v s) / ∴ [s v (r v q)] · [(s v (r v p)]

2.   [~(~ p v ~ q) v r] v s   Association 1

3.   [~(~ q v ~ p) v r] v s   Commutation 2

4.   [(~~ q · ~~ p) v r] v s   De Morgan 3

5.   [(q · p) v r] v s   Double Negation 4

6.   [r v (q · p)] v s   Commutation 5

7.   [(r v q) · (r v p)] v s   Distribution 6

8.   s v [(r v q) · (r v p)]   Commutation 7

9.   [s v (r v q)] · [s v (r v p)] Distribution 8

Notice the following points about this demonstration:

i   Only one rule is used in moving to a further line in the proof.

ii   Changes can be made within parts of the propositions as long as the sense of the proposition is not altered because we are here dealing with equivalences rather than inferences. Where the rules of inference are employed this kind of move is not possible. There whole lines are used as premisses for further lines consequent upon them.

Try the following examples which follow a similar pattern of increasing difficulty to the examples completed earlier when you were learning to employ the Rules of Inference (see p. 84-86).

7)   Give justifications for each line in the following proof of validity.

1.   (s v t) v p   /   ∴   ~[~ t · (~ p · ~ s)]

2.   p v (s v t) _____

3.   ~~ [p v (s v t)]_____

4.   ~ [~ p · ~ (s v t)]_____

5.   ~ [~ p · (~ s · ~ t]_____

6.   ~ [(~ p · ~ s) · ~ t]_____

7.   ~ [~ t · (~ p · ~ s)]_____

8)   Complete the following demonstration.

1.   ~ (p · q) v ~ (r · s)   /   ∴   ~ (p · s) v ~ (q · r)

2.   _____ De Morgan 1

3.   ~ [p · (q · r) · s]_____

4.   _____

5.   ~ [(q · r) · (p · s)]_____

6.   _____

7.   _____ _____

9)   Provide a demonstration of the validity of the following argument
        using no other rules than Rules 1 - 5 of Replacement

$$(p \lor q) \lor r \quad / \quad \therefore \sim (\sim r \cdot \sim p) \lor q$$

We are now ready to turn our attention to the use of Rules of
Replacement 6 - 10 (see pp. 66-67). In the examples which we shall use
in this section most of the moves made are by means of these rules. Here
and there, however, some of Rules 1 - 5 of Replacement will be needed.

Consider the following proof of validity.

1. $\sim p \lor q$

2. $(r \cdot \sim p) \supset \sim q$

3. $r \quad / \quad \therefore p \equiv q$

4. $r \supset (\sim p \supset \sim q)$ Exportation 2

5. $r \supset (\sim\sim q \supset \sim\sim p)$ Transposition 4

6. $r \supset (q \supset p)$ Double Negation 5

7. $q \supset p$ Modus Ponens 6 and 3 (this of course is a
                                     Rule of Inference)

8. $p \supset q$ Material Implication 1

9. $(p \supset q) \cdot (q \supset p)$ Conjunction 8 and 7

10. $p \equiv q$ Material Equivalence 9

Look carefully at each line and compare the moves made with
the formal rules as set out on pages 66 and 67. You should then be
ready to tackle the following examples which are once again set out in
order of increasing difficulty.

10)   Provide justifications for each of the lines of the following demonstration.

1.   (p · q) ⊃ r   /   ∴ q ⊃ (~ r ⊃ ~ p)

2.   p ⊃ (q ⊃ r)_____

3.   ~ (q ⊃ r) ⊃ ~ p _____

4.   ~ (~ q v r) ⊃ ~ p _____

5.   (~~ q · ~ r) ⊃ ~ p _____

6.   (q · ~ r) ⊃ ~ p _____

7.   q ⊃ (~ r ⊃ ~ p) _____

11)   Complete the following proof of validity.

1.   (p · q) ⊃ (r v s)   /   ∴ (q ⊃ r) v (p ⊃ s)

2.   _____

3.   _____ De Morgan 2

4.   [~ p v (~ q v r) v s]

5.   _____

6.   _____

7.   _____

12)   Provide a proof of the validity of the following argument.

(p ⊃ q) v r   /   ∴ p ⊃ (~ q ⊃ r)

_____

Use of Both Sets of Rules Together

You have now covered the use of the Rules of Inference and the Rules of Replacement in the demonstration of the validity of arguments. However, you have enjoyed some measure of guidance as to which rules were likely to be useful in the examples you have tackled. The following examples are intended to test your grasp of the rules without the benefits of such guidance. They are ordered in similar fashion to the sets of exercises which have occurred at each stage of our coverage of the rules.

13)   Provide a justification for each line of the following demonstration.

    1.   p ≡ q

    2.   (s v t) · ~ p   / ∴ t v ~ q

    3.   (p ⊃ q) · (q ⊃ p) _____

    4.   (q ⊃ p) · (p ⊃ q) _____

    5.   q ⊃ p _____

    6.   ~ p · (s v t) _____

    7.   ~ p _____

    8.   ~ q _____

    9.   ~ q v t _____

   10.   t v ~ q _____

14)   Complete the following proof of validity.

    1.   (p v r) ⊃ (s · t)   / ∴ p ⊃ s

    2.   _____

    3.   (~ p · ~ r) v (s · t) De Morgan 2

    4.   _____ _____

5.   (~ p · ~ r) v s   Simplification 4

6.   _____

7.   (s v ~ p) · (s v ~ r) _____

8.   _____

9.   _____   Commutation 8

10. _____

15)   Provide a proof of validity of the following argument:

~ (p v q) / ∴ p ≡ q

_____

III   Employing the Rule of Conditional Proof

This is a method of proof which makes life much easier for us when dealing with certain kinds of arguments. The rule is of more general use than that to which we shall put it though its application in these other contexts is a little more complicated.

We shall simply use it in demonstrating the validity of arguments whose conclusion is an hypothetical proposition.

Consider the following example:

p ⊃ q

r ⊃ s / ∴ (p · r) ⊃ (q · s)

If you compare the lengths of the two proofs of validity which follow you will see how much simpler the one which employs the conditional proof is. In most cases too it is shorter.

Standard Proof	Conditional Proof

Standard Proof

1. p ⊃ q
2. r ⊃ s / ∴ (p · r) ⊃ (q · s)
3. ~ p v q M.I. 1
4. ~ r v s M.I. 2
5. ~ p v q v ~ r Addition 3
6. ~ r v s v ~ p Addition 4
7. ~ p v ~ r v q Commutation 5
8. ~ p v ~ r v s Commutation 6
9. (~ p v ~ r) v q Association 7
10. (~ p v ~ r) v s Association 8
11. ~ (p · r) v q De Morgan 9
12. ~ (p · r) v s De Morgan 10
13. [~ (p · r) v q] · [~(p · r) v s]
    Conjunction 11 and 12
14. ~ (p · r) v (q · s) Distribution 13
15. (p · r) ⊃ (q · s) M.I. 14

Conditional Proof

1. p ⊃ q
2. r ⊃ s / ∴ (p · r) ⊃ (q · s)
3. p · r Assumption C.P.
4. p Simplification 3
5. r · p Commutation 3
6. r Simplification 5
7. q Modus Ponens 1 & 4
8. s Modus Ponens 6 & 2
9. q · s Conjunction 7 & 8
10. (p · r) ⊃ (q · s) C.P.3-9

You will see that the procedure is to assume the truth of the antecedent of the conclusion and proceed to deduce the consequent of the conclusion.

Call the premisses P, the antecedent of the conclusion A and the consequent of the conclusion C and the argument is as follows: $P \supset (A \supset C)$.

By exportation this is equivalent to $(P \cdot A) \supset C$ which is precisely the relation demonstrated in the conditional proof.

16)   As a final exercise in this chapter use the conditional proof
        method to demonstrate the validity of the following argument:

$$p \supset q$$

$$p \supset (q \supset r)$$

$$q \supset (r \supset s) \quad / \quad \therefore \quad p \supset s$$

To show the value of this method you may like to try a demonstration of
the standard variety!

_____

Examples

1.   Provide justifications for the lines of proof (a) and a
        proof of validity for argument (b) using Rules of Inference
        7, 8 and 9.

(a)   1. $\sim t \cdot (p \supset q)$
        2. $t \vee s$ $/ \therefore (t \vee s) \cdot (\sim t \vee s)$
        3. $\sim t$
        4. $\sim t \vee s$
        5. $(t \vee s) \cdot (\sim t \vee s)$

(b) $(p \vee s) \cdot \sim q$
        r $/ \therefore r \cdot [(p \vee s) \vee t]$

II.   Using any or all of the Rules of Inference 1-4 and 7-9
        provide justifications for each line in proof (a), complete
        proof (b) and provide a proof of the validity of argument (c).

(a)   1. $(\sim p \vee q) \supset (r \supset s)$
        2. $(\sim t \cdot \sim u) \supset (s \supset v)$
        3. $(p \supset t) \cdot (t \supset p)$

4. $(\sim t \cdot \sim u) \cdot \sim w \ / \ \therefore \ r \supset v$

5. $\sim t \cdot \sim u$

6. $s \supset v$

7. $\sim t$

8. $p \supset t$

9. $\sim p$

10. $\sim p \ v \ q$

11. $r \supset s$

12. $r \supset v$

(b)   1. $(p \ v \ q) \supset \sim r$

2. $r \ v \ q$

3. $(q \ v \sim p) \supset s$

4. $p \ // \ \therefore \ s \ v \sim q$

5.

6. $\sim r$ M.P. 1 & 5

7.

8. $q \ v \sim p$ Addition 7

9.

10.

(c)   1. $(p \ v \ q) \supset (r \ v \ s)$

2. $[(r \ v \ s) \ v \ t] \supset (u \ v \ v)$

3. $(u \ v \ v) \supset \sim r$

4. $s \supset \sim u$

5. $p \ / \ \therefore \ \sim p \quad v \sim t$

III.   Use any of the Rules of Inference to provide justifications
for each line in proof (a), complete proof (b) and provide
a proof of the validity of argument (c).

(a)   1. $p \supset (q \cdot r)$

2. $\sim p \supset [(s \supset t) \cdot (u \supset v)]$

3. $(q \cdot r) \ v \ [(\sim p \supset s) \cdot (\sim p \supset u)]$

4. $\sim (q \cdot r) \cdot \sim (v \cdot s) \ / \ \therefore \ t \ v \ v$

5. $\sim (q \cdot r)$

6. $\sim p$

       7.   (~ p ⊃ s) · (~ p ⊃ u)
       8.   ~ p v ~ p
       9.   s v u
    10.   (s ⊃ t) · (u ⊃ v)
    11.   t v v

(b)   1.   (p ⊃ q) · (r ⊃ s)
       2.   (q ⊃ t) · (s ⊃ u)
       3.   (~ p ⊃ t) · (~ q ⊃ s)
       4.   ~ t   / ∴ ~ r v ~ q
       5.
       6.   D.D. 2 & 5
       7.
       8.
       9.   M.T. 8 & 4
    10.
    11.   Addition 10

(c)   1.   p ⊃ q
       2.   r ⊃ ~ s
       3.   t ⊃ s
       4.   u ⊃ ~ q
       5.   u v r / ∴ p v ~ t

IV.   Using any of the Rules 1-5 of Replacement and any of the
       Rules of Inference provide justifications for the lines of
       proof (a), complete proof (b) and provide a proof of the
       validity of argument (c).

(a)   1.   (p · q) · (~ r v s)
       2.   ~ s · (p ⊃ r)   / ∴ s v ~ (p v r)
       3.   (~ r v s) · (p · q)
       4.   ~ r v s
       5.   ~ s
       6.   ~ r
       7.   (p ⊃ r) · ~ s
       8.   p ⊃ r

9. ~ p
10. ~ p v s
11. s v ~ p
12. s v ~ r
13. (s v ~ p) · (s v ~ r)
14. s v (~ p ·~ r)
15. s v ~ (~~ p v ~~ r)
16. s v ~ (p v r)

(b) 1. [s ⊃ (t · r)] · q
2. ~ t v (~ q v ~ r)   / ∴   ~ s
3.   Commutation 2
4. (~ t v ~ r) v ~ q
5.   De Morgan 4
6.   Double Negation 5
7.
8. q   Simplification 7
9.
10.   D.S. 6 & 9
11.
12.

(c) 1. q v (s · t)
2. r · ~ (p v q) / ∴ (~ q v ~ t) ⊃ (~ p v ~ s)

V. Using any of the Rules of Inference and Replacement
provide justifications for the lines of proof (a),
complete proof (b) and provide a proof of the validity
of argument (c).

(a) 1. (p ⊃ q) · (r ⊃ s)   / ∴ (p · r) ⊃ (q · s)
2. p ⊃ q
3. ~ p v q
4. (~ p v q) v ~ r
5. ~ p v (q v ~ r)
6. ~ p v (~ r v q)
7. (~ p v ~ r) v q
8. (r ⊃ s) · (p ⊃ q)

9. r ⊃ s
10. ~ r v s
11. (~ r v s) v ~ p
12. ~ p v (~ r v s)
13. (~ p v ~ r) v s
14. [(~ p v ~ r) v q] · [(~ p v ~ r) v s]
15. (~ p v ~ r) v (q · s)
16. ~ (p · r) v (q · s)
17. (p · r) ⊃ (q · s)

(b)   1. (p ⊃ q) · (r ⊃ s)
        2. (q v s) ⊃ t
        3. ~ t   / ∴ ~ (p v r)
        4.
        5.   De Morgan 4
        6. ~ q   Simplification 5
        7.
        8.
        9.
       10.
       11. r ⊃ s   Simplification 9
       12.
       13.
       14. p · r   Conjunction 8 & 13
       15.

(c)   1. p ⊃ (q v r)
        2. s ⊃ (r v t)
        3. ~ r   / ∴ (~ q · ~ t) ⊃ (~ p · ~ s)

VI. Using the Rule of Conditional Proof provide proofs of the
     validity of arguments:

                II(a); V(a);   V(c).

VII.   Determine the validity or invalidity of the following arguments. Where an argument is valid provide a formal demonstration of its validity

(a)   If either Liverpool or Manchester United reach the cup final then Wolves will not reach it. Either Wolves reach it or Manchester United do. If either Manchester United reach it or Liverpool do not then Spurs will. Liverpool will reach the final. Therefore either Spurs reach it or Manchester United do not.

(b)   If Labour win the election they will introduce more nationalisation. Therefore if they win the election and continue to enjoy the support of the unions then they will introduce more nationalisation.

(c)   If people insist on justice then more will enjoy liberty if criminals are caught. If criminals are caught and more do not enjoy liberty then some malfunction has occurred. If either more enjoy liberty or some malfunction occurs then no-one can blame the system. Therefore if people insist on justice no-one can blame the system.

IN OR OUT:

Relations between Groups

Chapter Eight: Getting Them all Sorted Out

One day the teacher comes into class and asks all the girls to sit on one side near the window, and asks the others to group themselves on the other side, near the door. Like this:

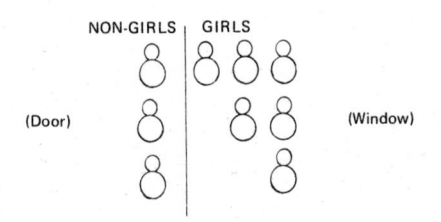

Then he moves to the back everyone who is wearing glasses, and brings the others to the front. He can do this without mixing up the girls with the others again:

It so happens, in this class, that those without glasses are all girls: i.e., that the non-girls all wear glasses. So the bottom left corner of the diagram is empty.

We shall mark an EMPTY compartment with a stick (e.g., a toothpick). This shows that such things (non-girls without glasses) are 'barred' or 'ruled out'. You can read the stick as 'There aren't any...': e.g., 'there aren't any non-girls without glasses in this class'.

This diagram also says that 'All of those without glasses (in this class) are girls'. Which 'stands to reason', as we say. For if none of the non-girls lack glasses, then none of those lacking glasses are non-girls -- so they must be girls!

To show a compartment OCCUPIED, we could go on putting a letter or sign for each of the people or items there. But sometimes that would be inconvenient, or impossible. For example, we might say with confidence that 'Most boys ride bicycles', but there are so many boys that we can hardly put a B for each, and we don't really want the bother of counting them. Again, we know that 'some prime ministers are women'. Is it three, or four? Even if we are not sure of the precise number, we can still say that SOME are. And that may be all we need to say, for purposes of argument. For the present, we shall not bother with the actual numbers. That means treating -

> Many wild flowers are good for medicine

as if it were

> Some wild flowers...

and

> 23 dentists had toothache last week

as if it were

> Some dentists...

and so on.

That is a waste of information, in a way. But if the specific information (How many dentists...?) is not needed for the purposes of argument, then there is little value in symbolizing or repeating it.

Instead of putting letters or signs for individuals, we shall mark an OCCUPIED compartment with one big blob (e.g., a pebble, or a coin). So the previous diagram will now appear like this:

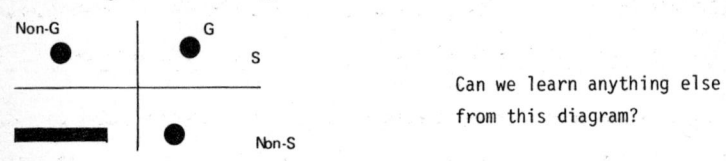

Can we learn anything else from this diagram?

If we look at the left hand side (non-girls) we can see that (i) there are some, and (ii) they are all in the rear (top) compartment, among those wearing spectacles.

So we can say: 'All non-girls (in this class) are bespectacled'.

Again, if you look at the bottom of the diagram, you can see that there are some people in the class without spectacles, and that all of them are girls: 'All those without spectacles are girls'. (Which is not at all the same as 'All the girls are without spectacles' - that is false, according to the diagram).

Please now draw a blank diagram (two lines) onto a fair-sized sheet of loose paper or card; and get together three coins, and three matchsticks (or toothpicks). Then, each time we show a diagram in the book, mark yours to match (G or non-G or whatever), and put in the sticks and coins to show which compartments are EMPTY and which are OCCUPIED. You will find that moving the 'sticks' and 'pennies' around the diagram gives you a quicker grasp of how the whole thing works.

You may think it was silly to keep writing 'non-girls'. Why not just put 'boys'? Well. suppose an adult woman, an inspector of schools, were sitting at the back of the class. She is not, strictly, a girl. and she certainly is not a boy! If you divide the class into 'girls' and 'boys' you would be leaving her out: your division would be incomplete. But if you divide it into 'girls' and 'non-girls' then you must have covered everyone - you needn't even look to see if an inspector is sitting in the class. A true DICHOTOMY (division-into-two) is always into A and non-A, so as to guarantee that it is complete or <u>exhaustive</u>, i.e., that no-one gets left out.

We can of course draw diagrams for other things besides boys and girls and spectacles. For example, someone may say 'No true democrat is against trade unions'. We mark the diagram with TD on the right, and non-TD on the left; and UH (union-haters) at the top, etc. Now the statement is about TD's who are UH; these folk will all be gathered into the top right corner.

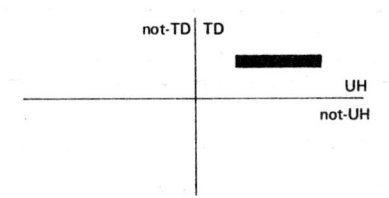

And what the statements <u>says</u> about such folk is: There aren't any. So we lay a stick in that corner, and bar out the possibility of union-hating true-democrats.

Again, if one said 'Some Company Directors are not slim', then keeping Directors to the right, and slim people on top, we shall find our way to the bottom right-hand corner, and put a coin or pebble there; for that corner contains non-slim Directors; and <u>there are some</u>! Or so the statement said.

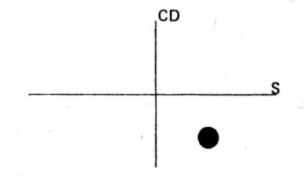

EXAMPLES

On your own diagram show the following state of affairs:

1. Right-thinking people never dance after midnight.

2. Some unborn children have the right to live.

3. Nobody likes to have his jokes not laughed at.

4. Research indicates the occasional occurrence of persons with incomes in excess of £1m. who are not in possession of a motor vehicle.

5. Down with motorways!

6. Oboists do not all like jazz.

7. All the same, some folks are funny.

8. Some like it hot and some do not.

9. I'm not saying anyone's a liar but someone is not telling the truth.

10. All teachers are not graduates.

Chapter Nine: <u>All and None</u>

Every nice girl loves a sailor. So they say.

How do we show this on our diagram? We can put the NG on the right (near the window); and keep sailor-loving people up above. Now the people we have in mind are NGs who are SL; and these people should all be penned up in the top right corner of the diagram. So do we put a stick there? No, that would mean that there aren't any. So do we put a coin, then? That would say that <u>some</u> NG are SL. But we want to say that they <u>all</u> are. So the coin won't do the job, either. Let's try again.

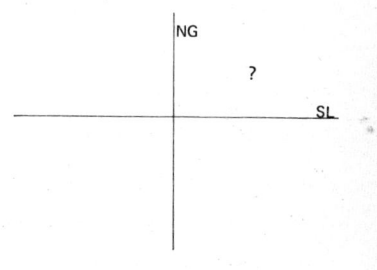

If all NG are SL, that means you can't find an NG who isn't SL: that no NG's are non-SL. And we do know how to diagram this statement: by a stick in the bottom right corner of the diagram.

A statement like 'Every nice girl...' is called <u>Universal</u> because it is about <u>all</u> the NG, not just some of them.

'No true democrat...' is another universal statement, for it is about all the TD (it says that they <u>all</u> are non-UH).

Every universal statement is shown in the diagram by a stick or bar. For 'No true democrat...' the bar is placed in the square TD/UH (top right).

For 'Every nice girl' the bar comes below, to rule out NG being <u>non</u>-SL:
for if no nice girls are non-LS, that means all the nice girls must be SL;
which .is what we meant to say.

<u>EXAMPLES</u>

Mark these statements on your diagram.

1.   All right-thinking people stop dancing before midnight.

2.   Every little counts.

3.   The motion was passed unanimously.

4.   You will never find a clover with four leaves.

5.   Except for the stars, all heavenly bodies are orbiting the Sun.

6.   Knowledge is power.

7.   Nothing is beautiful but truth.

8.   No-one is always happy.

9.   Nothing is good for you if you have too much of it.

10.   All the plays of Shakespeare cannot be read in one day.

Chapter Ten: Does <u>All</u> imply <u>Some</u>?

Some people say that 'Every nice girl loves a sailor' is not quite the
same as 'No nice girl fails to love a sailor' (which is what we represented
in the diagram). For the first statement is positive, it says what the nice
girls are doing: while the second is negative, concentrating on how many
of them fail to do that thing. (How many? None).

To mark this difference, some people want to put a coin in the top right
of the diagram (as well as the bar at bottom right): which means 'and there
are some NG'. And you may think there are some. Maybe I do too. But the
question is, if someone (Bill) says 'Every nice girl loves a sailor', has
Bill <u>said</u> that some girls are nice?

On this question, different people hold quite different views. So what
shall we do about our diagram?

Policy I

We could say that each person should decide this point for himself, with
each 'All-'statement that he comes across. This should keep everyone happy,
and busy, but we shall sometimes be uncertain how to read each others'
diagrams.

Policy II

We all come to an agreement about what to do, and then this is done by
everyone every time they put an All-sentence into a diagram. On this policy,
we shall all know what to do, and what a diagram means, but some may feel
that certain statements are not presented very faithfully.

Almost all students-of-arguments (logicians) favour Policy II, because the results are more predictable. Unfortunately, they are not all agreed which agreement or 'convention' should be made.

Here are two possible conventions:

1. Always put the coin in.
2. Don't.

Until the last century almost all logicians favoured 1. Now most of them favour 2; and this is what we shall follow in this book. I shall give just one reason for it, now.

If you interpret 'Every nice girl...' to mean only 'No nice girls fail to...' (and put a bar at bottom right), then you are free to add, if you like, 'Some girls are nice' (coin, top right). So you can say anything you might want to say, on Convention 2.

On Agreement 1, however, 'Every nice girl...' would already include 'Some girls are nice'. So if you happen to hold that, while all NG are SL, maybe there aren't any NG, you will have some difficulty in showing this on the diagram.

In a diagram, it is easier to say less, and then add more if you want to, than to say more and then start trying to cancel bits of it.

That's my reason for favouring Agreement 2. Other reasons can be found in other books.

(If you prefer 1 very strongly, you could work through the book on that basis, provided that you stuck to it all the time. It would make some difference, but not a lot, to the final results.)

<u>EXAMPLES</u>

Take these statements in turn, and ask yourself:

(a) Would the ordinary man think it had existential import?

(b) If so, what must you add (on our conventions) in order to say what he would take it to say?

1. All fairies are fancy-free.

2. Footballers always wear boots.

3. Policemen are not allowed to strike.

4. Now is the time for all good men to come to the aid of the party.

5. Trespassers will be prosecuted.

6. No-one is always happy.

7. The motion was passed unanimously.

8. No hawkers, no circulars.

9. Passengers must cross the line by the footbridge.

10. All graduates are not teachers.

Chapter Eleven: Two-ended Arguments

We have decided that all sorts of 'All...' statements can be shown by bars (i.e., have no existential import): that 'Most...' and 'Many...' and 'Few...' and '23...' can, for our purposes, be treated just like 'Some...': and that 'Only X are Y' means 'No non-X are Y'. So we can now make a grand simplification: THERE ARE ONLY FOUR TYPES OF STATEMENT left!

Here they are, with a diagram for each, and the code-letter tradition has allotted to each one: -

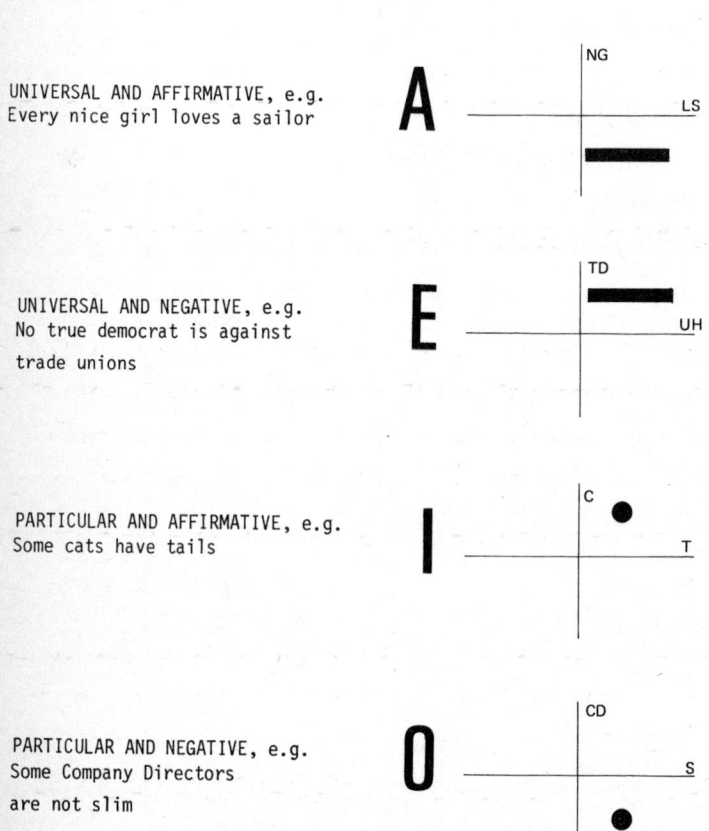

UNIVERSAL AND AFFIRMATIVE, e.g.
Every nice girl loves a sailor

UNIVERSAL AND NEGATIVE, e.g.
No true democrat is against
trade unions

PARTICULAR AND AFFIRMATIVE, e.g.
Some cats have tails

PARTICULAR AND NEGATIVE, e.g.
Some Company Directors
are not slim

As you can see, universal propositions are (all) indicated by a stick or bar, and so have no existential import; while particular propositions are shown by a coin, and do imply existence. 'Some cats have tails' actually says that there are some cats.

You may also notice that the sticks and coins all appear on the right-hand side. What would it mean if one came on the left? Well, this one says that 'some non-cats have tails' (e.g., dogs, tigers and elephants). Now we could always take this as a statement about items called 'non-cats' or 'other animals': in which case it turns into an ordinary I proposition and is shown by a coin at top right. This suggests that we shall not discover any really new types of statement, by looking at the left-hand side.

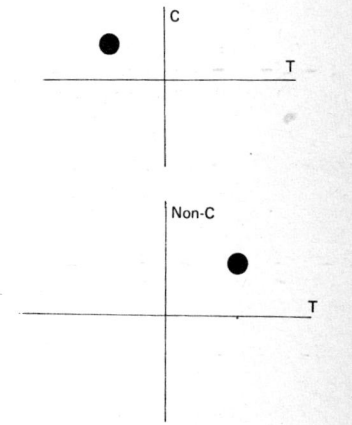

We are now in a position to symbolize, or picture, in our criss-cross diagram, some very simple arguments. After a bit of practice we shall be able to make the diagrams do the arguing for us (so that we ourselves can have a rest). Or, we may ask the diagram-method to check someone else's argument, and see if it is logically sound.

Consider first:

Some pigs are sows

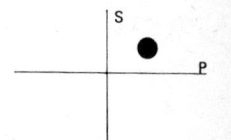

If we rub out or forget the horizontal line this diagram tells us that the part marked 'S' is occupied, i.e., 'There are some S', or 'Sows exist'. If we rub out the vertical line instead, then the same spot now tells us that 'there are P', i.e., 'pigs exist'. So from the I proposition 'some pigs are sows' we can infer two statements about existence: 'Sows exist' and 'there are pigs'.

Some people say that all politicians are rogues. Now suppose we meet an honest politician, called Smith. Smith is an example of a politician who is not a rogue. So the class of non-R.P (non-rogue politicians)

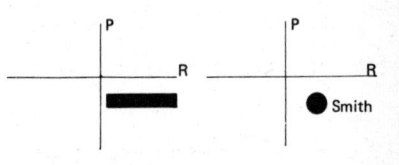

is occupied, and to show this we must put a spot in the bottom right corner. Now, can you have both a bar and a spot in the same space? The bar is a notice saying 'this space is empty'. The spot says 'this space is occupied'. If both notices refer to the same space at the same time, then they cannot both be right. And this gives us our argument:

> If all politicians are rogues
> Then it is not true that Smith is an honest politician

And: If Smith is an honest politician
> Then it cannot be true that all politicians are rogues.

And this time the diagram really did do the arguing for us.

Let us call our two statements DUM ('all politicians...') and DEE.[*] So far we have shown, that if one of these is true, then the other must be false. You may like to work out that, if one of them is false, then the other must be true. Statements which are linked in this see-saw relationship are called 'contradictories'.

---

[*]In Lewis Carroll's book Alice Through the Looking Glass, the two fat boys Tweedledum and Tweedledee are always 'contradicting' each other.

EXAMPLES

A.   Diagram each of these statements and try to draw some inference from it:

1. All sows are pigs.

2. Some pigs are not sows.

3. Smith is a dishonest politician.

4. It is not true that all politicans are rogues.

5. Only rogues are politicians.

B.   Using the diagrams, work out the contradictory of each of the above statements 1-5.

Chapter Twelve: Three-Sided Arguments

Dewi Thomas is a Welshman, so he must be fond of rugby.

Why?

Well, all Welshmen are, pretty well. Everyone knows that.

In this argument, two statements are put together and a conclusion drawn
from both of them:

All W are LR

DT is W
∴ DT is LR

There are three main items in the argument, labelled W, LR and DT. (We call
such items TERMS). Now on a diagram each term will need a line to itself, for it
marks a division: Welshmen from non-Welshmen, lovers of rugby from the rest of
us. So far, our diagram only has two lines (and drawing a diagonal won't help).

One solution is to make the third
line curl around the centre, marking
off everything inside the circle from
everything outside.

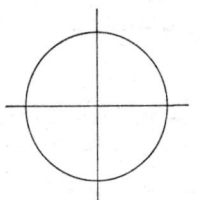

If you study the three statements in that argument you will find that
each term occurs exactly twice in different statements. So there must be
one term (Welshman) which does not come into the conclusion at all, but
only into the other two statements, the starting-points or 'PREMISSES'.
To keep things straight, we shall make it a rule to show this term inside
the circle; so in this case we mark the circle with a W. (This item is
called the 'middle term' because it
comes in between the other two and
links them together).

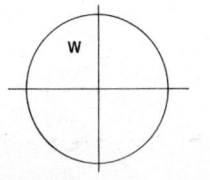

The subject of the conclusion (DT) goes beside the vertical line; the
predicate (LR) goes on the
horizontal one.

If we stick to these rules
we should always know how
to 'read off' our results.

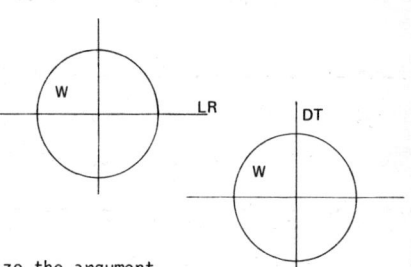

Now at last we can symbolize the argument.

All Welshmen love rugby

The lower half of the circle
is 'barred', i.e. empty (to
rule out Welsh non-lovers).
The bar lies across the
vertical line (to show it
applies to DT and to all
other Welshmen).

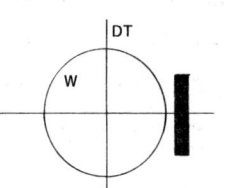

Dewi Thomas is a Welshman

(all of Dewi is inside the
circle, so there is a bar
outside.)

and finally

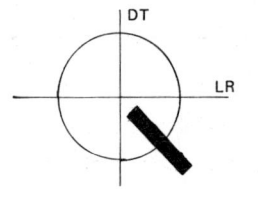

He (DT) must be fond of rugby

('must be' comes to the same
as 'therefore he is'.)

Now comes the test: if we put the first two diagrams together, does that provide the information required for the third diagram? Can you get that answer out of them?

Let us try. The two premisses together tell us that

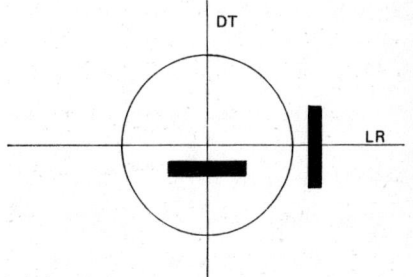

(a) the bottom right-hand corner is completely empty

(b) in the bottom left, the inner part is empty

(c) in the top right, the outer part is empty.

Now our conclusion (that <u>Dewi Thomas loves rugby</u>) simply states, (a) that the bottom right corner is empty. So the two premisses put together do <u>justify</u> you in asserting the conclusion. So the argument is sound and reliable.

EXAMPLES

Diagram the following pairs of statements, and decide from the
diagram what conclusion, if any, can be drawn:

1. All altruists are benevolent, and all the benevolent are
   charitable folk.

2. No bibulous person is a worthy candidate for this exalted
   post. All the applicants are bibulous.

3. All burglars are athletic criminals.

4. All athletes, like all criminals, are burglars.

5. No artists are bishops, or canons either if it comes
   to that.

6. All cannons are guns, and no bishops are canons.

7. All arguments are boring, which criticism never is.

8. No aspidistra is a bathing-machine, and none of these
   is a clavichord.

9. All bicycles are cycles, and all two-wheeled cycles are
   bicycles.

10. Civic dignitaries, like artists, are all bearded.

NOTE: You may overlook the fact that some of these statements are false.

Chapter Thirteen: Barring it all Out

You may have noticed, in the diagrams in Chapter Twelve, that every bar lies across a line. Why is this?

Each bar represents one statement, which connects two terms but not the third Thus 'Dewi Thomas is a Welshman' says nothing about rugby. You can't discover from this statement whether Dewi Thomas is a rugby lover, or not. So the bar representing this statement has to lie across the rugby-lovers' line, barring out items impartially on either side of it. In effect, we have put a bracket into the statement, and made it read:

Dewi Thomas (who may or may not love rugby) is a Welshman.

Then we proceed with the argument, which may well show us what D.T.'s attitude to rugby really is.

You will also find that the two bars which stand for premisses are always at right angles. This results from the rule we made: always to attach the middle term to the circle and the other two to the two straight lines. Now each premiss connects the middle term to one of the others; so the resulting bar will lie across the other straight line. Thus, 'All Welshmen love rugby' relates W (circle) to LR (horizontal line) so the bar lies across the third, vertical line (DT). The bars for the two premisses will thus lie across both straight lines; and so will be at right angles to each other.

Where will the conclusion come? It does not concern the circle (middle term), only the two straight lines. So the conclusion must be shown by a mark in one of the four main quarters (quadrants) of the diagram. But it will not do if the bar just comes into the quadrant, and bars out only part of it.

Consider

Smith likes cheese but not pickles.

'Smith likes cheese' gives
a bar below:

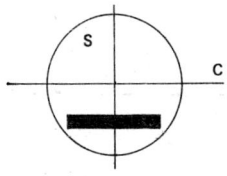

'Smith likes pickles' gives
a bar on the left:

and when these two are combined
they jointly bar out parts of
three quadrants, without any
one quadrant being completely
barred out. In particular,
we cannot conclude that
'there is no-one who likes
pickles but no cheese'
(bottom right), for the
premisses say nothing
about other people's likes
and dislikes, only Smith's
(the 'other people' are
all <u>outside</u> the circle).

Then how are we to get a conclusion? We must see to it that some quadrant is completely barred out. Now each premiss-bar will either be (all) inside the circle, or outside. And part of each quadrant is inside the circle, and part outside. So to bar out the whole of a quadrant we shall need one (premiss) bar inside the circle, and one outside. There is a discovery! Let us write it up on a notice, and remember it:

THEOREM I   Two bars yield a conclusion if, and only if, just one of them lies inside the circle.

EXAMPLES

In 1-5, diagram the pair of statements given, and then use Theorem I to decide whether any conclusion can be drawn from them (you need not say what it is):

1.   All policemen are sensible.
     No M.P's are policemen.

2.   No M.P's are policemen.
     All peers are M.P's.

3.   All policemen are sensible.
     No sensible people are M.P's.

4.   No M.P's are policemen.
     No M.P's are sensible.

5.   All policemen are sensible.
     All M.P's are sensible.

In 6-10, you are given one premiss (P_1) and a conclusion (C). Diagram these (use a dotted line, or different stick, for C), and work out what you would need as second premiss, to prove that conclusion (you can use Theorem I).

6. P_1 All artists are bearded

    P_2

    C   ∴ No artists shave

7. P_1 All burglars are lawbreakers

    P_2

    C   ∴ All burglars are criminals

8. P_1 No aspidistra is a bicycle

    P_2

    C   ∴ No aspidistra is a two-wheeled cycle

9. P_1 All archbishops are bishops

    P_2

    C   ∴ No canons are archbishops

10. P_1 All alcoholics are bleary-eyed

    P_2

    C   ∴ No-one who can read small print is an alcoholic

Chapter Fourteen: Matchpenny Arguments

What happens if one of the premisses is represented by a coin?

(A) All men are mortal

(I) Some mortals are millionaires

(I) So some millionares are men

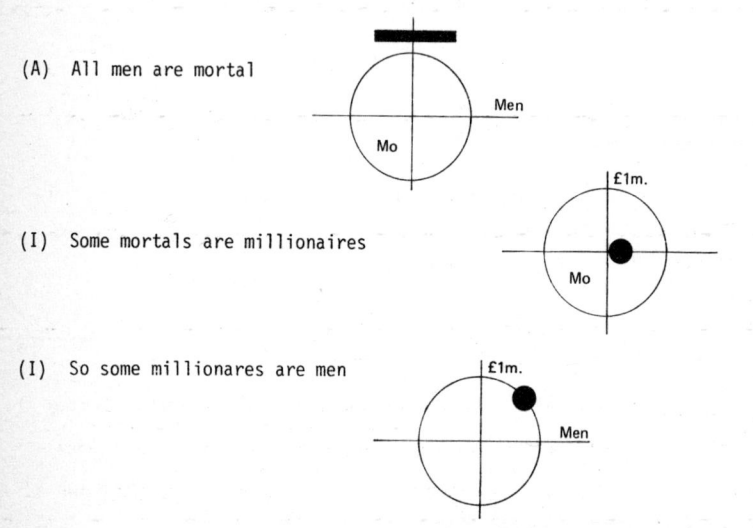

Notice that each coin lies on a line (just as the bars did). But while a bar across a line meant 'both sides of this line are unoccupied', a coin on a line means 'one side or other of this line is occupied'.

Now, the conclusion given above says that some part of the top right quadrant is occupied. Do the premisses show that this is so? The second premiss says that the inner part of either the top right or the bottom right quadrant is occupied. But which? We do not know, and the first premiss does not clear the matter up. So the most we can say is that MAYBE the top right quadrant is occupied, i.e., PERHAPS some millionaires are men. But MAYBE and PERHAPS are just not good enough in arguments. The conclusion has NOT been justified.

Let us try another argument:

(I) Some cows have horns

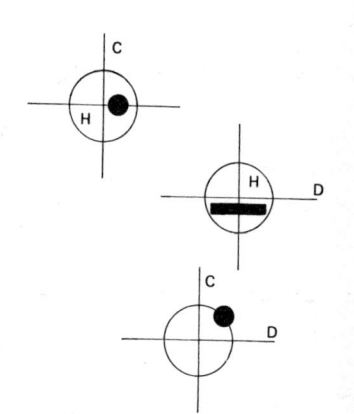

(A) All animals with horns have
     divided hooves

(I) Therefore some cows have
     divided hooves

Here the first premiss gives a coin on the horizontal line, showing
that <u>some part of</u> the right-hand side of the circle is occupied. But the
second premiss gives a bar in the lower half of the circle. So it cannot
be the bottom right part of the circle that is occupied, it must be the top
right (i.e., the cows with horns must be having divided hooves). So the
top right quadrant is definitely occupied, and the conclusion is justified:
some cows have divided hooves.

In this argument, the bar <u>pushed</u> the coin off the line (like 'getting
off the fence', i.e. moving from uncertainty to a definite decision).
And we could make this a rule for matchpenny arguments: that the bar must
push the coin off its line. Now this can happen only if both lie in the
same space.

THEOREM II: A bar and a coin will yield a conclusion if both come inside
the circle, or if both come outside, but not otherwise.

Can two coins yield a conclusion? No, for each will lie on one of
the straight lines, and there will be nothing to push either off.

For example:

Some filmstars are beautiful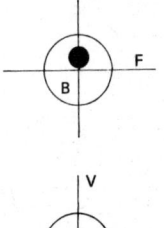

Some beautiful people are vain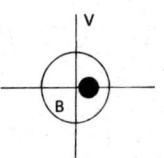

Now it may well be that some filmstars are vain: EITHER because some of those filmstars who are beautiful are vain (the top spot moving off the line to the right) OR because some of the beautiful vain people are film-stars (the lower spot moving upwards off the line). But we don't <u>know</u> that either of these things are so. MAYBE they are. MAYBE they aren't. And MAYBE won't do in the conclusion of an argument.

THEOREM III: Two coins don't lead anywhere.

EXAMPLES

In 1-5, diagram the pair of given statements, and use Theorem II
to decide if any conclusion can be drawn from them.

1. All men are mortal.
   Some men are vain.

2. Some Company Directors are not slim.
   All slim people are healthy.

3. No fairies are graduates.
   Some graduates are teachers.

4. Some folk are fat and some are musical.

5. All butlers wear tail-coats, some unwillingly.

In 6-10, you are given one premiss and a conclusion. Work out,
with the aid of Theorems I and II and a diagram, what you would
need as second premiss, to prove that conclusion (remember:
a coin across a line means that <u>one</u> side of it is occupied.)

6. P_1 Some Company Directors are not slim

   P_2
   ___
   C   ∴ Some Company Directors are not healthy

7. P_1 All wrestlers are fat

   P_2
   ___
   C   Some fat people are not musical

8. P_1 All burglars are agile

   P_2
   ___
   C   Some agile people are criminals

9. P_1 All policemen wear blue uniform

   P_2
   ___
   C   No M.P's are policemen

10. P_1 No M.P's are policemen

    P_2
    ___
    C   Some who bear blue uniform are not M.P's

Chapter Fifteen: <u>Different Diagrams</u>

The English mathematician JOHN VENN devised a three-circle diagram for checking arguments.

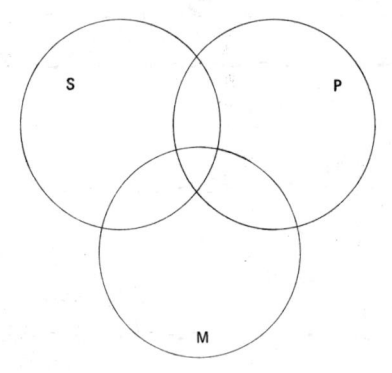

The premisses were represented by shading the parts that stood 'empty', and ticking those that were 'occupied'. The diagram was then inspected to see if the proposed conclusion was already shown by the shading and the ticks.

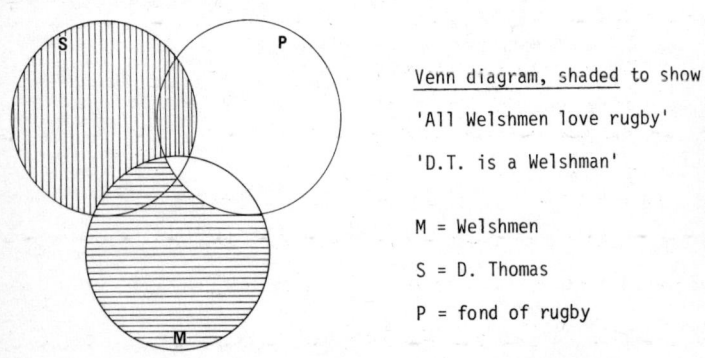

Venn diagram, <u>shaded</u> to show
'All Welshmen love rugby'
'D.T. is a Welshman'

M = Welshmen
S = D. Thomas
P = fond of rugby

The parts of circle S <u>outside</u> circle P are all shaded (= 'empty'), so the premisses prove that 'D.T. loves rugby'.

This method is really just the same as ours. The diagrams can be made to look the same (by making circle M smaller and blowing up the other two). The shading can be replaced by our bar, and the tick by our coin.

The essential point is that each diagram has eight distinct spaces, to represent the eight possible terms in an argument

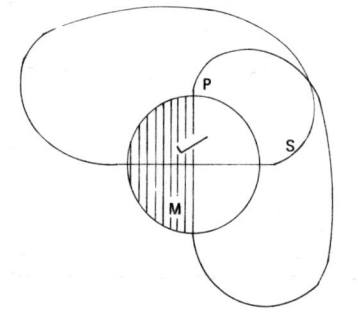

S = cows
P = hoof-dividers
M = horned animals

Venndiagram, squashed to resemble ours, and shaded to show 'Some cows have horns' 'All horned animals divide the hoof

P = hoof-dividers
S = cows
M = horned animals

The shading in circle M cancels part of the tick, so 'some cows' must be in circle P; so it follows that some cows divide the hoof.

Why eight? Well, suppose you had an argument about Saints (or non-Saints, if it comes to that), and Priests (or non-Priests), and Martyrs (or non-Martyrs, as the case may be). There are just eight things that anyone who comes into your argument could be:

1	Sainted Preistly Martyr	S P M
2	Sainted Priestly non-Martyr	S P M´
3	Sainted non-Priestly Martyr	S P´M
4	Sainted non-Priestly non-Martyr	S P´M´
5	non-Sainted Priestly Martyr	S´P M
6	non-Sainted Priestly non-Martyr	S´P M´

7	non-Sainted non-Priestly Martyr	S´P´M
8	non-Sainted non-Priestly non-Martyr	S´P´M´

> (We could write non-M by putting a stroke
> right through the M .., but in print it
> looks clearer as ... M´)

Now a diagram with eight spaces (marked SPM, SPM´... etc.) will cater for
all the people who could possibly come into such an argument. Let us
mark them in, and see where they all come:

Venn Diagram   Our Diagram

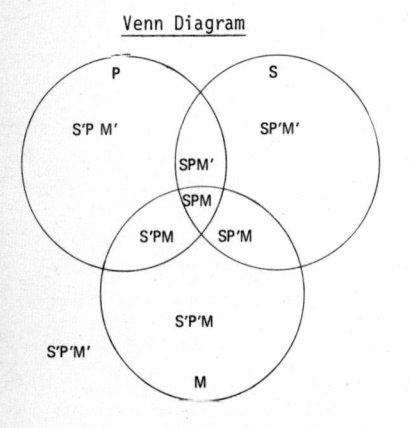

in Venn, the 8th space goes
right round outside

NOTE: Lewis Carroll used a square box, instead of a circle, in the middle
of his diagram. If you read his book, remember that for him 'All fairies
are feminine' actually says that fairies exist: so each A proposition is
shown by a bar AND a spot -- see Chapter Ten above.

EXAMPLES

Draw a Venn diagram to illustrate each of the following pairs of premisses, and work out what conclusions (if any) can be drawn from them:

1. All poets are soft-hearted.
   No matter-of-fact people are poets.

2. No mayors are poachers, but a Lord Mayor is a mayor.

3. Portrait-painters are invariably self-employed, and they can't be employees.

4. No miners are either prelates or saints.

5. Pirates, like admirals, are all sailors.

6. Women are human, no doubt, but some of them are vain.

7. Fat people are jolly, but some shareholders are not fat.

8. Grandmothers -- not a flighty lot at all -- indeed some of them will not touch a drop.

9. Among fliers you will find some fanatical and some morose.

10. Beachcombers are just treasure-hunters, really, but some are unsuccessful in their search.

(Note: one of your given statements connects A with B, the other connects B with C, and you have to work out, if you can, how A is connected to C - that is your 'conclusion'.)

Chapter Sixteen: <u>Argument Codes</u>

We could check an argument by the letters alone, without even looking at the diagram. For instance, consider this argument:

> Policemen must be strong, for they all eat meat, and people
> who eat meat are always strong

The first premiss says that the number of policemen who don't eat meat is zero. So we take our bar (meaning 'empty' or 'none') and put it over those letters: $\overline{M'P}$. This says that there are no vegetarian policemen; neither strong ones, nor any other sort. So in place of $M'P$ we could write $S\ \overline{M'P}.S'\overline{M'P}$ (here the dot between the two lots of letters stands for AND).

The second premiss is treated the same way:

> All meat-eaters are strong, i.e., none are weak, $S'\overline{M}$

> i.e. there are no weak meat-eaters at all, neither $\underline{policemen}$
>   nor peers nor parents nor procrastinators ... $S'\overline{M\ P}.S'\overline{M\ P'}$

Now put the premisses together, and see if we can extract a statement connecting S and P

$$S\ \overline{M'P}.S'\overline{M'P}$$
$$\overline{S'M\ P'}.\overline{S'M\ P}$$

(combining the codes on the right) $S'\overline{P(M.M')}$

Which says that 'no policemen are weak (neither meat-eaters nor any other sort)'. That is, no policemen are weak. $S'\overline{P}$.

To extend this method to a matchpenny argument, we must make some new rules for our code:

(i)   if you write a group of letters (without the bar), it means that
there are some, thus   SP   means

'there are some strong policemen/swindling politicians/stupid
poltroons ... (or whatever it may be)'

(ii)   M/M´ means 'who are either M or M´'.

Now let us try:

> Some patriots are maniacs,   M P
>
> No maniacs are safe companions, $\overline{\text{S M}}$
>
> Therefore some patriots are not
> safe companions.   S´P

Does this follow?   Well, some may be safe companions and some not, among
the patriotic maniacs. So M P = S M P/S´M P. And maniacs are unsafe as
companions, whether they are patriots or not. So S M = S M P.S M P´.

Putting these together, the second   S M P / S´M P

premiss rules out one of the $\overline{\text{S M P}}$. $\overline{\text{S M P´}}$

alternatives, S M P, in the first,
leaving the other, S´M P.

That is, premiss 1 admits, at first, that there may be some safe maniacal
patriots (S M P) but premiss 2 then rules this out. That leaves premiss
1 (not admitting but) asserting that there are some unsafe maniacal patriots.
From this it follows that some patriots are not safe companions.

We can work out rules for this letter-code, corresponding to Theorems I
and II for the diagram.

1.   TWO-BAR ARGUMENTS

    One premiss connects M with P. We expand this by adding (S.S´), i.e.,
'neither those that are S nor those that are not'. In the same way, the
second premiss, about M and S, is expanded by adding (P.P´). Now, to get

a conclusion connecting S with P, we need to pair up two letter-groups which are the same in S and P (e.g., both are SP´), one from each premiss; one of these must have M and the other M´, so that these go into a bracket as alternatives and disappear.

Thus in the one about policemen:

Premiss 1 : $\overline{M}$´P expands to S $\overline{M´P}$. S´$\overline{M´P}$

Premiss 2 : $\overline{S´M}$ expands to S´M $\overline{P´}$. S´M $\overline{P}$

Combine the groups on the right: S´$\overline{M´P}$. S´$\overline{M\ P}$

     Bracket the M's: $\overline{S´P (M.M´)}$

i.e. No policemen are not strong (neither the meat-eaters nor the others)
  = All policemen are strong   S´P

THEOREM I   In a valid two-bar argument:

(i) just one premiss contains M, and one M´

(ii) S must appear the same in both premiss and conclusion; and so must P.

MATCHPENNY ARGUMENTS

Here one premiss provides alternatives, and the other premiss has to rule out one of them. In the one about patriots: -

Premiss 1: M P - maybe safe or not = S M P / S´M P

Premiss 2: S $\overline{M}$ - whether P or not = S M $\overline{P}$. S M $\overline{P´}$

To make this work the M must stay the same.

THEOREM II   In a valid matchpenny argument:

(i)   the M's must either both be primed, or both plain

(ii)   (as in Theorem I).

To my mind the diagram method is easier to begin with, and it helps you to see how two-bar arguments work. The code-method is of course easier to type or print, and it helps you to see how matchpenny arguments work. It also helps you to remember that patriotic maniacs are either safe or not, that safe maniacs are either patriots or not, and that safe patriots must be either maniacs or not, etc., which is the underlying principle of this whole ring-a-ring-a-roses that we call the syllogism.

EXAMPLES

Check by the letter-code method your results for the following examples:

Chapter Fourteen, Nos. 2, 5;

Chapter Fifteen, Nos. 2, 4, 5.

Chapter Fourteen, Nos. 7, 9, 10;

Chapter Fifteen, Nos. 8, 10.

Chapter Seventeen: Going by the Book

People have tried, in the past, to draw up a list of rules which every good argument must obey. It would certainly be handy to have such a list; then if someone puts forward an argument we can easily check if his argument is reliable.

Here is a set of rules designed to produce the same results as our diagrams: -

RULES FOR ARGUING

1.   A syllogism must contain three propositions, and three terms.

2.   At least one premise must be universal.

3.   At least one premise must be affirmative.

4.   If one premise is particular then the conclusion must be so too;
     and if the conclusion is particular then so must one premise be.

5.   If one premise is negative then the conclusion must be so too.

6.   The middle term must be distributed exactly once.

7.   A term distributed in the conclusion must be so in the premisses.

('Distributed' are the subjects of universal propositions, and the predicates of negative propositions.)

Now, if we check an argument against these seven rules, and find it obeys them all, we shall declare it to be VALID: if it disobeys any ONE rule, we call it invalid. This shows that for arguments (as for people) there are different ways of being wrong. Some of these 'fallacies' have special names (just as human failings do: greed, meanness, bullying...).
For example, consider: -

All footballers have two legs

All human beings have two legs

Therefore some footballers are human

This syllogism disobeys rule 6; although the conclusion happens to be true (I think), it does not follow from the premisses. For it might be that the class of two-legged creatures had the footballers all in one corner, and the humans in another, without overlap. In which case the argument <u>would not prove</u> that any footballers were human.

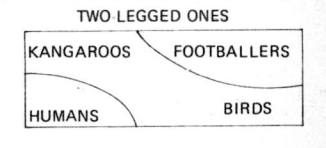

(If you don't like that example, try putting 'birds' in place of 'footballers', and follow the discussion through again.)

An argument which disobeys rule 6 is said to have an UNDISTRIBUTED MIDDLE.

A different fallacy is hidden in this argument:

All mountain people are stocky and good climbers,
so all stocky people are good climbers

Here the conclusion makes a statement about ALL stocky people, though the premisses only mentioned SOME (those who live in mountainous country). So this argument disobeys rule 7: it is said to suffer from ILLICIT PROCESS.

EXAMPLES

Check arguments 1-5 by ALL seven rules:

1. All men are mortal, and some mortally offended people are MP's, so some MP's, at least, must be men.

2. Some men are broad and hairy, therefore some hairy things are broad.

3. Every judge has to be a lawyer, and some lawyers wear wigs, so judges all wear wigs.

4. Some grocers, unlike policemen, wear aprons, so policemen must wear something else.

5. No dogs are cats, or pigs either, therefore no pigs are cats.

6. If you find an argument disobeys one rule, do you need to check it against the other six as well?

In 7-10, construct an argument for the conclusion given, but so as to violate the rule mentioned in brackets:

7. All men are selfish (Rule 4)

8. Some dogs eat meat (Rule 5)

9. All tigers eat rabbits (Rule 6)

10. All lapdogs eat chocolate (Rule 7)

Chapter Eighteen: Who Checks the Rules?

We illustrated the rules by producing arguments which (a) were obviously
bad, and (b) did disobey some rule. But that hardly shows that EVERY argument
which disobeys a rule is invalid; and it does not even suggest than an argument which obeys all seven rules must be a valid one. Of course, that was the
intention of the man who made the rules! But was he successful? Do the seven
rules single out ALL and ONLY those arguments whose conclusions really do
follow from their premisses?

We can give no general answer to that question at this stage. But we can,
of course, re-check by some other method any argument which we have checked
against the rules. Let us take
the one about footballers and
draw a matchpenny diagram: the
two bars neither evacuate nor
occupy any whole quadrant so no

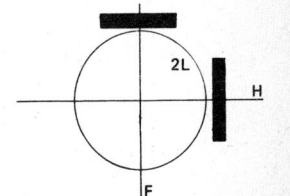

conclusion can be drawn. (This example shows, by the way, that the rule about
where the bars come has something to do with distribution.) If we now accept
that the argument is invalid (because of what we saw on the diagram), then we
are really relying on the diagram as the first test, and are using the rules
just to get an indication when we should refer to the diagram. If so, we
should use the rules only if they are much quicker and easier. If they are
not, it will be best to go straight to the diagram.

Another checking procedure is available. First we make a list of all the
valid TYPES of argument, then we make up some jingle or catch-phrase to help
us remember this list. Finally we check any given argument against the jingle

to see if it is of a type listed as valid. That sounds more trouble than it is worth, but it does actually work: firstly because others have done most of the work for us, long ago; and secondly because the list of types of valid argument is reasonably short.

We saw earlier that all statements or propositions could be regarded as belonging to one or another of four types, A (universal and affirmative), E (universal and negative), I (particular and affirmative) and O (particular and negative).
To remember these, put them on a double-division diagram (those diagonally opposite are contra-dictories).

Affirmative   Negative

A | **E**

I | **O**

Universal
Particular

So a particular type of argument can be shown by writing down three letters: two for the premisses, and then one for the conclusion. Thus the example about footballers is of type AAI. This is called a MOOD of the syllogism.

This little symbol, however, does not tell you quite enough, for 'All footballers have two legs' is rather different from 'All two-legged persons play football': yet the 'A' says only that it is one or other of these two. Fortunately, there are only four such arrangements, or FIGURES, in a syllogistic argument.

Taking the conclusion as fixed (S - P), we put the premiss containing P (the MAJOR premiss) on top (i.e., first); and the MINOR premiss, containing S, under iv.   Then we study the pattern made by the middle term (which comes twice, once in each premiss). There are four possibilities:

I	II	III	IV
M - P	P - M	M - P	P - M
S - M	S - M	M - S	M - S

(To remember the official numbering, think of the dotted lines as a ship - or as a jumper going through a polevault.)

Now, we have three propositions, each of which may be A or E or I or O: that makes 64 different possible moods. Each of these can come in any one of the four figures (depending on the arrangement of the terms), so altogether there are 256 different types of syllogistic argument. Fortunately for us, most of these are invalid! The traditional list of valid moods contained 19 items (sometimes 24), and these were set out in a jingle, Latin in parts, and referred to by its first two words:

I.   bArbArA cElArEnt dArII fErIOque prioris;

II.   cEsArE cAmEstrEs fEstInO bArOkO secundae;

III. tertia dArAptI dIsAmIs dAtIsI fElAptOn
      bOkArdO fErIsOn habet: quarta insuper addit:

IV.   brAmAntIp cAmEnEs dImArIs fEsApO frEsIsOn.

      (Vowels standing for proposition-types have been
       put in capitals).

      For an English jingle, see p.154.

To check a syllogism you see what sorts of proposition it contains (A.E.I.O., thus giving the mood) and where the middle term comes (figure); then you look under that figure, in the rhyme, to see if that mood occurs in any of the words. Thus the example about footballers is AAI in II, but no AAI word comes in the second line: so this syllogism is not a valid one (according to our list).

EXAMPLES

In arguments 1-5, work out the mood and figure, and then see if that type of argument is listed as valid in the rhyme. If so, give the code-word from the rhyme.

1. All usherettes are prim and sweet, so some prim people are sweet.

2. All usherettes are prim and some are sweet, so some prim people are sweet.

3. Any donkey can get through our front door but no camel can, so no donkeys are camels.

4. Any donkey can get through our front door, and no camel is a donkey, so no camel can get through our front door.

5. All perfect pianists are monks and all monks are serious, so some serious people are perfect pianists.

In examples 6-10 construct a syllogism in the mood mentioned, for the conclusion given:

6. Sportsmen are invariably fit and healthy (Barbara)

7. No St Bernard is a lapdog (Celarent)

8. Not every politician is a Member of Parliament (Baroko)

9. Some dogs are not fond of children (Ferison)

10. Some sailors are drunkards (Disamis)

Chapter Nineteen: Doing Without Fairies

Must there be some fairies, to do whatever it is that fairies do?

On the convention adopted in this book, universal statements carry no suggestion that their subjects actually exist:

> All fairies are flighty
>
> All trespassers will be prosecuted
>
> All persons more than a mile high must leave the court

These are taken to mean:

> All fairies (if such there be) ...
>
> All trespassers (if any) ....
>
>   and so on

That is why we represented an A (or E) proposition by a single bar or stick in the diagram. We did not use a stone or coin as well. (See Ch. IV).

Now the people who picked out the 19 valid moods (from 256), and who gave them names in that jingle, did all their working by the other convention. They held that 'All fairies are flighty' actually _says_ that there are some fairies: and if they had used our diagram they would have put a coin (as well as a bar) in representing it.

On their view, then, you could move from

	All fairies eat cheese	A
to	Some fairies eat cheese	I
and from	No leprechauns are married	E
to	Some leprechauns are not married	O ;

inferences which would be invalid on the conventions adopted in this book.

The result was that those people recognized as valid some types of argument which, on our convention, must be treated as <u>in</u>valid. Let us draw a diagram for one of our examples (XII. 5).

All perfect pianists are monks
All monks are serious
∴ Some serious people are perfect pianists

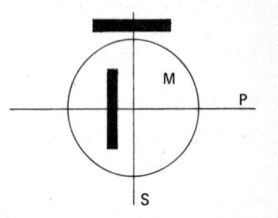

What those premisses prove is that no non-serious people are perfect pianists, i.e., all perfect pianists are serious. They do <u>not</u> show, as claimed, that some serious people are perfect pianists (which would require a coin at top right).

Which syllogisms are valid on their convention, but not on ours? Look at Darapti (III), Felapton (III) and Fesapo (IV), and Bramantip (IV); these all have two universal premisses and a particular conclusion, as do five more not listed in the code. (See our rule 4, which was specially drafted to exclude these moods.)

Darapti, Felapton and Fesapo are also peculiar in having the middle term distributed twice. With them eliminated we can write rule 6 in its new (amended) form: '... distributed exactly once'.

What do these arguments lack that makes them invalid? They lack a clear statement that so-and-so really do exist. If you supplement Darapti, Felapton or Fesapo with the extra premiss 'There are m' you obtain a valid argument (though not a syllogism, which can only have <u>two</u> premisses). In the same way, Bramantip needs supplementing by the extra premise 'There are p'.

Apart from these four moods, now reckoned invalid (because of a change of convention) the three systems coincide. That is, the same syllogisms are classed as invalid by matchpenny diagrams, by the rule book, and by the doggerel: and the same moods are classed as valid by all three. So we can use any method we please, and still reach the same result; or use one method to check results obtained by another one.

EXAMPLES

Consider whether the following arguments are valid (a) by the conventions adopted in this book and (b) by the alternative convention. (On (a) universal propositions do not imply the existence of the subject; on (b) they do.)

1. Fairies are all spiritual, but not paraboloid, so some spiritual beings are not paraboloid.

2. Fairies are all spiritual, but not paraboloid, so no paraboloids are spiritual beings.

3. All flawless epic poems are written by dunderheads, and things written by dunderheads are not worth reading, so some flawless epic poems are not worth reading.

4. Policemen are all above medium height, i.e., more than 5'6", so some persons more than 5'6" in height are policemen.

5. Sheep are all woolly, which means they won't have long teeth.

6. Wizards, who all wear pointed hats (a sure sign of rascality) are some of them rascals.

In each example found valid by convention (b) but not by convention (a), work out what extra premise would be needed to establish the proposed conclusion.

7. Find the five missing moods, valid on the old convention, but not listed in the code.

Chapter Twenty: Swopping Arguments

Out of 256, the old logicians selected 2**4**, or even 19, as reliable. We
have brought this down to 15. Can these results be further simplified?

It is easy to see that some of the moods are equivalent. Consider:

> All men have deep voices, and some schoolteachers
> are men, so some schoolteachers have deep voices

This is in Darii, figure I. But we could turn the minor premiss round, to
read 'some men are schoolteachers', yielding the same conclusion, but in
Datisi, figure III. In the same way, Cesare (II) can be 'reduced' to
Celarent, while Festino, Ferison and Fresison all boil down to Ferio (or
you could say, Ferio boils down to them).

By juggling of this sort all the other moods can be 'reduced' to those
of the first figure, except for Baroko and Bokardo. In these two cases we
could (if we wanted) establish their conclusions 'indirectly', showing by
means of another syllogism (in Barbara) that the stated conclusion could
not very well be false if the premisses were true. Consider

All politicians are mudslingers	A
Some sensible folk are not mudslingers	O
Therefore some sensible folk are not politicians	O

II

(Baroko)

Now just suppose for a moment that

All sensible folk are politicians	A

(which contradicts the conclusion given). If we combine this with the given major premiss, then by a syllogism in Barbara

All politicians are mudslingers	A
All sensible folk are politicians	A
Thefore all sensible folk are mudslingers	A I

We arrive at a conclusion which contradicts the minor premise of the original syllogism. But _that_ was given as true. Well, then, _this_ (second conclusion) must be false, so its minor premiss must be false. So the original conclusion (which that minor premiss contradicted) must have been true after all. (This rather back-to-front method is called Indirect Proof.)

This shows, that if you were not allowed to use any arguments except those of the first figure, you could still eventually arrive at all the conclusions to which those of the other figures lead: just as, if your hands were tied behind your back, you might still manage to dig the garden with a penknife! But it does not quite show, that all other arguments reduce to those of the first figure.

The moves involved in 'reduction' are easy to follow on the diagram. Consider an argument in Barbara:

All men eat potatoes

All soldiers are men

Therefore all soldiers eat potatoes

Now we could say 'does not abstain from potatoes' instead of 'eats potatoes'. This makes the argument look negative: and moves one stick to another position on the diagram.

No men abstain from potatoes

All soldiers are men

Therefore no soldiers abstain from potatoes

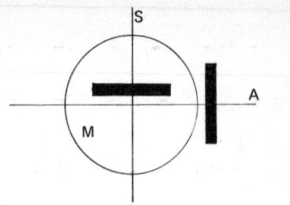

Now we could turn this conclusion around ('convert' it), thus making the major premiss into the minor one:

All soldiers are men

No men abstain from potatoes

Therefore no persons who abstain from potatoes are soldiers

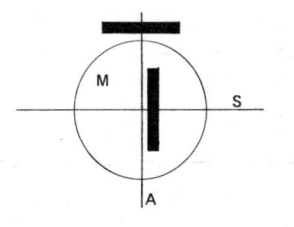

These arguments are all the same, really: they are 'equivalent'. (They look slightly different because of our rigid rules about where to enter the major and minor terms on the diagram.) By changes like this we can work our way around to all five valid moods with two universal premisses (Barbara Celarent Cesare Camenes Camestres); and to all eight two-stick diagrams which have one stick in the circle and one outside.

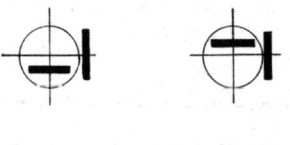

etc

Much the same applies to matchpenny arguments. There are eight which have both inside the circle, representing Darii/Datisi, Dimaris/Disamis, Ferio/Festino/Ferison/Fresison, Bocardo. Then there are eight more with match and penny outside the circle, and one of these bears a traditional name, Baroko. Once again, one can move from one diagram or mood to another, just by swopping terms around or by finding a negative way to express the predicate.

If most of these moods are equivalent (as these correspondences suggest), there can only be two basic types of (syllogistic) argument: two-stick and matchpenny.

EXAMPLES

Construct a syllogism in each of the following moods:

1. Celarent
2. Festino
3. Camenes
4. Dimaris
5. Fresison

Now change your syllogisms as follows, and find the code names for the new syllogisms thus obtained:

1. Convert major premise
2. Convert minor premise
3. Convert conclusion
4. Convert conclusion
5. Convert major premise: replace p by p´ (negative term)

Chapter Twenty One: Two Basic Arguments

I   TWO-STICK   (conclusion and both premisses universal)

Ia S, as all of them are M (all of which are P), are all P.
    e.g., Sailors, being all married men (who, of course, are
    penniless), are therefore all penniless.   Barbara

    Now at last we can see how the argument works! M hands on the S to
P, like a runner in a relay race. He must hand on <u>all</u> the baton, not just
a bit of it: so the bracket must say '(<u>all</u> of which are...)'. That is
why 'the middle term must be distributed' (rule 6).

    If the conclusion is negative, so will one premiss be:

Ib S, as all of them are M (all of which are P´), are all P´.
    e.g., Sports all involve muscular strain (which is never
    free of pain), so they are not free of pain.   Celarent

    If we turn the conclusion around (in Ib) we get another variant:

Ic P being all M (who all are S´) are all of them S´.
    e.g. Padres being all men (who are none of them
    spinsters) are none of them spinsters.   Camestres

II MATCHPENNY   (conclusion, and one premiss, particular)

IIa S, some being M (which are all P) are some of them P.
    e.g. Secret ceremonies, being some of them magical
    (and all magic is perilous) are some of them perilous.   Darii

    Then a negative version of this:

IIb S, some being M (which are all P´) are some of them P´.
    e.g. Saints, of whom some are mothers (who are none
    of them princes) are some of them not princes.   Ferio

(also)   S, some being M´(which are all P´) are some of
        them P´   Baroko

   In both cases we can turn the conclusion around, obtaining: -

IIc (from a) P some being M (who are all S) are some of them S.
IId (from b) P´, some being M (which are all S) are some of them S.

   IIc is Dimaris, IId is Bocardo. See if you can make up examples
to fit: try Patients, Males, Shirt-wearers for IIc
            non-passengers, Moustachioed, Sockwearing for IId

   Thus all sorts of valid syllogism boil down to two simple patterns
of argument, one to establish a particular point, the other more universal
or general.

(I)   TWO-STICK ARGUMENT (Universal conclusion)

(Ia)   S, all being M (which are all P) are therefore all P   (Barbara)

          Variations on this theme

(Ib)   S, all being M (which all are P´) are therefore all P´   (Celarent,
                                                                     Cesare)

(Ic)   P, all being M (which all are S´) are therefore all S´   (Camestres,
                                                                     Camenes)

(II)   MATCHPENNY ARGUMENT (particular conclusion)

(IIa)   S some being M (which all are P) are therefore some
          of them P
                                                                    (Darii
                                                                     Datisi)

          Variations on this theme

(IIb)   S some being M (which all are P´) are therefore   (Ferio
          some of them P´   Festino
                                                                      Ferison
                                                                      Fresison)

(also)	S some being M´ (which all are P´) are therefore some of them P´	(Baroko)
(IIc)	P some being M (which all are S) are therefore some of them S	(Disamis Dimaris)
(IId)	P´ some being M (which all are S) are therefore some of them S	(Bocardo)

An English version of <u>Barbara Celarent</u> (but omitting the moods we regard as invalid, Darapti, Felapton, Fesapo, Bramantip; see Ch. XIII):

Abraham debated his duty, an animist due for a pension;
He had watered his flocks in peace and afoot up there
                          in Bedlinog,
Now bailiffs. Could an invalid live on potato at Meifod?
Mistaking venison for beef, he put mustard for Kathleen.

(There are many better waiting to be writ)

EXAMPLES

Try to rearrange the following arguments into one of the patterns just provided. If you cannot, then test it by a letter-code or a Carroll diagram.

1. It said so in the paper, but the papers all tell lies, so it was a lie.

2. All ignorant people are vain, but no professors are ignorant, so none of them are vain.

3. Eagles can all fly but some pigs cannot, so some pigs are not eagles.

4. All philosophers are logical, an illogical man is always obstinate, so some obstinate people are not philosophers.

5. It was a bad day for Dai Bloggs. He had set off with his team,
   the Whitchurch Wanderers, for a match in Bristol. At St. Mellons
   their minibus packed up. A hasty dash to the station. As they
   passed the barrier, a whistle went on Platform 2. Up the stairs!
   A friendly porter held the door open and they piled in. Crawling
   from underneath the scrum, Dai thought, 'Well we made it at last -
   they're all on the train and its going to Bristol, so they'll get
   to Bristol all right'. As the train jerked forwards, he picked
   his way to the window and saw the goalie and one linesman puffing
   up the stairs. 'Oh, well', he thought, 'they're mostly on the train,
   so they'll mostly get to Bristol as that's where the train is going'.
   Just then he saw the destination indicator: SWINDON and PADDINGTON
   ONLY. 'Looks like its Swindon they'll mostly get to, not Bristol
   after all'. He stood up to review his battered troops, 10 and
   himself, but that linesman had the togs. Oh well, why tell them?
   He wandered down the train to the buffet car, and found linesman
   and goalie enjoying an early beer. That changed things. The
   team was complete, so none of them would get to Bristol for the
   game! He sank into a seat and tried to think of something else.
   Are fairies married? Well, leprechaun's aren't, and all of them
   are fairies, so... He saw a sign saying BRISTOL PARKWAY, leapt
   up, and pulled the communication cord.

   Disentangle five arguments used by Dai, and evaluate.

6. No misers are unselfish and no-one else saves egg-shells,
   a thing, it follows, which unselfish people never do.

7. A song that lasts an hour is tedious, but his songs never do,
   so they aren't.

8. Some thieves get found out, for some dishonest people are,
   and no thief is an honest man.

9. As no mathematician has squared the circle, no-one who has
   achieved that is a mathematician, so they are all non-
   mathematicians. So there is some non-mathematician who
   has squared the circle.

10. Every valid syllogism distributes the middle term once at
    least, as this one does. This syllogism, therefore, is
    a valid one.

Chapter Twenty Two: Mary, Mary ...

We have studied various ways to move from one statement to another, safely and reliably. But sometimes we need to stand still, and give an account of their relationship -- which is not always as easy as it looks.

Given two statements, in what various ways could they possibly be connected, as regards truth and falsity? And if their relation is known, what can we work out, given the truth or falsity of one, about the truth-value of the other one? Let us call our statements p and q: -

SUPPORTIVE STATEMENTS

Suppose first that p and q are along the same lines, and tend to show similar truth-values: that one of them supports the other in some way.

(1)   p being true requires or ensures that q is also true: p IMPLIES q
(for example, p = It was wet all week, q = Wednesday was wet)

(2)   p being false requires or ensures that q is also false: p IS IMPLIED BY q
(for example, p = it rained last week, q = Wednesday was wet)

These two relationships are quite distinct: neither follows from the other one. For 'p implies q' does not require that also 'p is implied by q', i.e. that 'q implies p', though that further relationship is not ruled out. (See the Mad Hatter's Tea Party, in Alice).

(3)   p being true (or false) requires or ensures that q also is
true (or, false, respectively):   p IS EQUIVALENT TO q
(p = it was wet all week, q = not one day was dry).

This third, double relationship combines the other two: here p IMPLIES and IS IMPLIED BY q. They sink or swim together, their truth-values will always

be the same. Equivalence is a 'stronger' (i.e. tighter) relationship
than implication; for 'is equivalent' <u>includes</u> 'implies' <u>and something</u>
<u>more</u> as well.

Given that p implies q, we can of course move from the truth of
p to the truth of q; and so we can also move from the falsity of q to
the falsity of p (for if q had to be true when p was, then p can't have been
if q was not). But there is no valid move starting from the <u>falsity</u> of p.
Arguing from the falsity of the if-bit is called Denying the Antecedent,
and is a common fallacy. Thus from 'If I sleep, I breathe', those who
are awake cannot safely infer that their breathing must have stopped.
But people do make that sort of imprudent inference, because they confuse
an IF with an IF AND ONLY IF, i.e. mistake Implication for Equivalence.

You may object that some implications <u>can</u> be turned around; given
'If today is Tuesday then tomorrow is Wednesday' we may also assert,
without further inspection of the calendar, that 'if tomorrow is Wednesday
then it must be Tuesday today'. But that is because we <u>understated</u> the
actual relationship (like referring to one's twin brother as 'a relative').
To be fully accurate we should have said '<u>if and only if</u> today is Tuesday
...'; and this fuller statement <u>would</u> justify the second inference.
Sometimes people clear it up by saying 'that cuts both ways', when they
are given the weaker relationship, but realise they are dealing with the
stronger one.

The fact remains that you cannot in general and safety argue
from the falsity of p, when given only that p implies q. Implication
is an arrangement for transporting truth, not falsity.

Similar restrictions apply when starting from 'p is implied
by q'. If that is all you are given, then you cannot argue from the
truth of p to the truth of q (fallacy of Affirming the Consequent).

OPPOSED STATEMENTS

Now consider the case of statements which go different ways,
which oppose each other, and tend to take different truth-values in a
given case.

(4)   p being true ensures the falsity of q: p and q are CONTRARY
        (p = today is Tuesday, q = today is Wednesday)

(5)   p being false ensures the truth of q: p and q are SUB-CONTRARY
        (p = some days this week were wet, q = some were fine)

Contrary statements cannot both be true (but may both be false). Sub-
contrary statements cannot both be false (but may both be true). So
these relationships are quite distinct, and neither follows from the
other one. Exclusive Either-Or alternatives are contrary: 'the red
token entitles you to tea or coffee' (but NOT both!). Exhaustive it's-
one-or-the-other alternatives are sub-contrary: 'overseas travel is by
boat or plane'.

(6)   p being true (or false) ensures that   (p = today is Sunday
        q is false   (or true) respectively   q = today is a weekday)

This last, double relationship combines the previous two: if p and q
cannot both be true AND cannot both be false, then they must take
opposite truth-values, and be contradictory. Contradictory statements
are always 'agin' each other, shouting Tisn't-Tis, Tis-Tisn't, like young
children short on points but still arguing; or like a see-saw, one up,

the other down. Contradiction is a stronger, stricter relationship,
and includes the other two.

We often notice that two statements are opposite, without making
clear whether their opposition is contrary or contradictory; and fallacy
can result from treating contraries as contradictories. Thus if today
is Tuesday then it is certainly not Wednesday, but we should not infer
that, if it is not Tuesday, it must be Wednesday that it is. That would
mean treating an exclusive alternative as also an exhaustive one. This
error is common, but has no common name. It could be called the Fallacy
of Missed Alternatives. The opposite error is perhaps less easy to
commit: from 'Jones travelled overseas by plane' few would infer that
he did not also go by boat.

If either statement 'controls' the truth-value of the other, it
must be in one or other of these six ways. If neither controls the
other, if the truth or falsity of one makes no difference at all to the
truth or falsity of the other, then the two statements are said to be
logically 'independent'. Independence of this sort is a special version
of irrelevance. If two statements have nothing to do with each other, and
do not affect each other in any way, we say they are irrelevant.
Independence is irrelevance-as-regards-truth-or-falsity. Thus 'Jane's
father has come home' and 'Jane has gone in to get on with her homework'
are independent, as far as we know, but do not look irrelevant: that is,
we can see some possible connection, but we cannot say that the truth-
value of one actually controls that of the other, in any way.

Each of the six relationships has the effect of excluding some
combination(s) of truth and falsity in the statements it relates:

independence excludes none, but leaves all the options open, all truth-combinations possible.

1. p implies q   means that you CAN'T have   (p true with q false)
2. p is implied by q   "   (p false with q true)
3. p is equivalent to q   "   (p,q taking different values)
4. p is contrary to q   "   (p,q both true)
5. p is sub-contrary to q   "   (p,q both false)
6. p is contradictory to q   "   (p,q taking same value)

Equivalence and Contradiction each exclude two truth-combinations. Independence is really a non-relation, not excluding anything.

It is particularly important to recognise the relations between different statements sharing the same terms; e.g. how does 'some folk like jazz' stand to 'others don't'?

*   *   *   *   *   *

Let us start with 'everyone likes George' (A). This clearly implies that 'some people like George' (I). Moreover the A proposition cannot be true at the same time as 'Nobody likes George' (E); they are incompatible. A is also incompatible with 'Some people do not like George' (O); in addition, these two propositions are strict alternatives: EITHER everyone likes George OR somebody doesn't, there is no third alternative. We thus obtain:

A implies I; A and E are contrary; A and O are contradictory.

Similarly, if we start with 'Nobody approves of Jane' (E), we shall find:

E implies O; E and A are contraries; E and I are contradictories.

Finally, we could start with a particular statement, such as 'some people like spaghetti'. We already know the relation of I to A and to E; but how is our statement related to 'some people do not care for it' (O)? Surely everyone either likes it, or does not, so these alternatives are exhaustive, and cannot both be false. But they can both be true; just because some people like spaghetti that does not hinder others from disliking it. I and O are sub-contraries.

These relations can be added to the diagram on p.130:

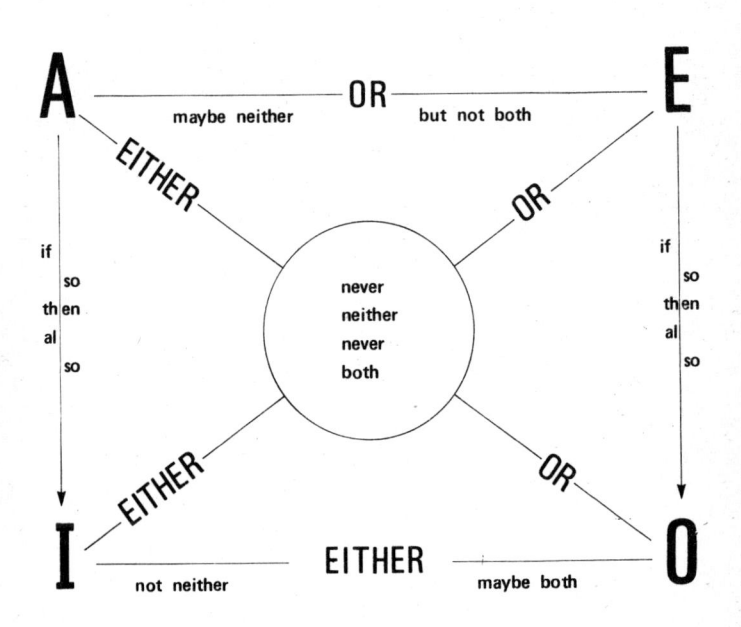

One caution is needed, however, before using this diagram for purposes of inference: most of it will work only on the assumption that there are some members of the subject-class. Consider the statements 'all fairies wear gossamer' (A) and 'No fairies wear gossamer' (E). Some would hold that, in the absence of fairies, both are true, so they are not strictly contraries. Again, some hold that 'All leprechauns have pointed shoes' does not actually commit the speaker to there being some such little men, whereas 'Some leprechauns have ...' is actually asserting that there are. On this convention, clearly, an inference from A to I is unreliable. In fact, all the outside of the diagram will disappear, under these conditions; and only the contradictions will remain. Some logicians wish to abolish the dear old 'Square of Opposition', on these grounds. You may prefer to retain it, and remember the conditions attached to using it: (i) if the subject-term has instances, then it all works, (ii) if not, only contradiction does.

EXAMPLES

1. Devise symbols for use in place of words in the Square of Opposition (e.g. put arrow for 'implies'), distinguishing directional relationships from those which work both ways.

2. Use Carroll diagrams to explain the relations stated in the Square of Opposition. Does the existential assumption it requires figure in your diagrams?

3. Starting from an I proposition, construct
    (a) a contradictory proposition with the same subject and predicate,
    (b) an equivalent proposition,
    (c) a sub-contrary proposition.

4. Find three pairs of relationships, one of which is stronger than and includes the other, and thence make up three understatements, suggesting contexts in which these might amuse or mislead.

5. Try to invent a new relationship between p and q, which excludes two truth-combinations (as contradiction does); or three. How many possibilities are there to investigate?

Chapter Twenty Three : <u>What Can Syllogisms do for us?</u>

At best, a system of logic will help us to see why some arguments are reliable, and some others unreliable. No system can do more than this; e.g. no system can <u>make</u> an argument reliable. Nor can any system do it for <u>all</u> possible arguments.

A system of logic works by classification and comparison. It shows us how to group together arguments which are similar in 'form'; and it then shows how each group of arguments can be assessed for reliability by comparing them with some very simple and obvious argument whose reliability (or otherwise) is very obvious. Both steps involve the assumption that two arguments which are really similar in 'form' -- which are the same <u>as arguments</u> although their terms and topics may be different -- must be equal in reliability, i.e. be both valid, or both invalid. We call this the 'Principle of the Parity of Reasoning'.

Perhaps we should try to assess or justify this Principle? Let us watch it working first:

'You should say what you mean', the March Hare went on.

'I do', Alice hastily replied: 'at least -- at least I mean what I say -- that's the same thing, you know'.

'Not the same thing a bit!' said the Hatter. 'You might just as well say that "I see what I eat" is the same thing as "I eat what I see"!'

'You might just as well say', added the March Hare, that "I like what I get" is the same thing as "I get what I like"!'

'You might just as well say', added the Dormouse, who seemed to be talking in his sleep, 'that "I breathe when I sleep" is the same thing as "I sleep when I breathe"!'

'It <u>is</u> the same thing with you', said the Hatter, and here the conversation dropped. (<u>Alice's Adventures in Wonderland</u>, vii)

These debaters argue 'if you're going to say A then you might as well say B' (as A and B are similar in form). This 'might as well' can work both ways:

(i) positively: 'once grant A, and you'll have to admit B as well'; here B, once dubious, is made acceptable by comparison with A.

(ii) negatively: 'don't grant A, for then you will be forced to admit B as well (though B is obviously wrong). The Hare and the Hatter were using this negative approach.

Our very first steps in logic (or in arithmetic) involve an appeal to this 'principle' of the Parity of Reasoning -- though we may not have said so, or even realized it, at the time. So there is not much hope of justifying it (showing it to be sound) by appeal to some logical principle that is even more basic and fundamental. The most we can do is to recognize that this is how we always work, in trying to assess and adjust our reasonings: that 'sauce for the goose is sauce for the gander too', when arguing. Logic just grows by seeing how 'Similar arguments must have equal force'; and that is that. (Our use of diagrams and codes also depends on this basic principle of logical comparison.)

The syllogism, then, offers us a system for showing some arguments valid, and others invalid, by tracing them back through logical comparison to other 'standard' arguments whose validity (or otherwise) is very obvious and is universally agreed.

Which arguments does the system of the syllogism deal with?

Syllogisms are arguments about groups of things: either to show indirectly that a certain item must (or cannot) belong to a given group; or to show that the whole of one group is included in a certain given group (or, cannot belong to it). The argument brings out the relations of inclusion between the groups of items referred to by its terms: e.g. the items called 'men' are all included in the class or group of 'mortal things', so we say 'All men are mortal'. The argument proceeds from these group-relations, as stated in the premisses, (not from relations between statements, as in Chapters 2-7 and 22).

The simplest such argument is an 'Immediate Inference'; here the conclusion is drawn from a single premiss, which it re-states or partially repeats. All other inference is called 'mediate', a difficult word to say distinctly (use 'indirect' instead). In the simplest indirect inference, the conclusion is drawn from two premisses, e.g. in a syllogism. Here the main task is to re-arrange the information given in the premisses, in the hope of extracting the conclusion desired. The test of validity could be stated thus: is the information which the conclusion offers contained in that which is provided by the premisses?

There are of course more complex forms of mediate inference, with three, four, five ... premisses. Sometimes these can be 'reduced' to a chain of simpler arguments:

Given: 1. Babies are illogical
        2. No-one is despised who can manage a crocodile
        3. Illogical persons are despised,

we can reach the conclusion 'Babies cannot manage crocodiles' by first concluding that 'all babies are despised' (from 1 and 2) and then combining this with 3 in a second syllogism.

Such a 'sorites' or 'heap of arguments' involves no new principle, provided it can be analysed into a chain of syllogisms.

The system of the syllogism was also extended to cater for 'if-then' and 'either-or' premisses (see Chapter 4).

There remain several types of valid deductive argument whose validity does not become more evident by reducing them to syllogistic form. Many such were examined in Chapters 2 to 7. In addition, there are arguments from comparison: 'John must be taller than Mary, being taller than James who stands head and shoulders above her'. There are also arguments about interlocking membership: 'Seven of the football clubs' ten members also belong to the cricket club, and six of them are on the PCC, so at least three PCC members are in the cricket club'. This is easily checked on a Venn diagram, but not easily re-stated in a syllogism.

Syllogisms, though very useful, and applicable to a great many everyday reasonings, do not enable us to assess for validity all forms of deductive argument.

TWO FOR THE PRICE OF ONE:

A Wider Theory

Chapter Twenty Four : <u>Arguments about Things in General</u>

<u>Outline</u>:

I   <u>What are Quantifiers?</u>

In this chapter we shall be thinking about arguments which employ the general terms 'all' and 'some'. You have already considered many arguments of this sort in your study of syllogisms. In this section we shall learn to use the symbols for these terms which we call 'quantifiers'. The use of these symbols and the rules which attach to them have considerable advantages over the symbolisation and analysis contained in Aristotle's system of logic. We shall study these advantages in our next chapter. But first let us see what these new symbols are and how we employ them to construct well-formed-formulae.

You will remember what a subject-predicate proposition is. It is a proposition where a property is ascribed to an individual, as in the example: Susan is pretty. We shall adopt the practice of using lower case (a...w) letters to stand for individuals (which may be human or otherwise, of course). Thus we could use s to stand for Susan. We shall use capital letters to stand for the properties ascribed to individuals. These property symbols will always precede the symbol for the individual. Thus the full symbolic expression of our example will be: Ps.

We could show the form or shape of this expression by means of a dash as follows: P_, but in line with our earlier practice we shall use x as the place-minder. Thus we get Px as the form of the expression. We could make the form even more general by using a place-minder for the space occupied by the property P. The Greek letters ϕ and ψ are used for this purpose. Thus we get the general form ϕx.

Thus 'Susan is pretty and intelligent' would be symbolised as: Ps.Is, whereas 'John is handsome and athletic' would be symbolised as: Hj.Aj. However, they would enjoy the same form, namely: $\phi x.\psi x$.

On the other hand the proposition 'Susan is pretty and John is handsome' would be symbolised as: Ps.Hj, and would be of the form: $\phi x.\psi y$.

1) Symbolise the following propositions. Then proceed to symbolise their logical form.

(a) The Prime Minister is both hardworking and famous.

(b) The jug is full but the bottle is empty.

(c) Either June is a hot month or it is wet and miserable.

(d) If rugby is a gentle game then the moon is made of cheese.

(e) If the Labour candidate is popular then the SDP candidate is neither optimistic nor popular.

We are now ready to introduce the general terms 'all' and 'some'. The Universal Quantifier is used to symbolise the term 'all'. It is written as (x) and can be read as: for all x. Thus if we wish to symbolise the proposition 'Everything is a gift' we would write (x)Gx; which reads, For all x, x has the property of being a gift. In other words, All things are gifts.

Now though we said that Gx would not be a proposition but rather the form of a proposition, (x)Gx is a proposition. Thus there are two ways of making a propositional form or function into a proposition. The first is to substitute specific instances for the place minders in the expression as with φx which became Ps in our example 'Susan is pretty'. The second is to quantify each of the variables in the x,y position to form a general proposition as in the example we have just completed, 'All things are gifts', where Gx became (x)Gx.

You now have enough equipment to symbolise the A and E propositions which played such an important part in the theory of the syllogism. You will remember that they were of the form: All S is P, and No S is P. Using the Universal Quantifier we can write the A proposition as follows:

$$(x)(Sx \supset Px)$$

How do you think we could represent the E proposition? Try to do this before reading on.

You might have been tempted to simply negate the A proposition as follows:

$$\sim(x)(Sx \supset Px)$$

This would not reflect the meaning of the E proposition however, because it would allow the possibility that some S's were P's. Rather the negation sign must be placed elsewhere as follows:

$$(x)(Sx \supset \sim Px)$$

This reveals that if anything is S then it is not also P.

2)   Symbolise the following propositions:

     (a) All cows eat grass.

     (b) No cows are bipeds.

     (c) Whenever cows are black and white they are Jerseys.

     (d) It is not the case that any cow is a member of the canine family.

     (e) No bipeds nor canines are cows.

The Existential Quantifier is used to signify the term 'some'. It is written as: $(\exists x)$ and can be read as: There is at least one x. Thus if we wish to symbolise the proposition 'Some things are precious' we would write $(\exists x)Px$; which reads, There is at least one x such that x is precious.

Given this piece of symbolism we are ready to formulate expressions for the I and O propositions encountered in our study of the syllogism. Remember that the I proposition is of the form: Some S is P, and the O proposition is of the form: Some S is not P.

How would you symbolise the I form? Be careful not to write the following:

$$(\exists x)(Sx \supset Px)$$

This expression does not convey the message of the I proposition. If you think about it you will see that it claims that there is at least one thing such that if it is an S then it is a P. By substituting actual properties in the S and P positions the error of the symbolisation should become clear.

Consider the example: Some above-average scholars are Tibetans.
According to the above symbolisation of the form of the I proposition
this example would be represented as:

$$(\exists x)(Ax \supset Tx)$$

But this means: There is at least one thing such that if it is an above-
average scholar then it is also Tibetan. Two situations only could make
this false. First the situation where there were no things, which is
manifestly not the case. Second, the situation where everything was an
above average scholar and nothing was Tibetan, which is impossible as
the notion of being above-average suggests that some things must be
other than above average. The proposition symbolised becomes trivially
true, that is it claims very little because it rules very little out,
if anything at all. But the proposition:

Some above-average scholars are Tibetans

is not trivially true. We know how to find out whether it is true or
false. It makes a real claim. We must therefore symbolise it differently.
It is correctly symbolised as follows:

$$(\exists x)(Ax.Tx)$$ which reads:

There is at least   one individual which is an above-average scholar
and that individual is also Tibetan.

You will not find it difficult to see that the O proposition is
symbolised as:

$$(\exists x)(Ax. \sim Tx)$$

which reads: There is something which is both an above-average scholar
and not Tibetan.

3)   Symbolise the following propositions using the Existential Quantifier:

    (a) Some apples are rosy.

    (b) It is not the case that some rosy things are apples.

    (c) Some rosy things are not apples.

    (d) Some rosy things are apples whilst some are not.

    (e) Some apples are rosy and sweet.

Relations between Quantifiers

Before we move on to examine the Rules of Quantification we need to
note that propositions containing the general term 'all' can be symbolised
by means of the Existential Quantifier and propositions containing the
general term 'some' can be symbolised by means of the Universal Quantifier.

If you look again at examples 2d and 3b this should become clear.
Though we have the word 'any' appearing in 2d you might find it natural
to express the proposition as:

$$\sim (\exists x)(Cx.Dx) \quad \text{where Dx means x is a canine.}$$

If you correctly symbolised it in the exercise designed to test
your grasp of the Universal Quantifier however, you will have written:

$$(x)(Cx \supset \sim Dx)$$

You may remember making similar moves when mapping out propositions in
the 'All and None' Chapter by means of bars. There All S's are P's was
transformed into, There is not one S that is also a non-P.

We can list the relations of this sort between Universal and Existential Quantifiers as follows:

$$[(x)\phi x] \equiv [\sim(\exists x)\sim\phi x]$$
$$[(\exists x)\phi x] \equiv [\sim(x)\sim\phi x]$$
$$[(x)\sim\phi x] \equiv [\sim(\exists x)\phi x]$$
$$[(\exists x)\sim\phi x] \equiv [\sim(x)\phi x]$$

4) Symbolise each of the following propositions by means of Universal and Existential Quantifiers:

(a) No giants are dwarves.

(b) Some angels blow trumpets.

(c) Giants are never delicate nor pretty.

(d) Some giants overeat.

(e) It is not true that giants are never considerate.

II   Rules of Quantification

These rules will enable us to prove the validity of arguments whose goodness depends upon the occurrence of the terms 'all' and 'some' in them. Within this class of argument lie the syllogisms with which you have already learned to deal in the traditional way. The Rules of Quantification extend the Rules of Inference and Replacement introduced in Chapters 4 and 5. As a result, the propositions which would otherwise resist the application of the earlier rules can be transformed and be seen to take their place in the context of truth-functional logic. More will be said about this extension in the next chapter.

First let us identify these new rules.

Two of them attach to the Universal Quantifier and two to the Existential Quantifier.

They are called: Universal Instantiation
Universal Generalisation
Existential Instantiation
Eixstential Generalisation

Universal Instantiation

The nature and value of this rule can best be grasped by considering a typical proof of validity of an argument involving quantifiers.

1. All who are ambitious are hardworking.

2. All hardworkers succeed.

Therefore all who are ambitious succeed.

Now it is clearly a valid argument. Yet we cannot demonstrate it to be so by means of the Rules of Inference and Replacement alone. This is because the propositions making it up are not truth-functionally related, each being non-compound.

To symbolise it without using quantifiers would be quite unsatisfactory producing the form: p

q / ∴ r

Now it is clear that (p·q) ⊃ r is not a tautology. Thus it might appear that the argument is not valid.

Then how can the Rule of Universal Instantiation help us?

Look at the first premiss. If it is true without restriction that everyone who is ambitious is hardworking, then it is true of absolutely anyone that

if he or she is ambitious then he or she is hardworking. For example,
it would be true of me, Margaret Thatcher, Mohammed Ali or anyone else
you cared to name. We might express this by writing:

$(x)(Ax \supset Hx)$ therefore $Ad \supset Hd$ and $At \supset Ht$ and $Aa \supset Ha$.

By employing just one of these instantiations in our proof we can provide
a demonstration of the validity of the argument in the following way:

1. $(x)(Ax \supset Hx)$

2. $(x)(Hx \supset Sx)$ $\therefore$ $(x)(Ax \supset Sx)$

3. $Ad \supset Hd$ Universal Instantiation 1.

4. $Hd \supset Sd$ Universal Instantiation 2.

5. $Ad \supset Sd$ Hypothetical Syllogism 3 and 4.

6. $(x)(Ax \supset Sx)$ Universal Generalisation 5.

We shall consider the move made in line 6 in a moment. But first
note the moves made in lines 3 and 4. Line 3 involves the move I described
a moment ago. If the general premiss is true then it is true of me, Don,
as representative of any individual. As the second premiss also expresses
a universal truth it is equally true of me. That is, I am entitled to pick
out the same individual of whom it is true as I selected in line 3.
The result is that in lines 3 and 4 I have the kind of complex propositions,
truth-functionally related, with which we learned to deal when we earlier
mastered the Rules of Inference and Replacement.

Now consider line 6 and the second Rule of Quantification, namely,

Universal Generalisation

This rule permits us to move from an assertion about a particular case to a general assertion. In our example the move was:

$$Ad \supset Sd \quad \therefore \quad (x)(Ax \supset Sx)$$

You may well suspect that there is something wrong with such a move. For example, we would not be entitled to move from the assertion that Mrs. Thatcher is red-haired, to the assertion that Everyone is red-haired. That would commit the fallacy of Hasty Generalisation, as you will learn later. Then why are we entitled to make the move in line 6 of the above proof?

The answer to this question lies in the context in which the move was made. It was made in the context of a demonstration where we had already _arbitrarily_ chosen an individual, d, of whom the premises were true. We were then able to conclude of this individual that if he was ambitious then he would be successful. But as he was arbitrarily chosen this would be equally true of Margaret Thatcher, Mohammed Ali or absolutely anyone else we had cared to mention. In other words, it would be true of everybody; which is what the rule states.

5) Give reasons for each step of the following proofs of validity. (These reasons will be drawn from the Rules of Inference and Replacement introduced in Chapters 4 and 5, and the Rules of Quantification.)

a)
1. $(x)[Ax \supset (Bx.Cx)]$
2. $(x)Ax$ /∴ $(x)Cx$
3. $Aa \supset (Ba.Ca)$_____
4. Aa_____
5. $Ba.Ca$_____
6. $Ca.Ba$_____
7. Ca_____
8. $(x)Cx$_____

b)
1. $(x)(Bx \supset Cx)$
2. $(x)(\sim Cx \lor \sim Dx)$
3. $(x)(Dx)$ /∴ $(x)\sim Bx$
4. $Ba \supset Ca$_____
5. $\sim Ca \lor \sim Da$_____
6. Da_____
7. $\sim\sim Da$_____
8. $\sim Ca$_____
9. $\sim Ba$_____
10. $(x)\sim Bx$_____

c) 1. (x)(Ax ⊃ Bx)
    2. (x)[Cx ⊃ (Ax.~Bx)]
    3. (x)(Dx ⊃ Cx)   /∴ (x)~Dx
    4. Aa ⊃ Ba_____
    5. ~Aa v Ba
    6. ~~(~Aa v Ba)_____
    7. ~(~~Aa.~Ba)_____
    8. ~(Aa.~Ba)_____
    9. Ca ⊃ (Aa.~Ba)_____
   10. ~Ca_____
   11. Da ⊃ Ca_____
   12. ~Da_____
   13. (x)~Dx_____

d) 1. (x)[Ax ⊃ (Bx v Cx)]
    2. (x)[(Bx ⊃ Ex).(Cx ⊃ Fx)|
    3. (x)Ax   /∴ (x)(~Ex ⊃ Fx)
    4. Aa ⊃ (Ba v Ca)_____
    5. Aa_____
    6. Ba v Ca_____
    7. (Ba ⊃ Ea).(Ca ⊃ Fa)_____
    8. Ea v Fa_____
    9. ~~Ea v Fa_____
   10. ~Ea ⊃ Fa_____
   11. (x)(~Ex ⊃ Fx)_____

Existential Instantiation

Remember that the Existential Quantifier is used for the general term _Some_. The rule with which we are now concerned enables us to transform propositions beginning with an existential quantifier into a form with which we can deal with our Rules of Inference and Replacement. There is a crucial difference in the manner of selection of the individual when this rule is applied. Quite clearly not absolutely any individual will do, as in the case of Universal Instantiation, as the particular nature of 'some' propositions introduces a restriction. As 'some' restricts our attention to part of a class of things we are not entitled to assume that the individual we choose is the same as any other individual already mentioned in the context of the argument. Consider the following example:

1. Mr. Callaghan was once Prime Minister.

2. _Some Prime Ministers are female._

   Therefore Mr. Callaghan is female.

Such an argument is clearly invalid. We are not entitled to conclude that the individual already named as a Prime Minister is part of the sub-class denoted by the terms 'Some Prime Ministers' in the second premiss.

For the same reason we cannot assume that any individual already named in the previous lines of a demonstration is an instantiation of an existentially quantified premiss. It is therefore important to remember that if you are going to apply this rule anywhere in a proof you do it before Universally Instantiating with respect to any given individual. If you bear this qualification in mind then the rule can simply be expressed in the form:

$$(\exists x)\phi x \quad \therefore \quad \phi a$$

Consider the following demonstration:

1. $(x)[(Ax \lor Bx) \supset Cx]$
2. $(\exists x)\sim Cx \qquad \qquad /\therefore(\exists x)(\sim Ax.\sim Bx)$
3. $\sim Ca$ _____ E.I. 2 _____
4. $(Aa \lor Ba) \supset Ca$ ___ U.I. 1 _____
5. $\sim(Aa \lor Ba)$ ___ Modus Tollens 4,3 ___
6. $\sim Aa.\sim Ba$ _____ De Morgan 5 _____
7. $(\exists x)(\sim Ax.\sim Bx)$ ___ E.G. 6 _____

Line 3 correctly applies the rule of E.I. because the individual a has not been named previously in the proof.

Line 4 applies the rule of U.I. to premiss 1 with respect to the same individual a. We are entitled to do this as the generalisation in this premiss is universal, meaning that we can arbitrarily select any individual as an instantiation. As the individual which already interests us is a then we choose it again producing a truth-functional relation between lines 3 and 4.

So we come to line 7 and the final Rule of Quantification, namely, Existential Generalisation.

This rule states that: Aa $\therefore$ $(\exists x)Ax$

This is probably the easiest of all the rules of quantification to understand for a proposition like $(\exists x)Ax$ is true when any substitution instance of it is true, for it claims that it is true of at least one individual that it has the property A. Therefore if a or indeed any other individual has the property A the general proposition is true.

6)   Provide justifications for each line of the following proofs:

a)
1. $(x)[Ax \supset (Bx.Cx)]$
2. $(\exists x)\sim Bx$ $/\therefore$ $(\exists x)\sim Ax$
3. $\sim Ba$_____
4. $Aa \supset (Ba.Ca)$_____
5. $\sim Ba \vee \sim Ca$_____
6. $\sim(Ba.Ca)$_____
7. $\sim Aa$_____
8. $(\exists x)\sim Ax$_____

b)
1. $(x)[(Cx \vee Dx) \supset Bx]$
2. $(\exists x)Cx$ $/\therefore$ $(\exists x)Bx$
3. Ca_____
4. $(Ca \vee Da) \supset Ba$_____
5. $Ca \vee Da$_____
6. Ba_____
7. $(\exists x)Bx$_____

c)
1. $(x)\{Ax \supset [Bx \equiv (Cx.Dx)]\}$
2. $(x)(Cx \supset \sim Dx)$
3. $(\exists x)Ax$ $/\therefore$ $(\exists x)\sim Bx$
4. Aa_____
5. $Aa \supset [Ba \equiv (Ca.Da)]$_____
6. $Ba \equiv (Ca.Da)$_____
7. $Ca \supset \sim Da$_____
8. $\sim Ca \vee \sim Da$_____
9. $\sim(Ca.Da)$
10. $[Ba \supset (Ca.Da)].[(Ca.Da) \supset Ba]$ _____
11. $Ba \supset (Ca.Da)$ _____
12. $\sim Ba$ _____
13. $(\exists x)\sim Bx$ _____

Before you end this chapter by attempting to provide your own proofs of validity for arguments involving quantifiers it is important that you be warned against two common errors. They are very similar to fallacies you encountered when studying the syllogism, viz. the fallacy of the Undistributed Middle and the fallacies of Illicit Process.

III Two Common Fallacies of Quantification

A. When you studied the Rules of the Syllogism you looked at examples of arguments which involved non-overlapping sub-classes: Consider the following example:

> Some men are clever.
>
> Some women are clever.
>
> Therefore some men are women.

The middle term 'clever' is not distributed in either premiss. That is, there is no way of knowing whether the sub-class of clever things referred to in the first premiss overlaps the sub-class of clever things referred to in the second premiss. We are certainly not entitled to assume that there is any overlap, as the conclusion in this case bears out.

We come up against the temptation to make such a move when we are faced with more than one existentially quantified expression in an argument. The golden rule is never to instantiate existentially twice with respect to the same individual in the same argument.

We can illustrate this fallacy by symbolising the above argument as follows:

1. $(\exists x)(Mx.Cx)$

2. $(\exists x)(Wx.Cx)$ $/ \therefore$ $(\exists x)(Mx.Wx)$

The fallacious demonstration would take the following form:

3. Ma.Ca   E.I. 1
4. Wa.Ca   E.I. 2
5. Ma   Simplification 3
6. Wa   Simplification 4
7. Ma.Wa   Conjunction 5 and 6
8. $(\exists x)(Mx.Wx)$ E.G. 7

As pointed out earlier, the error occurs in line 4. We have no right to assume that the individual 'a' which occurred in the sub-class of clever things in premiss 1 also occurs in the sub-class of clever things referred to in premiss 2.

Remember then that if you have used the rule E.I. once in a proof and you are tempted to use it again, be careful not to use it with respect to the same individual.

B. You will remember the fallacies of Illicit process studied in your consideration of the syllogism.

Such fallacies occurred when a term which was not distributed in the premisses was distributed in the conclusion. In other words an unjustified jump was made from 'some' to 'all'. Remember the example:

All mountain people are stocky and good climbers, so
all stocky people are good climbers.

The premiss only mentioned those stocky people who lived in the mountains whereas the conclusion mentions all stocky people.

A similar error is committed in demonstrations where one universally generalises from an expression like φa where the variable a has been introduced into the proof by means of existential instantiation.

This danger really is a threat when multiple quantification is employed. As we shall not be proceeding to such complicated cases the fallacy in question will not be such a pitfall as the first one mentioned above.

7)   Provide justifications for each line in the following proofs:

a)
1. (x)[Ex ⊃ (Fx v Gx)]
2. (∃x)(~Fx.~Gx)   /∴ ~(x)(Ex)
3. ~Fa.~Ga_____
4. Ea ⊃ (Fa v Ga)_____
5. ~(~~ Fa v ~~Ga)_____
6. ~(Fa v Ga)_____
7. ~Ea_____
8. (∃x)~Ex_____
9. ~(x)Ex_____

b)
1. (Ex)[(Fx ⊃ Gx).Hx]
2. (x)(Gx ⊃ Ix)   /∴ (∃x)
        [(Hx.~Fx) v (Hx.Ix)]
3. (Fa ⊃ Ga).Ha_____
4. Fa ⊃ Ga_____
5. Ga ⊃ Ia_____
6. Fa ⊃ Ia_____
7. Ha_____
8. Ha.(Fa ⊃ Ia)_____
9. Ha.(~Fa v Ia)_____
10. (Ha.~Fa) v (Ha.Ia)_____
11. (∃x)[(Hx.~Fx)v(Hx.Ix)]____

8)   Complete the following proofs:

a) 1. (∃x)[Ax.Bx.Cx]
    2. (x)[Cx ⊃ (~Ax v Dx)|
    3. (∃x)(Dx)   /∴ (∃x)(Dx.Bx)
    4. _____
    5. _____
    6. Ca   Simplification 4
    7. ~Aa v Da_____
    8. _____
    9. ~~Aa_____
    10. Da_____
    11. _____
    12. _____ Conjunction 10 and 11
    13. (∃x)(Dx.Bx) _____

b) 1. (x)[Ex ⊃ (Fx.Gx)]
    2. (∃x)(Hx.~Fx) /∴ (∃x)~Ex
    3. _____
    4. _____
    5. _____ Simplication 4
    6. _____ Addition 5
    7. ~(Fa.Ga)_____
    8. _____ Modus Tollens 7 & 3
    9. _____

9)   Provide proofs of validity of the following arguments:

a) 1. (x)[(Wx v Sx) ⊃ Tx]
    2. (∃x)(Wx.Vx)
    3. (∃x)(Wx.Rx)
    4. (x)(Tx ⊃ Rx)   /∴ (∃x)(Vx.Rx)

b) 1. (x)[Wx v Sx) ⊃ Tx]
    2. (∃x)(Wx.Vx)
    3. (∃x)(Wx.Rx)
    4. (∃x)(Sx.~Tx) / (∃x)(Vx.Rx)

Chapter Twenty-Five : <u>New Rules for Old</u>

Outline:

    I.   The limitations of earlier systems

    II. The scope of the new rules

    III. The problem of existential import.

I.   <u>The Limitations of Earlier Systems</u>

     In Chapters Two to Seven you learned to analyse arguments by means of the rules of the Propositional Calculus. Such arguments as you could cope with by means of these rules ranged from the most simple arguments of all to quite complex arguments. However, they all shared an important feature, namely that their validity or invalidity depended on the relations between the truth and falsity of their component propositions taken as simple (i.e. unanalysable) units. This enabled you to make fairly straightforward truth-functional calculations. For example:

     If p and q are true and r and s are false, then the truth value of

$$(p.q) \lor (r.s)$$

could be calculated as follows:

$$
\begin{array}{cc}
(p \cdot q) & \lor \ (r \cdot s) \\
T\ T & \quad F\ F \\
T & \quad\ F \\
& T
\end{array}
$$

     If an argument form expressed as an 'if...then' proposition yielded the value T for all possible values of p,q,r and s as in

$$[(r \supset s) \cdot q] \supset (p \lor \sim p)$$

it was described as being a tautology. All such argument forms were said to be _valid_. (At this point you might wish to review some of the discoveries you made when you played the third of the Logicon games 'Must and Can't'.)

Sadly, however, having mastered this system of analysis, you discovered that many good arguments could not be tested by means of it. Syllogisms depended on different considerations for their validity, as is shown by the following example:

> All good students of logic understand this Chapter.
> Some pupils do not understand this Chapter.
> Thus some pupils are not good students of logic.

If we symbolise the argument in the mode of the Propositional Calculus we get the form:

$$(p \cdot q) \supset r$$

Now this is clearly a contingent proposition, not a tautology. Yet the argument is perfectly valid.

In Chapters 8 to 21   you learned to test the validity of such arguments. The tests involved an analysis of the structure of the component general propositions (i.e. those employing the terms 'all', 'some' and 'none') in terms of subject-predicate relations rather than truth-functional relations. These all fell into the categories of A,E,I or O propositions.

By means of this kind of analysis you were able to determine the combinations of such propositional forms which produced valid argument forms.

Most recently, in Chapter Twenty Four, we extended the Propositional Calculus by adding the Rules of Quantification. This extension, as we saw, enables us to deal with the whole range of arguments catered for by the Propositional Calculus and the Syllogistic taken together. This not only has the advantage of theoretical tidiness but also illuminates the importance of truth-functional considerations in syllogistic arguments. Valid syllogisms are also tautologies, necessary truths.

There is a further and more important advantage gained by this extension. Some valid arguments which depend upon class considerations and truth-functional relations for their validity escape the net of the Propositional Calculus and the Syllogistic taken together. These arguments cannot escape the more powerful analytic apparatus of the extended Propositional Calculus which is usually called the Predicate Calculus. We shall examine some examples of these arguments in the next section.

II.   The Scope of the New Rules

The addition of the Rules of Quantification to the Propositional Calculus enables us to analyse what are sometimes called asyllogistic arguments. These are arguments which contain one or more general terms like 'all' or 'some' but which cannot be forced into the Standard Form of the syllogism without distortion.

You will no doubt remember from Chapters Seventeen and Eighteen, that Standard Form Syllogisms contain three propositions each of either the A,E,I or O category and three terms, S,P and M, with the M term occurring in each premiss, the P term in the major premiss and conclusion and the S term in the Minor Premiss and the conclusion. Various rules concerning the distribution of these terms and the positive or negative nature of the propositions govern the validity of arguments in the syllogistic form.

In our previous chapter we learned that the A,E,I and O forms of propositions can be represented in terms of quantifiers by the expressions:

$(x)(\phi x \supset \psi x)$; $(x)(\phi x \supset \sim \psi x)$;

$(\exists x)(\phi x \cdot \psi x)$; $(\exists x)(\phi x \cdot \sim \psi x)$.

This formulation makes it clear that the general terms 'all' and 'some' qualify the propositional functions:

$\phi x \supset \psi x$, $\phi x \supset \sim \psi x$, $\phi x \cdot \psi x$ and $\phi x \cdot \sim \psi x$

If actual propositions can be transformed into such models without altering their sense then all is well. The arguments containing them can be presented in Standard Form all other things being equal. Look at the following example.

It is not the case that all logicians have fun.

<u>Only people who have fun live happy lives.</u>

Therefore it is not the case that all logicians live happy lives.

Symbolised straightforwardly, the argument would look like this:

1. $\sim(x)(Lx \supset Fx)$

2. $(x)\cdot(Hx \supset Fx)$ / $\therefore$ $\sim(x)(Lx \supset Hx)$

But the premiss 1 is not an A,E,I or O proposition as it stands. However
it can easily be transformed into acceptable form without changing its
sense. The same is true of the conclusion. Consider the premiss:

It is not difficult to show that $\sim(x)(Lx \supset Fx) \equiv \sim\sim (\exists x)$
$\sim (Lx \supset Fx)$ according to the equivalences listed on page 176.
The right hand side can be further transformed as follows:

$(\exists x) \sim (Lx \supset Fx)$	Double Negation
$(\exists x) \sim (\sim Lx \vee Fx)$	Material Implication
$(\exists x)(\sim\sim Lx \cdot \sim Fx)$	DeMorgan's Theorem
$(\exists x)(Lx \cdot \sim Fx)$	Double Negation

This latter formulation is of course the standard form of an O proposition.

Some arguments contain propositions which cannot be so
transformed and yet they are still valid. These propositions contain
a minimum of three terms at least two of which are bound together in
either the subject or predicate part of the proposition. Consider the
following argument which contains two such constituent propositions and
which is valid.

Whenever one comes across a politician one confronts
an ambitious extrovert.

Sometimes generous and warmhearted people are politicians.
Therefore some warmhearted people are extroverts.

I think you will agree on inspection that this is a valid
argument. Yet neither of its premisses can be forced into an A,E,I
or O category without obscuring this validity.

Imagine that we press the first premiss into the A category. This can only be done by running the properties of being ambitious and being an extrovert into one joint property which we could call the property of being <u>both</u> ambitious and extrovert.   We might thus symbolise the premiss:

$$(x)(Px \supset Bx)$$

where Bx means x has this combined property.

But what happens when we come to symbolise the conclusion? This combined property does not appear there. The predicate term of the conclusion covers only part of the combined property.

Similarly with the second premiss. The subject term of this premiss involves the combination of a number of terms. It is made up of those who are warmhearted and generous together. Only by combining terms in this way can we represent the second premiss as a proposition of the I category. It would be symbolised as:

$$(\exists x)(Tx \cdot Px)$$

But again the term T does not figure as the subject term of the conclusion.

Expressed in terms of quantifiers, if we allow the premisses to be represented as suggested above, the argument would be of the form:

$$(x)(Px \supset Bx)$$
$$(\exists x)(Tx \cdot Px) \quad /\therefore (\exists x)(Wx \cdot Ex)$$

When expressed thus it becomes obvious that the relation between the truth of the conclusion and the truth of the premises is completely obscured. As we have already agreed that the argument is valid then we must conclude that forcing the premises into the A,E,I or O categories has distorted the argument. Indeed we have not merely failed to produce a valid syllogism by this means, we have failed to produce a syllogism at all for the symbolised argument contains five terms rather than three.

By employing the new Rules of Quantification we can deal with such arguments with ease. We can unpack all of the terms and exhibit their relations in the following way:

1. $(x)[Px \supset (Ax \cdot Ex)]$
2. $(\exists x)(Gx \cdot Wx \cdot Px)$ / $\therefore$ $(\exists x)(Wx \cdot Ex)$
3. $Pa \supset (Aa \cdot Ea)$ U.I.1.
4. $Ga \cdot Wa \cdot Pa$ E.I.2.
5. Pa Simplification 4
6. $Aa \cdot Ea$ M.I.3.
7. Wa Simplification 4
8. Ea Simplification 6
9. $Wa \cdot Ea$ Conjunction 7 & 8
10. $(\exists x)(Wx \cdot Ex)$ E.G.9.

Exercise

(i)   Decide which of the following arguments can be proved valid without employing the Rules of Quantification.

(ii)   State whether the arguments in question can be handled by means of the Propositional Calculus or the Syllogistic.

(iii)   Provide a proof of validity for every argument in the list.

Argument 1: Either politicians are ambitious or they are public-spirited.
             It is not the case that they are public-spirited. Therefore
             they are ambitious.

Argument 2: Some politicians are ambitious and public-spirited.
             Therefore some ambitious people are public-spirited.

Argument 3. All politicians are ambitious while some are public-spirited.
             Therefore some ambitious people are public-spirited.

III.   The Problem of Existential Import

        You will remember that the problem of existential import arose
in Chapter Ten when we made the choice to assume that A and E propositions
did not assert the existence of any members of their subject class.
For many centuries the opposite convention was adopted. It would be
a mistake to think that either assumption was right or wrong. Sometimes
when we employ universal propositions in our arguments they do have
existential import and sometimes they do not. This is usually determined
by the context of the argument.

        You were given a reason for our assumption at that time.
The reason was one of convenience. It was that if we assume universal
propositions yield no information either way about the existence of
members of their subject class we can, if needs be, write in such
existence in a Carroll diagram by employing a dot in a suitable
quadrant. If however we assume the universal proposition to assert
existence then there would be no way of marking out the case where it

manifestly does not. Remember the example of every nice girl loving
a sailor:

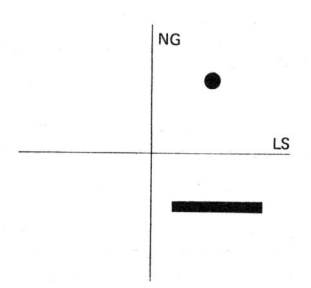

By means of the bar we show that the proposition declares that no nice
girls fail to love a sailor. By means of the dot we can declare that
there are some nice girls. The trouble which arose at that point was
that the standard form of the syllogism could not accommodate such
existential propositions.

When we employ the new Rules of Quantification however, we
can write in the information carried by the dot in the Carroll diagram
above by using an existential quantifier in the following way:

$$(x)(Nx \supset Lx) \cdot (\exists x)(Nx)$$

As there is no longer any worry about having to find only three
propositions of the A,E,I or O forms to make up a proper argument
this existential proposition can play its rightful role in the argument.

So it is still true that we assume that propositions involving
the universal quantifier do not have existential import. But it is
now easy for us to incorporate such import where it is clearly present

in an argument. In other words we now have a system flexible enough to allow us to make precisely the move which was suggested as being necessary in such cases at the end of Chapter Nineteen.

Consequently some arguments which fit into the Darapti, Bramantip, Felapton or Fesapo categories (see Chapter Nineteen) may be shown to be valid by means of the Predicate Calculus, while others will be seen to be invalid.

Compare the following examples:

1. All fairies are fleet-footed.

    All who are fleetfooted are physically fit.

    Therefore some who are physically fit are fairies.

2. All Olympic sprinters are fleet-footed

    All who are fleet-footed are physically fit.

    Therefore some who are physically fit are Olympic sprinters.

These arguments are of the same mood and figure, namely Bramantip. We know enough about the subject to be assured that there are Olympic sprinters and that the second argument is not about imaginary or unlikely characters. It is easily shown to be valid by means of the Predicate Calculus as follows:

1. $(x)(Ox \supset Fx) \cdot (\exists x)(Ox)$

2. $(x)(Fx \supset Px)$ / $\therefore$ $(\exists x)(Px \cdot Ox)$

3. $(x)(Ox \supset Fx)$ Simplification 1.

4. $Oa \supset Fa$ U.I.3

5. $Fa \supset Pa$ U.I.2

6. $(\exists x) Ox$ Simplification 1.

7.	Oa	E.I.6
8.	Fa	M.P.4 & 7
9.	Pa	M.P.5 & 8
10.	Pa · Oa	Conjunction 9 & 7
11.	(∃x)(Px · Ox)	E.G.10

In the case of the argument involving fairies we would not be entitled
to write in the conjunct (∃x)(Fx) in the first premiss. As a result
there would be no possibility of instantiating existentially in the
course of the demonstration. To draw an existential conclusion, as
the argument does, would then involve a contravention of the stringent
conditions which attach to the Rule of Existential Generalisation.

Further Examples

(i)   Decide which of the following arguments can be proved valid
        without employing the Rules of Quantification.

(ii)   State whether the arguments in question can be handled by
        means of the Propositional Calculus or the Syllogistic.

(iii)   Provide a proof of validity for each of the arguments in
        the list.

Argument 1: Gamblers are adventurous and foolish. Some of them are
             also ruthless. So some who are adventurous are ruthless.

Argument 2: Sometimes gamblers are adventurous but they are always
             foolish. Therefore some fools are adventurous.

Argument 3: If all gamblers are adventurous and foolish then so are
             mountaineers. But not all mountaineers are adventurous
             and foolish. Therefore not all gamblers are adventurous
             and foolish.

Argument 4: All gamblers are foolish. Thus either they are all foolish or they are all adventurous.

Argument 5: To be a gambler is to be foolish. Sometimes it is adventurous to be a gambler. It is therefore true that it is sometimes adventurous to be foolish.

Argument 6: Some adventurers are foolish gamblers, but they are all brave. Thus some fools are brave.

Chapter Twenty Six : <u>Arguing from Instances</u>

In a valid deductive argument, the conclusion <u>must</u> be true if the premisses are so, for the information which those premisses provide <u>includes</u> the point which that conclusion makes. The argument simply <u>shows</u> that this is so. This means we can rely on the conclusion, even if we cannot check it directly, for the argument <u>guarantees</u> its truth, on the basis of the given premisses (see Chapter 1, ii).

Among arguments which do not guarantee their conclusions in this way, some are just failures: intended deductions which turn out to be invalid, and so tell us nothing about how their conclusions are related to their premisses. Such arguments, once detected, should be simply thrown away. Some others, however, are not meant as deductions, but operate in quite a different way. Such an argument makes no claim to <u>guarantee</u> its conclusion as true, but only to make it somewhat likelier.

Important among such likely-fying reasonings are those which review the available members of some class in the hope of finding some further property common to all of them:

> This donkey has long ears. So has that. And the one
> over there. And that one you rode at the seaside,
> remember? ... I think they <u>all</u> have long ears.

Sometimes the argument moves only to some further, uninspected member of the class:

> I bet Jane's donkey has long ears, for mine has, and so
> has Amanda's, and Catherine's, and all those in the
> programme that we saw last night.

These are both 'arguments from instances', one moving to the class (or a 'rule'), the other to another of the instances. Both arguments 'go beyond the evidence', as given in the premisses, so they are clearly not deductive arguments. The question is: Can such arguments make their conclusions likelier, and if so, how?

If the instances in question are all available for inspection, and the results of inspection are all given in the premisses, then we may be able to reach a rule with certainty. Thus if we are interested in the general statement 'All romantic poets wore flannel shirts', we may discover from biographies that Wordsworth wore them from July to June, on Dorothy's advice, that Keats wore them in Scotland, Byron when on active service in mountainous country, and Coleridge when attending funerals ... As the class of 'romantic poets' is now regarded as fixed and closed it may well be possible to make quite sure about a statement describing all of them just by checking it in each and every case.

Most of the classes we deal with are less fixed and definite than the class of English romantic poets. Many classes are far too big for us to go through all their members one by one: think of trying to check up on a statement about 'English dogs of the nineteenth century'. Quite apart from their number, most of those dogs are now dead and inaccessible. And suppose someone made a statement just about 'English dogs'. Here the inaccessibility gets worse, for many such dogs have not yet been born. A class which cannot be checked right through because its membership is not yet complete is said to be 'open'. Arguments to an open class from some of its members will surely be uncertain, as 'going beyond the evidence'. They may also be interesting, for it is with just such classes that we need the help of inference. To say anything at all about dogs in general, we shall have to 'generalize' from a comparatively small proportion of the instances.

Generalizations are always unsafe, for they go beyond the evidence. Are they always unwise? They are often dismissed as 'hasty', perhaps too hastily and generally. But if no-one had ever 'gone beyond the evidence' in assuming that fire (generally) burns, or that the next tiger may be a maneater like the last, then this race of logical purists would have died out long ago. A tendency to generalize is probably an aid to survival, on the whole, even if this tends to select those who tend to generalize too much, too hastily.

Many of man's oldest and firmest generalizations are registered in the languages he has developed, for each general name (man, dog, sunset, thunder, milk, meat, anger, pride ...) stands for many individual things which he has grouped together by their similarities, and each such thing is taken to have many further features in common, observed in some instances and then generalized: e.g. a man has two legs, thunder goes with rain (see Chapters 35-37). It is their membership of such recognized and 'predictive' classes that makes things into 'instances' for purposes of generalizing argument.

We are not however here concerned with generalizing as a natural human tendency, which may have helped man down from the trees and into trousers and mortgages. Our concern is rather with how to assess or evaluate the generalizing inferences that are made. What makes the bad ones bad, and the good ones good, and how good can the good ones really be?

We all already hold that some generalizations are better than others. The next chapter tries to spell out what makes the better ones

better, by considering why some 'analogies' carry more weight with us
than others do. The question is then considered from the other end.
Supposing there is some connection, some hidden rule linking together
different phenomena (e.g. malaria with mosquito bites), what sort of
patterns should we look for, in the instances, to make out that
connection and establish it? Mill suggested certain definite methods
for discovering rules and confirming them by the instances.

Chapter Twenty Seven : <u>Analogy and Argument</u>

Outline:

 I Describing and Arguing by analogy

 II Criteria for evaluating analogies

 III Application of criteria of evaluation

I. <u>Describing and Arguing by Analogy</u>

You will already be familiar with analogies. We use them regularly in everyday conversation. Sometimes they serve useful purposes. Sometimes they are no more than a decoration. They may provide a useful means of emphasising a particular point, as for example when we describe someone's reactions as being quick as lightning. They may, on the other hand, provide useful food for thought in helping us to reach conclusions or make decisions. We shall be concerned to ask how it is that analogies function in this latter way, for such talk at least resembles arguing.

In this section of the Chapter we need to make a simpler but necessarily prior distinction. How do we distinguish between uses of analogy which do resemble argument and those which do not? I hinted at the answer to this question a little earlier. Sometimes analogies are intended to be no more than descriptive. That is not to say that they cannot be evaluated as more or less successful. We could try to devise criteria for evaluating analogies used in this way, though it is not an easy task. For example we might suppose that the number of respects in which the items compared are thought to be similar will have some bearing

on the success or otherwise of the analogy. Thus to use the description
'quick as lightning' employs the one feature of lightning relevant to
speed, viz., the momentary nature of a flash. What happens if we combine
two such comparisons as in 'quick as greased lightning'? As parts of a
machine will move more quickly if well lubricated, the suggestion is that
whatever is described is even swifter than lightning as such. However
the story is not as straightforward as our example suggests.

Consider the opening of Dickens' 'A Christmas Carol'.

> Old Marley was dead as a door-nail.
> Mind! I don't mean to say that I know, of my own knowledge,
> what there is particularly dead about a door-nail. I might
> have been inclined, myself, to regard a coffin-nail as the
> deadest piece of ironmongery in the trade. But the wisdom
> of our ancestors is in the simile; and my unhallowed hands
> shall not disturb it, or the country's done for. You will,
> therefore, permit me to repeat, emphatically, that Marley
> was as dead as a door-nail.

Here, clearly, the greater number of similarities between the items
compared does not succeed in adding to the force of the analogue.
What gives it force is not easy to discover. Even if there was once
an explanation it has long been lost in the mists of the wisdom of our
ancestors. The simile is familiar, it has a ring about it which makes
it apt. But this is simply a matter of usage and learning.

We might well expect more success when we search for criteria
for evaluating analogies which are supposed to form the basis of
certain conclusions we are expected to reach. If such analogies do
constitute reasons of some sort for the conclusions then the connections
between them and the conclusions should be apparent. We shall attempt
to isolate such criteria in the next section of this Chapter.

1.   Think of some examples of similes and try and decide what it
     is about them which makes them useful.

     Before moving on to find criteria of evaluation, let us think
about the manner of our distinguishing between analogies whose role
is purely decorative or expressive and those which appear to constitute
some form of argument.   You may remember that we considered an example
of a so-called argument from analogy in Chapter 1 when we briefly looked
at inductive arguments (see page 4).   There the analogy was drawn
between the behaviour of rats and the expected behaviour of humans in
certain conditions.   Maybe we could elaborate the argument somewhat to
make it more impressive.   Both rats and humans are sentient creatures.
Rats may also be considered to be intelligent creatures in that they can
be trained to respond to various stimuli and consequently behave in ways
which at least resemble rational behaviour (in that they can make correct
choices as to which path of the maze to take in order to reach food, and
so on).   Rats, it might be asserted, also enjoy a certain social structure
or organisation.   Lack of space and provisions can be shown to exert
stresses on this organisation.   All of these features may be identified
in human beings and their life together.   Thus, if beyond certain limits
of crowding, rats begin to destroy each other, it seems reasonable to
conclude that human beings will do the same.

     Whether or not this argument is sound or unsound, we can use it
to illustrate the form of such reasonings.   Two kinds of things are
compared (in other cases it may well be that many more individuals or
cases are compared) in a number of respects.   That is, we have identified
a number of characteristics shared by the samples in the analogy.   We

then note that one of these samples possesses a further characteristic. On the strength of this we conclude that the other sample is likely to share the additional characteristic. Whether or not such considerations as the shared features constitute reasons for concluding that the samples will share the extra features is a question which we shall leave until the end of this Chapter. Let us assume for the moment that they do and that the propositions taken together do constitute an argument.

The form of the argument is something like this:

A and B share the properties w, x and y.

A also has the property z

Therefore B has the property z.

If, when an analogy occurs, you can present the matter in this form then you will have marked it off from those cases where it performs a purely decorative or expressive function.

2. Decide which of the following uses of analogy constitute an argument in the sense outlined above:

(a) Time and tide wait for no man so it is foolish to put off until tomorrow what you can do today.

(b) Never walk under a ladder nor use two spoons to stir one cup of tea because it is unlucky to walk under ladders and it is unlucky to have two spoons in one saucer too.

(c) Men and women perform equally well in degree examinations so it is reasonable to suppose that they enjoy the same career opportunities.

(d) Both trees and people are living things. Neither can survive without oxygen or moisture. Trees cannot survive without light and it is probably the case that people cannot either.

(e)   The institution of marriage ought to be protected because,
        as the song so rightly argues, love and marriage go together
        like a horse and carriage.

II.   Criteria for Evaluating Analogies

        We have already noted that it is not easy to provide tests
for determining the effectiveness of analogies which are used simply
as descriptive devices. Can we do any more to provide tests for
assessing arguments by analogy?   Well, logicians have certainly tried
to do so. I shall leave it to you to decide whether or not they have
been successful when we have considered some of the tests they have
suggested.

        (i)   The most obvious is the one which we tried out on the
purely descriptive analogies, namely the number of respects in which
the items figuring in the argument are compared. We shall call the
criterion SIMILARITIES.

        You will have noticed that this was the way in which we made
the argument employing the analogy between rat behaviour and human
behaviour more impressive on page 205. By lengthening the list of
similarities between rats and humans we made it appear more likely
that they would be alike in the further respect in question, namely
that as rats turn upon each other violently in certain circumstances,
so human beings will in similar circumstances.

3.   Employ the above means to make the following arguments from
        analogy more impressive.

(a)   This pair of trousers will wear well because I bought them
        in the same store as the blue pair and they have given me
        excellent service.

(b)   Traffic wardens and policemen are public servants. The former
        are rather unpopular so it is not surprising to learn that the
        latter are also unpopular.

(c)   Reckless driving and drug peddling are illegal activities.
        If there are high penalties for the former offence then
        there should be high penalties for the other offence.

(ii) The second test which can be applied to analogical
arguments fairly easily could be called ANALOGUES. This would be
a short way of referring to the number of items which are compared.
We might express this in the general form: If two things have a
number of properties in common then we might expect that they have
a further specified property in common if it is known that one of
the things possesses it. How much more likely it seems that if one
hundred things have the same number of properties in common and
ninety nine of them are known to have the further property in common
then the hundredth thing will have the further property also.

If we apply this criterion to our example about the rats
then we find that it employs the least possible number of items
which can be compared, namely, two. By increasing this number we
make the argument yet more impressive. For example, if it could be
shown that the phenomenon in question occurs not only in colonies
of rats but also amongst mice, gophers and hamsters, then it seems
more likely that it will also happen amongst humans.

4.   Use the device of ANALOGUES to strengthen the arguments
        contained in Exercise 3.

(iii)   The third criterion by which we might wish to test the
strength of arguments from analogy may be called DISSIMILARITIES.
Here we are interested to concentrate on the number of ways in which
the items compared in the premisses of the argument are different from
each other. The greater the number of differences between these items
then the more telling the argument will be because the likelihood of
the item in the conclusion being dissimilar in all respects to those
in the premisses will be reduced.

To illustrate this point, let us attend to the argument about
rat and human behaviour again. In the last section we strengthened
the argument by increasing the number of items compared with the item
in the conclusion. However, the longer list of analogues was still
entirely made up of rodents. Maybe rodents behave differently from
other groups in this respect. If so then if we included all examples
of this category of creature we would have missed a crucial consideration.

If when we lengthened the list we varied the creatures included
in it to cover reptiles, marsupials, carnivores and birds, then we
would have succeeded in making the conclusion more likely.

5.   Use the device of DISSIMILARITIES to strengthen the arguments
        contained in Exercise 3.

(iv)   The fourth criterion by which we may assess the strength
of an argument from analogy is negative in character. That is, unlike

the three criteria which have gone before the more the number of
instances of this criterion are to be found in an argument the <u>weaker</u>
it becomes.

We may call the criterion <u>DISANALOGIES</u>.

Look once again at our argument about rat behaviour and human
behaviour. Can you think of any disanalogies between rats and human
beings which discredits the inference at all? Perhaps the first to
occur to you would be that human beings have the dimension of morality
built into their social order whereas rats do not. This is a crucial
disanalogy between the two kinds because, for obvious reasons, the
business of moral consciousness has important bearings upon the
killing of others. No doubt you could think of other disanalogies
which would call the inference into question. It is fairly clear that
the more such differences you can discover than the less impressive
the argument appears to be, isn't it?

6.   Use the criterion of DISANALOGIES to cast doubt upon the
        quality of the arguments contained in Exercise 3.

There is one further criterion by which we may endeavour to
assess the degree of probability with which the conclusion is likely
to be true. It concerns the <u>weight of the conclusion</u> with respect to
the premisses. For convenience let us call the test the test of <u>BALANCE</u>.

It is not difficult to understand that the stronger the claim
made by a conclusion then the stronger the premisses need to be to
maintain the impressiveness of the argument. The strength of a conclusion
may be increased in various ways. For example, it may be made more precise.

If in our argument about rats and human beings we had concluded that because at a certain density of population rats began to kill each other at a rate of one per half hour then human beings would kill at precisely that rate given precisely the same density of population, then the argument would have been considerably weakened. But it would not be as weak as the argument which consisted of the original premiss and the new conclusion would it?

Similarly, if one weakens the strength of a conclusion then one may well make the argument relatively stronger. For example if we concluded that given the levels of density of population in question in our argument about rats and humans, then human beings will, at least on very rare occasions, become violent towards each other, the chances of breakdown between the premisses and the conclusion are lessened. We could weaken the conclusion even further and hence strengthen the argument, by saying that given such density of population human beings will sometimes be tempted to become violent towards each other.

7.   Use the technique of BALANCE to first strengthen and then weaken the arguments in Exercise 3.

III.   Application of the Criteria of Evaluation

First of all we should notice that these so-called criteria we have been identifying are best seen as aids to thought. That is we can improve our reasonings, we can make our investigations more fruitful by employing the techniques concerned.

This is rather different from the activity of employing criteria to compare the strengths of various arguments. In fact this latter exercise is not one which we engage in often with respect to arguments from analogy. It is not a matter of much interest or indeed of any use to enquire whether a particular argument from analogy about human behaviour is better or worse than another argument from analogy about the movement of heavenly bodies. What is a matter of importance is how we can best strengthen such an argument or how we can best reveal fatal flaws it may contain. This observation brings us to a fundamental question about analogical arguments. Can the considerations so far listed forge reasonable links between premisses and conclusions?

If we answer yes then we shall be justified in calling the examples we have been considering in this chapter arguments. If not then we may well wish to call such ways of thinking something other than argument. For example, we may simply wish to say that they are suggestive or illuminating ways of thinking.

Well what answer are we going to give? Some logicians who do wish to call these ways of thinking arguments suggest that we employ a further criterion in order to assess their force, namely RELEVANCE. I myself feel that this begs the very question at issue. Whether or not certain considerations count as reasons for other considerations is at least partly a question of whether they are relevant to each other. If we simply say that RELEVANCE is one test amongst others, even if we say that it is the most important test, then we are assuming that a form of thinking which fails this test is simply a bad argument. It would be better in such cases to say that it is not really an argument at all.

This can be illustrated simply by inventing three propositions which could not be connected in any sensible way in terms of their truth conditions and slotting them into the apparent form of an argument.

It is raining.

Black cats are beautiful.

Therefore tomorrow is Saturday.

It is not simply the case that the 'conclusion' does not follow from the premisses but rather that no conclusion of the sort could ever follow from 'premisses' of this sort. No tests to discover whether in fact the one proposition follows from the others are necessary. There is not even a prima facie case to be made for saying that the form constitutes an argument. The matters concerned in each proposition are totally irrelevant to each other.

We can understand this matter more clearly by going back to our example of the analogy between rat behaviour and human behaviour. Imagine that we retain the enhanced list of similarities presented on page 205. On the basis of all the criteria mentioned in the last section the 'argument' which makes a certain 'conclusion' about the behaviours of rats and humans could be no better than one which concluded that as rats are quadrupeds human beings must have four legs also. But this is obvious nonsense. We may well ask what being sentient, intelligent, social etc., has got to do with the number of legs a being has.

You are no doubt wondering how it is that we can decide whether one consideration is relevant to another. We shall simply say at this point that such decision procedures cannot be put into any general formal rules, and that they are bound up with our knowledge of the characters of the things which are related in the 'argument'. We shall expand this rather terse observation in the next chapter.

Finally, we ought perhaps to note that it does not matter very much whether we agree to call analogical ways of thinking argument or not as long as we realise that what goes on there is very different from what goes on in formal reasoning for example. Where analogies are helpful in furthering our knowledge of things, that is where considerations cited in 'premisses' are relevant to those cited in 'conclusions', little will be gained by an insistence that no argument is occurring. The crucial point to remember is that whenever you are presented with such moves of thought application of the five criteria listed in Section 2 of this chapter will not confer authority on the moves. You will always have to decide whether or not the 'reasons' cited for the 'conclusions' are really reasons, i.e. relevant considerations.

Chapter Twenty Eight : <u>What Did It? Some Tips</u>

When Alice fell down the rabbit-hole she found a whole maze of
passages, like an underground house, but some of them much too small for
her. Then she found a little bottle marked DRINK ME, and being a
foolishly obedient child, she did, and found herself getting smaller
and smaller, 'shutting up like a telescope'. That meant she could
get through the tiny door and into the magic garden beyond, but it
also got her mixed up with the mice and lizards, and almost drowned
in her own (previous, big-size) tears. So she wished she were bigger;
and in due course came across another bottle, quite unmarked, but
this time thought 'I know <u>something</u> interesting is sure to happen,
whenever I eat or drink anything' so she took a swig -- and soon had
to lie down with one arm through the window and one foot in the
fireplace... Finally she came on some little cakes, and ate just
enough to become the right size once again -- that is, the size she
always used to be, before she started varying. (<u>Alice in Wonderland</u>,
I-IV).

Alice noticed, in this story, that her size changed when she
drank or ate certain things. She assumed, quite naturally, that it
was what she ate or drank that made her bigger or smaller. She even
came to suppose, after a short course of such experience, that
<u>whatever</u> she ate or drank would bring about some striking change in
size.

We say 'That's silly', meaning it has never happened to us or
to any real person we have heard about. <u>We</u> don't expect to get longer
or shorter, just by drinking things, or indeed by thinking things

(Matthew 6.27); though we are quite accustomed to people changing their circumference by dietary means.

We agree with Alice, then, in thinking that some events are brought about by other, previous events; that changes need causes, and that knowing the cause may enable us to control the change: e.g. 'anyone needing to put on weight should eat plenty of chocolates and chips'.

We all reason in this way: that known causes will continue to have their usual effects; and that some cause must be found to account for any new or unusual effect. And of course Alice's mind also was working on those lines. Perhaps each of us would have reached her conclusions, had we been in her shoes. It would have been unsettling, certainly. But would we be right to argue in her way? Are any inferences to or from a cause at all reliable?

This question falls into two parts. First, are so-called 'causes' sure to go on having their 'usual' effects? Will bread nourish us tomorrow? Will the next match I strike burst into flames? Our own experience in these matters is so limited. You, dear reader, may not yet have seen seven thousand yesterdays, or matches. How can you generalize from that tiny bit of evidence to ALL matches, ALL our tomorrows? Even if you add in all the past experience of mankind, that can hardly guarantee what the future holds for us.

This is a puzzle of the sort called 'philosophical'; one which has been argued over for centuries without any one answer commanding general assent. So if you and I don't know the complete answer -- and I don't -- at least we are in good company. And we shall have to do the best we can without it, like everybody else. Which means we shall go on making causal inferences, and relying on them, at least to some extent. Indeed, I doubt if you could stop, even for as long as you can hold your breath.

The elements in this first question have been explored in earlier chapters: sequence of instances, analogy, generalization, probability; and we shall return to them briefly in the next. We shall not pursue this question further here, because we want to concentrate on the second one.

The second question works the other way: Given an event, which happens quite often but in various circumstances, how can we pick out or detect the 'cause' of the event? In a detective story the reader has to make out 'Who Done It?'. In this detective story we are to make out What Did It? How can we select the most likely candidates?

WHICH CAUSE IS THE CAUSE?

Sometimes we find a whole chain of causes leading to some thing. Indeed, if each and every change has a cause, then that cause also had been caused, and that one too ... so that each and every event is just the latest item in some beginningless causal chain which stretches ever back and back ... perhaps that is too metaphysical, too much for us to think about. Let us look at just one, shortish causal chain:

> For lack of a nail a shoe was lost,
> For lack of a shoe, a horse was lost,
> For loss of the horse, the rider was lost,
> For loss of the rider, a battle was lost,
> For loss of that battle, the war was lost ...

The poet suggests that the war was lost because of that nail missing from a horse's hoof. Yes, that was a cause, but surely it was too remote? So many other steps came in between, and so many coincidences were required, for that one lack at each stage to be the crucial one. Just so, a tennis match ends with one point which is 'game, set, and match'; but that rally is the crucial one only because all the other rallies concluded as they did, making this the last, crucial, decisive 'match point'.

We can't say the match point was the whole match, because it was made decisive by all the points that went before. Nor can we say that losing a nail lost the war, because so much else had to happen afterwards. But we could perhaps pick on the final stage -- in its whole context -- as 'the cause'. The loss of the battle was the immediate and -- in the situation at that time -- the full cause for losing the war. The score-so-far made that last point into 'match point', so that deciding it (on that score) was 'the cause' which decided the whole match.

Finding the last cause in the chain may not be enough, for there may be more than one. In order to catch cold, you need to inhale some viruses which, for some reason, your bodily defences do not at once eliminate. In addition, you have to breathe. Of course, you do that all the time, so you rightly do not think of it as 'the cause'. But it has to be there, and should be included in a complete account.

The cause we are looking for must be the immediate cause, and all of it. To help us find it, we must study the <u>logical</u> relationship which it involves.

NOT WITHOUT, AND ALWAYS WITH

When you strike a match it bursts into flame. But what is 'the cause' of the flame? Clearly, you need a match, to begin with: a little wooden stick with some chemicals on one end. Then you need something suitable to strike it on, e.g. a matchbox (if it is a safety match then you must have the right box, with one side coated with particular chemicals, essential to the incendiary effect). Both match and striker need to be dry. And you need some oxygen, to allow the match to burn; if the match is struck into some other, inert gas, the flame will very quickly die (try carbon dioxide, from a bottle of pop). Now, was the flame caused by the oxygen, or the dryness, or the striking, or the chemicals? Clearly all these factors were needed; each one has to play its part.

Any such factor, essential to some process or operation (to 'make it work') is called a 'necessary condition'. Thus, if you want to stick a stamp on an envelope, the gum will <u>have to be</u> moistened first. So moistening is a necessary condition of sticking on the stamp. You may moisten it by licking; if you think that unhygienic, you can use a little sponge. So the licking is not a necessary condition, for the stamp can be moistened in some other way. But the moistening is necessary: the stamp will stick <u>only if</u> it has been moistened first.

Of course the stamp is not bound to stick just because it has been licked. Sometimes the gum dries up and refuses to be stickified. Some over-enthusiastic young lickers lick all the gum off and then there is nothing left to stick. Licking, we say, is not a sufficient condition of the stamp sticking to the envelope; for sometimes it does not work. A sufficient condition is one which is enough, all by itself, to 'make it work'. For example, jumping off the top of a cliff is enough to make you fall right down, until you hit something. Just one little jump is enough. Nothing further is required.

Some conditions are necessary but not sufficient (moistening the stamp); some are sufficient but not necessary (jumping off cliff -- there are other ways to fall!). Can we find some conditions that are necessary AND sufficient? That is like looking for an IF AND ONLY IF (see Chapters 3 and 22):

IF a plane straight-sided figure has 3 sides then it has 3 corners

ONLY IF a plane straight-sided figure has 3 sides then it has 3 corners

so a plane straight-sided figure has 3 corners IF AND ONLY IF it has 3 sides, i.e. having 3 sides is a NECESSARY AND SUFFICIENT CONDITION for a plane straight-sided figure to have 3 corners. Not that anyone will say that 3-sidedness <u>causes</u> 3-corneredness, in triangles. But every true cause will show some 'necessary and sufficient condition' (such as we have just explained for triangles).

It is said that smallpox has now been eradicated from the world. That is, as no-one now suffers from this disease, no-one is harbouring the particular germs by which others might be infected with it: there are no germs left, because there is nowhere left for them to live. Like the dodo, the smallpox virus has become extinct. So travellers no longer need to be vaccinated against it, or to carry certificates to that effect. Clearly the doctors suppose there is only one cause for this disease (an infective organism),

and that it will cause the disease in persons infected with it, unless
there is some countervailing, protective factors in those individuals
(the 'immunity' which vaccination gives). So they think they know a
necessary and (more or less) sufficient condition for people catching
smallpox; and that this knowledge has enabled them to get rid of it.
In this example, we know pretty well what we mean by 'the cause' of
smallpox; and we can see that whatever is 'the cause' in that strict
sense will be a necessary and sufficient condition of the disease.
(We had to put in 'more or less' because no infections are 100%
'successful': some people show signs of the disease, and some others
don't. But this may be because the body was warded off the infection
before any recognizable symptoms appeared.)

Every true cause is a necessary and sufficient condition, in
this way (though we saw that the converse does not always hold). So
when we are looking for a cause, if we can pick out the whole
necessary and sufficient condition for that effect, that should reveal
the cause that we are looking for. Several ways to track down necessary
and sufficient conditions have been devised, and canonized as official
'Methods' by Mill.

FINDING THE COMMON FACTOR

Suppose you are interested in some event E, and you want to find
out what is the cause of it. That means, you think there must have been
some previous event or other, C; and that C caused E. This involves
a logical relation: C is the necessary and sufficient condition for
E, i.e. E could happen only if C happened first (necessary), and, if
C did happen, then E was bound to follow afterwards (sufficient).

So, given that C was the cause of E, we are assured of two quite general
relationships:

> E only if C (necessary condition), so whenever E, there C.

> if C, then E (sufficient condition), so whenever C, there E.

It is these two 'whenever' statements that may help us track down C.

Look first at the necessary condition, E only if C. This means
that C must be there every time that E occurs -- for E cannot happen
without it. Now if we only see E happen once, e.g. just one man
suffers from malaria, then everything else that happened about that
time might be the cause of it. Maybe he saw a black cat, and quarrelled
with his relatives, and there was an R in the month, and a heavy thunder-
storm, and a seafood supper at the club. Any or all of these factors
might be responsible for that one case of malaria. But as soon as
we look at a run of cases, we can begin to narrow down the candidates.
For the cause must be something that happened every time the malaria
occurred. It has to be a constant companion of the effect; just like
a chaperone.

If there is only one circumstance in which all the instances of
the effect ('the phenomenon') agree, then that one circumstance is the
cause of them. If there are several such constant companions, then
the cause is one or more of them. Because the instances have to
'agree' in containing that phenomenon, this is called the Method
of Agreement. It simply means the cause is something that effect
never happens without; the cause is a necessary condition of that
effect.

To see this method at work we need to examine a number of instances, and tabulate our results. We need a column for each of the attendant circumstances, and one for the effect or phenomenon they were 'attending' on. By putting a tick for each instance in which these were found, we can soon see in which circumstances all the instances 'agree'.

Let us suppose that the health authorities are investigating an outbreak of food poisoning. The first thing is to find the dish or course concerned. All the victims are questioned as to what they ate that day:

Instance (pupils)	Circumstances, i.e. dishes eaten							Effect, i.e food poison
	Chips	Pie	Gravy	Peas	Ice Cream	Apple Tart	Milk	
George	✓	✓	✓	✓	✓			✓
Ann	✓	✓		✓	✓	✓		✓
Jane		✓	✓		✓			✓
Peter	✓	✓	✓	✓	✓		✓	✓

On this evidence, the cause must lie in either the Ice Cream or the Pie, for these are the only dishes which all the victims took. To decide which is the real culprit, we need to find a further victim, who took only one of them.

In this example we only studied the victims, those pupils who did get food poisoning. But those who were spared may also be important evidence. The cause is supposed to be a sufficient condition of obtaining the effect: that is, IF the cause is present, then the effect MUST be present too. Now (turning this around) if we find some cases where the effect did NOT occur, then the cause must have been ABSENT on those occasions. So the non-victims will show us circumstances which were NOT the cause, and so help to narrow down the field. From this, Mill derived his 'Method of Difference': if an instance differs in only one way from a non-instance of the effect, then that peculiar circumstance must be responsible for that effect. To illustrate this, add one more pupil to the table just given: Miranda took chips, pie, gravy, peas and milk and did NOT suffer from food poisoning

Miranda	✓	✓	✓	✓		✓	—

Miranda's diet was just like Peter's, EXCEPT that only Peter took ice cream, so it must be ice cream that gave him the bug but spared her from distress. That was the vital 'difference'.

The true cause is both a necessary condition for the effect to occur, and a sufficient one: so we can use both methods together. The cause must be something which always happens when the effect occurs, and never otherwise. Mill listed this separately, as the 'Joint Method of Agreement and Difference'; which is a bit like saying that accounting involves adding, taking away AND adding and subtracting TOO. Agreement and Differences are just two sides of the same requirement; and the Joint Method (so-called) has already been illustrated in our example of food poisoning.

THAT LITTLE EXTRA

Sometimes the 'effect' whose cause we seek is a matter of degree. Maybe I always get warm walking to the station, but some days I get very very hot, and I wonder why. It is clearly not due to the distance walked, for that is the same every day; so we 'subtract' the warming which happens anyway and everyday, and put on one side the factors which always accompany that part of the effect: my wearing shoes, and carrying a bag, progressing uphill, now and then looking at my watch. Presumably the cause of my regular warm-up lies among these constant circumstances of the walk. The cause of my 'over-heating' must lie in some special circumstance. It isn't the weather, for that is sometimes hot and sometimes cold, sometimes clear and sometimes close. Nor is it the timing. Sometimes I start a bit late, and have to go faster; but I also overheat on some days when time is plentiful. After much research I track it down to the nylon lining in a certain coat. Whenever I wear that coat, I overheat, but not otherwise.

This research followed just the same lines, of looking for agreement and difference, i.e. searching for the constant companion of the effect. But it applied these methods only to a 'residual' effect, to the over-heating which occurred only sometimes and in addition to a regular warming from the walk. So Mill called it the Method of Residues. It plays a large part in science, since phenomena do not usually present themselves to us neat and 'on a plate', textbook-style, for us to investigate, but will arrive all mixed up and intertwined. It was by this Method of Residues that the planet Neptune was discovered: the observed movements of Uranus were not quite explained by the pull of the other known planets and the sun.

MORE MEANS WORSE

Where both cause and effect are matters of degree, we expect them to vary together in size or in intensity: if eating ice-cream should make you fat you'd expect to get fatter the more you ate of it. In such a case, if we study instances showing varying degrees or amounts of the effect we may be able to spot a circumstance which varies accordingly, and put it down as cause. Thus in a study of men with 40" waists, 42", 44", ... up to 56", if we found that the 40-inchers drank one pint of beer each night, the 42-inchers two pints, the 44-inchers three, and so on up to nine nightly pints for the 56"-waisted men, we should certainly suspect a connection between indulgence in beer and obesity. Wherever there is a causal connection, you would expect that more of the cause would produce more of the effect, and less produce less. This does not always work; you may take more and more of something you like without your enjoyment always increasing proportionately (or at all): think of peppermint creams, or Bach cantatas, or George's company. But where there is variation in the effect there must be some reason for this, so there must be something which varies in the cause. Mill formulated this as the 'Method of Concomitant Variation'. It is of course just a further application of our original principle: where C is the necessary and sufficient condition of E, they will vary together in amount _if_ both C and E admit of degrees; and we know of no other relation that will make two things always vary together in amount.

This Method is particularly useful where several causes are involved, which it is impractical to isolate and study separately.

We may be sure that the Sun and the Planets have some effect on tides;
but there remains a large variation which keeps step with the movements
of the moon; so we say the tides are partly or mainly due to the
movements of the moon. The method is also of help in cases where a
cause does not always have a (noticeable) effect. We can't say that
everyone who smokes will get lung cancer; if only because many of them
will die of something else first. But if more of those who smoke more,
or for longer, do come down with the disease, this concomitant variation
will persuade many that smoking has something to do with that disease
(here 'many' includes most non-smokers, almost all doctors, and everyone
who understands the statistical use of evidence). But this Method
(like the others) serves mainly to exclude: a constant factor cannot
be the whole cause of a varying effect.

DO THE METHODS WORK?

The four or five Methods are all drawn from our original description of 'the cause' or a phenomenon as the necessary and sufficient
condition for its happening. They are so many dodges for spotting
a necessary and sufficient condition, if there is one around. They
are very useful in that way, and they do help us to understand quite
a lot of scientific research and reasoning. It is perhaps only
natural that the man who had, as he thought, first formulated them,
should have over-estimated the benefits we can receive from them.

These Methods serve for discovery but not (as Mill supposed)
for proof. That any given happening _must_ have some cause, some
necessary and sufficient condition for its happening, has never yet
been proved. We all get along quite happily assuming it, but assumption

is not proof. Then again, if the Methods point to a certain circumstance
as cause, we cannot be quite sure of this result, because we can never
be quite sure that we have examined all possibly relevant circumstances.
We can of course try out the supposed cause, and see if we can manufacture
further instances of the effect; (thus applying one of the Methods over
again); but can never be sure even so that the cause is the item we have
identified, and not some hidden invariable concomitant of it (perhaps
people smoke to relieve tension, and that tension has an effect upon
their lungs?).

The Methods are developed and explained in relation to very much
simplified 'textbook' instances. Real life is more complex; and we may
have to modify the methods to allow for this. Statistical inference
can be seen as modifying Mill's Methods to cope with causes which
'do not always work'. Alternatively we often pretend that the facts
are simpler than they are, just to get a hold on them. In studying the
weather or the motion of a boat we have to jettison a lot of detailed
given facts, at the outset, in order to make any sense at all of the
phenomena. It remains true that Mill's Methods do explain and describe
the essential elements of most of our enquiries into Cause.

It is sometimes said that deductive reasoning is all theoretical,
and that all reasoning regarding facts is inductive in character. But
Mill's Methods do not involve generalizing from a series of instances;
but rather divining from instances a connection which may run through
all of them. Our moves from 'the cause' to 'necessary and sufficient
condition' and from there to each of the Methods were all deductive
in character.

EXAMPLES

1. Study a fairy-tale which involves unusual causes and effects, to see if the author has achieved <u>regularity</u> (do those causes always work?). Also note any explanation given, and see if you can devise a different one, from the information given.

2. Consider any TWO miracles recorded in the Gospels, and suggest possible 'natural' causal explanations.

3. Could a miracle be described as a Cause which almost never works?

4. Which of the following ideas would you need to jettison if you really and consistently believed that 'every event has a cause':

    fate, co-incidence, invisible forces, luck, guardian angels, equality of the sexes, prayer, democracy.

5. Plan out a tale of how 'one thing leads to another' resulting in (one of):
    Discovery of penicillin, Newton's Theory of Gravitation, Kubla Khan (poem), Schubert's Unfinished Symphony, Julius Caesar's visit to Pevensey, Columbus in the Caribbean.

    Consider which items in your 'chapter of accidents' was a necessary condition for the final outcome, and whether any set of them was sufficient.

6. Apply the Method of Difference to investigating the cause of the sanctuary fire recorded in I Kings 18. (Draw up a table to present the evidence.)

7. Which of the following conclusions might have been reached by the Method of Concomitant Variation:

    (i)   More money does not always make one happier
    (ii)   Thou has put gladness in my heart since the time
           that their corn and wine and oil increased
                            (Psalm 4, prayerbook version)
    (iii) Boiled eggs take longer to cook the higher up you are
    (iv)   Heating water makes it boil.

8. Consider any one tale of scientific discovery, to see if any of Mill's Methods were employed (see popular-science books, e.g. medicine or astronomy)

9. Smith drinks scotch and soda one night, brandy and soda the next, then rum and soda, gin and soda, finally soda and vermouth. Each morning he wakes with a headache. He has vowed to keep off soda in future. Can you fault his reasoning?

10. Analyse (a) a fault-finding chart (car/washing machine/etc), or (b) a table for chemical analysis, to see how far these rely on the Methods of Agreement and Difference.

11. Driving along, you hear a new and nasty noise from somewhere in the car. Consider how, making use of the Method of Concomitant Variation, you might without stopping trace the noise to (a) engine, (b) bodywork or (c) final drive and wheels.

Chapter Twenty Nine : Is Maybe Good Enough?

'The trouble with people is, they will generalize'. This natural
tendency to move on from case to case is not disgraceful, and may even be
of use to us in 'real life'. It is certainly useful to have standard,
certified ways of finding and checking a theory or hypothesis to cater
for a given set of 'instances'. For these agreed methods should help us
agree in finding theories, or at least suggest an agreeable way to
proceed, when we disagree.

Granted that these methods help us to agree, do they also ensure
that we will get the answer right? No, it takes a deductive argument to
ensure that the right conclusion is drawn from given premises. The
methods just explained do not ensure a right answer, or establish a
suggested answer as certainly correct. At best, they will select
one answer as 'more probable'.

To show that they do even this, one would need to go into the
theory of 'probability'. Most of us have met this in some form;
"Suppose I have six socks in a drawer, and know that all are grey or
brown. I need a grey pair, but the light has fused. Three times
I take a pair downstairs and find them to be brown. What is my chance
of picking a grey pair next time? How likely is it that they are all
brown? And what do we here mean by 'likely' or 'probable'?" Guidance
on the first two questions will be found in books on 'mathematical
probability'. Some of these also attempt answers to the third
question, which is 'philosophical'. But all three questions are
beyond the scope of the present book.

Granted, then, that a good argument from instances will make its conclusion 'more probable' (whatever that may precisely mean) and so more acceptable to us, is that all that such arguments can do for us? No, for the methods described will also serve for diagnosis or discovery. In deduction, we used arguments mainly for proof, to establish the given conclusion as certainly correct, as safe to rely on even if it could not be verified independently. But by the same methods we could also work out _what_ conclusion to draw from given premisses; we could _diagnose_ the consequences those premisses must have. This diagnostic function is more important, in arguments from instances. For one thing, such arguments very rarely achieve proof, but only 'confirm' their conclusion more or less. But that conclusion is more often open to an independent check. If we can check up on it directly, then we need no longer rely upon the argument by which we came to it.

Arguments from instances are mainly used in matters of observation -- by which we get the 'instances'. As the further instances we infer will, (as other 'instances' of X) be similar, they are usually observable and so able to be verified on their own account, once we know where to look. Malaria could have been due to so many things, that we might never have hit upon the cause for it, without some way to narrow the field of things to check up on. The 'instances' served to point to the cause: once located, it could be verified independently without relying on the instance-inference.

We can verify the 'further instances' only one by one. So if our argument leads just to several particular instances, we could verify them all and then throw away the argument. Thus if I argue 'the next policeman we meet will be wearing a helmet, for the last three were', the single instance inferred may be settled for good just down the street. But if I had inferred that 'all policemen must be helmeted', no amount of walking around to have a look will ever be enough to dispose of the matter finally.

No general statement (or 'theory') is every fully established by 'positive' instances (except in those few cases, like Romantic Poets, where the class is closed and limited and known). At best, more and more positive examples will help to confirm the theory more and more. But 'more and more' can go on forever without ever getting there (try taking a number and adding half and half again ...). However, one negative instance or 'counter-example', e.g. one case of malaria in Antarctica, is enough to destroy the general rule. There is even a theory that scientists should concentrate on looking for counter-examples, trying their hardest to smash the theories they took a fancy to. At least failure should improve their confidence (cp. Shorter Truth Table Method, in Chapter 6).

DEFINING TERMS TO ARGUE WITH.

Chapter Thirty: Words, Words, Words ...

We all use words, all the time, but never stop to wonder how they work for us. And then we wonder why they let us down. Thoughts can so easily get mangled or mislaid, while on their way in words from Smith to Brown; and then a pretty Miss Understanding may come dancing in and set them both at loggerheads. For anyone in the business of thought-transference, some study of the mechanics of language seems advisable.

Language is one of the more remarkable achievements of mankind: invented by no-one, though all are contributing to its development: an 'institution', like cookery or courts of law, with its own conventions and special words and ways of doing things, indeed its own 'inner logic' ... like a railway.

You may travel by train every day and not bother with couplings and crossings and sleepers and signalling, so long as somebody is bothering. And some people do travel by talk every day and never give a thought to defining terms and avoiding ambiguity and detecting fallacy. But in this case no-one else can bother for you, if you don't. So you may end up colliding with yourself, or get stuck halfway through an argument, or go huffing and puffing down a branch line to Nowhere-in-Particular.

Word-mastery can come by studying grammar: making out those parts of speech we have always used and never realised, taking sentences apart to see what is inside, listing idioms and cataloguing oddities. But straight thinking also is required, for talking straight, so logic does come into it, and especially the logic of classification: how to divide things up, for labelling, and how to pin them down, for purposes of argument.

Consider this argument:

No peers are children, for no M.P's are, and all peers are M.P.'s
That seems to follow; children cannot be M.P.'s, and that includes the peers. But now look at this one:

No peers are clergymen, for no M.P.'s are, and all peers are M.P.'s

That can't be right, for there are bishops in the House of Lords. Yet both the premisses are true, so only the reasoning can be at fault. But how can this argument be bad, if the one about children, which ran parallel, was sound?

The House of Lords and the House of Commons together make up 'Parliament', of which both lords and commoners could be called 'members'. But the term 'M(ember of) P(arliament) is by custom restricted to elected members, of the lower house. So all peers are M.P.'s only in the first or wider sense, while no clergymen are M.P.'s only in second and restricted sense. So the argument is a bogus one, trading on a double meaning in a vital term.

Detecting an ambiguity is enough to stop an argument. You need not decide which of the meanings is 'correct'; you just require the arguer to choose. If he plumps for elected M.P.'s, the first premiss is true but the second one is false; if he prefers the inclusive variety then that does include the peers, but some of them are clergymen.

A relay race might be easier to win if the second runner kept a spare baton up his sleeve. But that would not be fair. So we don't let him win with a baton which just looks the same; it has to be the very same one that was carried at the beginning of the race. The same applies in arguments. To prevent cheating, a strict and even pedantic umpire is required. Let us write a rule into his little book, to outlaw shifty arguing:

> RULE 42: No arguer is allowed to change terms in the middle of an argument.

To enforce this rule properly, the umpire will need to understand how words and terms apply to things: and how to divide, and rank in classes and define; and he had better study some common ways to cheat, in arguing, by misuse of terms.

EXAMPLES

1. Think of jobs (a) dealing mainly with things, (b) with words, (c) with both. List five of each. Which group is, on the whole, (i) best thought-of, (ii) best paid, (iii) most useful, in our society?

2. From literary texts collect ten instances of double meaning and/or misunderstanding of words. Classify into (a) puns, (b) double entendre, (c) uncertain reference, (d) malapropism.

3. 'Words are wise men's counters, they do but reckon with them, but they are the money of fools' (HOBBES Leviathan). Expand this thought to half a page, in the same style, bringing in either the dangers of too much learning or the advantages, to negotiators, of obscurity.

4. Write a five-line story to bring off any two of these puns (in some form):

   a. Get these shoes soled and give those to Oxfam to be sold.
   b. He had the whole of his savings hidden in that hole in the wall.
   c. We rode to the lake and then rowed across.
   d. The knight sat up all night.
   e. George took both crews on a cruise.
   f. Bill bought a bill-hook, and paid the bill.

g. Do you mean to take the arithmetic mean as 'average'?
    That's rather mean.

What is it that makes some puns funny?

5. Read Browning's _A Grammarian's Funeral_. Do you agree that life
    can begin only when learning finishes?

6. Trawl the dictionary for words with more than 5 distinct senses
    (each). Can you see why just those words should come to mean
    so many things? In which cases can you see real danger of
    misunderstanding, in consequence?

7. Consider J. Thurber's 'Here lies Miss Groby' (in _Thurber
    Carnival_: Penguin). What was Miss Groby's mistake, as a
    teacher of literature? Does a similar fate dog the footsteps
    of the student of logic?

Chapter Thirty One: <u>Hangers-on</u>

Now gentlemen, let us have the truth.
It was when George left that I realized
what friendship is.
Handsome is as handsome does.

Truth, friendship and good looks are not to be met with on this
earth. They don't take up space on buses or on supermarket shelves. You
can't weigh them or buy them or bump into them, for they are not <u>things</u>.
Yet we come across true statements every day, and friendly folk, and
some good-lookers too. So where do Truth, Friendship and Beauty come
in? -- not to mention Shame, Honour, Wit, Greed, Wisdom and Ability?
What are all these capitalized abstractions doing in our books and
in our thoughts?

Every thing you come across is individual, particular, just
one more item in the endless print-out of the Universe: George, Jane,
this pen, that table, Shetland, yesterday ... And each of these
individual things will show certain specialities: George is strong,
the sky is cloudy, that table was polished and is now covered with
crumbs and marmalade. Now the sky would still be the sky if there
were no cloud in sight, and George would still be George if weakened
by hunger or disease. But <u>strong</u>, <u>polished</u> and <u>cloudy</u> cannot go round
in public unaccompanied. <u>Strong</u> has to go with George (or somebody),
more or less leaning on his arm; <u>polished</u> depends on <u>table</u> or some other
piece of furniture; <u>cloudy</u> never comes out at all without a chaperone.
<u>Strong</u>, <u>cloudy</u>, and <u>covered-up-with-crumbs</u> are not independent
individuals, but everlasting hangers-on: not 'Substances' but
'Qualities'.

Most qualities are found hanging-on to several different things: milk is white, so is paper, so is snow. So why not think about <u>white</u> on its own, and forget the various items it may decorate? As a first step, give it a solid-sounding name, <u>Whiteness</u>; make a noun out of it, as though it were a thing. Disregarding the real-life chaperones is called 'abstracting from'; and the quality thus thingified for us is called an 'abstraction', and often honoured with a capital.

Some abstractions are stored up ready-made in dictionaries: Scholarship, Science, Seniority, Sensitivity, Solidarity and Sex. Others can be made up as we go along: Polished-ness, Facticity, With-it-ery. But most would draw the line at Covered-with-crumbs-and-marmalade-ness; though some languages seem to revel in Meccano-style compounds like crumbs-marmalade-obscurity. But we can always get round the problem with a paraphrase: 'the state of being covered in crumbs and marmalade'.

The actual messy state of this here breakfast-table is not just an object of thought, but a real sticky fact which can be wiped up with a cloth. 'In the concrete', we say, 'this table is a sticky mess'. In the abstract, it can serve as an instance of that whole side of life, unsung by poets but much described by J-P.Sartre, Sticky-Messiness. Every abstraction has some concrete instances, from which we have abstracted it (i.e. forgotten them, to concentrate on it). 'What is Truth, said jesting Pilate, and would not stay for an answer'. What is Strength? we may ask, and get a convincing answer just by poking George.

Abstractions can be a help to saying things more generally: Beauty is skin-deep, Attack is the best form of Defence, Work is Prayer. To convey the same more concretely might take a whole row of instances: Take Jane, she's a good-looking girl, but quarrelsome, and then there's Amanda, a smasher but eaten up with jealousy, and Felicity ... And there are some facts about very general facts which cannot be exemplified: Truth is great, Peace is indivisible. Very often, however, an abstraction is used because it sounds grander, and a concrete instance might be clearer. To make sure you are understanding what you read, try supplying concrete examples for the generalities and abstractions that you come across. If it cannot be done, that may show the writer has lost himself in the higher waffle, or is padding out emptiness with pompous ponderosities.

EXAMPLES

1. Take a page in some textbook and write down the first ten qualities mentioned. Write down the corresponding abstractions, if given in the dictionary. If none is given, try to make one up, in a word or by paraphrase.

2. Make up sentences giving concrete instances for these abstractions (e.g. for blueness give blue sky):
reverence, consciousness, idiocy, diplomacy, visibility, loquacity, relativity, inconsequence, irrelevance, autonomy.

3. Alice (in Wonderland) was puzzled to see a Grin without a Cat. Suggest five other unlikely Unaccompanieds, and work one of them up into a short story, Alice-like.

4. Explain, using concrete terms and instances:
anti-cyclone, cold front, reflation, restrictive practice, revolution, state of war, go-slow, rallentando, naturalism, idiosyncracy, wordliness.
Which of these do you regard as abstractions?

5. Select three rather different newspapers (highbrow, pinkish, tabloid) and compile for each an 'abstraction index' (number used per 100 words) for (a) straight news (b) chat columns (c) leaders.

6. In Hamlet, consider how Polonius' speeches indicate his character, especially his (a) hammering the obvious, (b) just prosing on, (c) using unnecessary abstractions, (d) otherwise.

7. Re-write one of the following, introducing abstractions as far as possible:
   (a) Antony's speech 'Friends Romans Countrymen', Julius Caesar III 2;
   (b) Churchill's 1940 speech 'We will fight on the beaches ...'
   (c) The Beatitudes, Matthew 5.3-11.

Chapter Thirty Two : <u>Groups and Individuals</u>

George Brown lives with his wife at 24 Coronation Street,
Milltown (Tel. 237) and runs a blue Cortina (ABC 384 V)

This statement links a particular man with a particular woman, house,
telephone line and car. Each of these has to be picked out or 'identified':
George by his name, Mrs. Brown by her marriage to him, the house by its
'address', the phone by the number you dial to connect with it, the car
by description and by the number on its registration plate.

Mr. Brown is just plain George at home, there being no others in
the household of that name. At work there are several, so he uses his
surname as well, so the wage-packet will not go astray. In Milltown
there are a number of George Brown's, so the police would use his address
as well, if they had to charge him with a motoring offence. Milltown
might have to go on to 4-digit numbers, if a lot more people subscribe
to the telephone. And car numbers are soon to start a new series, once
the year-letter gets to the end of the alphabet. Why do we use so many
systems of identifying reference?

The telephone reference-system looks the tidiest; but soldiers
and convicts resent being 'mere numbers', as though each were the same
as everybody else. The naming system seems the nicest, and people name
their houses, their boats, their cars, their bicycles ... as an old
familiar friend, or a real cuss, but at least an individual. But names
could not cope with really large numbers, and are more troublesome to
mechanize.

A name is a word or words somehow linked to just one individual, and used to refer to him or her or it: George, Jane, Big Ben, Mount Everest. Reference numbers and codes, and descriptive phrases ('his wife') also serve as names, intended to pick out just one item or person which the reader or hearer can identify. Sometimes, of course, the reference is not precise enough; or the situation may lead the hearer to 'get it wrong', to mis-identify. A great deal of dramatic comedy is based on such 'mistaken identity'. But the mistake can always be cleared up, by adding a further name or extra reference.

Most words and phrases are not names. 'Cortina' does not pick out any one motor-car, but a type or 'model'. 'Street' refers to any made-up road with houses down one side or both; 'wife' applies to any woman married to a man; 'blue' is a colour shared by sky and sea, sometimes, and some books and eyes; and so on. All these words are general in their reference.

To see the difference, imagine some of the words had been rubbed out. If the names are left, we shall know who the statement was about- but 'street' and 'wife' could come in anywhere. We have to see them in their 'context', i.e. in that whole sentence, to make out which street and which wife they are referring to.

If we want to refer to a lot of individuals at once we may treat them as a bunch:

The whole street was decorated for the Royal Wedding.

This refers to some particular street (already mentioned) and really means 'all the houses in that street ...'. The members of any group can be referred to 'collectively' like this:

The crew took to the lifeboats (i.e. all the seamen did).

The line of police linked arms and pushed back the crowd.

But there are some actions only a group can do, not the members individually:

The eight went past, keeping perfect time.

Parliament sat till 5 a.m.

Of course, Parliament cannot sit after all the members have gone home.
But the members could sit on and chat after the Speaker had adjourned
the sitting: so 'Parliament sat' is not just a collective description
of what the members did. Of course there are awkward borderline cases too:

The Paintstrippers Union is on strike.

A strike is some workers not working by agreement: it requires many
members collectively not-working, plus an official decision by their
union to call them out on strike. In the same way, we distinguish between
hostile actions however concerted and numerous, and declaration of a
State of War.

If very unwary, one might be led into logical error by a slide
from a general to a collective use of terms:

A   Five and Six are odd and even

B   Five and Six are thirteen

C   So Thirteen is odd and even

'Too silly', you say. Yes, in this case the mistake is obvious enough
for us to see just where it is: A takes 5 and 6 separately, and says
5 is odd but 6 is even (a funny way of saying it!), but in B these

numbers are taken together. Hence the fallacy. Now try this on a slightly
less stupid mistake:

No jury verdict is safe, as every juryman is liable to err.

Yes, each and every individual juryman may err. Or may not. Which does not
show that any whole jury will. 'May err' is true of the jury 'distributively'
but not 'collectively'. So the 'Fallacy of Composition' has occurred.

The same mistake can also be made the other way:

George should like tripe. After all, he is a Yorkshireman.

Perhaps enough Yorkshire people do share a liking for this delicacy, for us
to state this truly and collectively; but it does not follow distributively
that every single Yorkshireman is partial to the stuff. So it doesn't
absolutely follow that George does: the Fallacy of Division has occurred.

These fallacies are obvious enough when we attend to them - like
burglary. So those in the trade need darkness or distraction, to assist.
Thus if an advertisement shows a handsome well-dressed yachtsman in
admiring feminine company, and smoking Slayers No. 9, none of those who
see it will concede this inference:

Handsome well-dressed yachtsmen with nice girls around
smoke No. 9, so if I smoke No. 9 I shall become a
handsome well-dressed yachtsman with nice girls around.

But unless people allowed their minds to move along those lines, there
would be little profit in publishing such advertisements.

Examples

1. Think of various 'bodies' you might belong to. List five of these, and decide which of them

    (i)   are mutually exclusive (if you're in A then you can't be in B)

    (ii)   nest (you may be in A and A may be in B but that doesn't mean you're a member of B)

    (iii)   are transitive (if you're in A and A's in B then you're in B).

2. Explain briefly what is meant by: novel, poem, play, sonnet, limerick, literary work; and mention an instance of each.

Which of these terms covers most instances? Is there one which covers all the instances of another, and then some? (like TOOL and HAMMER). If so, derive a universal statement from this fact.

3. Your house has a number, your car may have a name; but not your flowers, coins, socks, teaspoons, cups of tea. Suppose you were giving evidence in court, and suggest how you could identify a particular one of each. Then consider how opposing counsel might attack your definite description, arguing that 'it might not be the same one'.

4. Read the story of 'the dinner-party that wasn't' (Luke 14). Consider what cause for complaint a host has if (i) some guests don't come to each of his parties, (ii) at each of his parties not all the guests come, (iii) some guests always fail to come to his parties (iv) at one of his parties, all the guests do not come.

    Do you think this host was wrong, to suspect a conspiracy?

5. 'England expects every man to do his duty'. Supposing this reducible to 'most English people expect ...', suggest suitable reductions for statements about your school, bank, building society, the MCC, the SDP. Are such reductions satisfactory?

Chapter Thirty-Three : <u>Which Ones do you Mean?</u>

'Do not drink poison' is very good advice, for a poison, we know, is something that may kill you if you swallow it. So bottles labelled 'Poison' had better not be drunk. But with an unlabelled bottle that advice is not much help. Knowing poisons are bad for you is mere book-knowledge, unless you know which things are poisonous to us, and can recognise them first: lead, ammonia, toadstools, household bleach. So it seems we can know what poison is and still not know what poisons are.

If you don't know what poison <u>is</u> you can 'look it up', and the dictionary will put the same thing in other words, and if you know what <u>they</u> mean then you can make out what poison is: 'substance that when introduced into or absorbed by a living organism destroys life or injures health' (C.O.D.).

To find out which substances are poisonous we might try an encylopaedia, or a textbook of biochemistry, or the schedules to the Drugs Acts. There we shall find a long list of things, most of them quite unknown to us, which do 'destroy life or injure health' if taken into the body. The word 'poison' is properly applied to all these things.

When we know what 'poison' means or 'connotes' we are ready to decide or discover which things it applies to or 'denotes'. The 'connotation' is a bit like a suit of clothes in the shop, ready-made for some-purchaser-or-other. The denotation is like the set of people whom that suit would fit.

A swan is 'a kind of large water-bird with long flexible neck, and in most species snow-white plumage, formerly supposed to sing melodiously at the point of death' (C.O.D.). So if we say (mistakenly)

All swans are white

our statement will be about all the animals which that term denotes. But if we say

Some swans are irascible

we would be speaking only about a part of the class denoted by that term. The connotation is the same, in either case: 'swan' means 'swan!' So by distinguishing what the word applies to from what it means we have helped to explain how a general or 'universal' statement differs from one more limited or 'particular': a universal statement is about all the items denoted by its subject term.

If someone says 'All Russian swans are white' he will refer to a smaller class of animal -- and perhaps stand a better chance of being right. Pursuing this line, he could restrict the subject to an even smaller class:

All ill-tempered Russian swans ...

Each added restriction or 'qualification' narrows the application, making the denotation smaller still. We might even get it down to one, or even less:

All ill-tempered Russian swans which broke a Volga boatman's arm on Tuesday last ...

As each qualification is added the subject-terms gets longer, and means more: hence the odd slogan 'Connotation and Denotation vary inversely'. That is, the more you specify your subject, the fewer things your stateme is about; conversely, the less precise it is, the more things will come into it.

Is a name a word denoting just one thing? And do names mean anything? Think of Dawn, and Violet, and Cook, and Carpenter. But Dawn, the girl, has no more to do with first-light than big Bill has to do with bills. It seems better not to ask what names mean, for they do not work like that. But one can put together words meaning this and that, so as to pick out a single item or person (as a name does):

the occupier (on a letter)
the first man up Everest
the millionth Mini
the only table spread produced from brewers' waste.

Each of these 'definite descriptions' describes an office which only one individual can hold, but it says nothing as to which individual is the holder, denoted by the phrase. That is a matter of fact, of history.

Examples

1. Consider the view that, as anything is bad for you if you eat
    enough of it, therefore all foods are poisons, more or less.

2. List 10 liquids kept in the kitchen, and 10 synthetic substances.
    Do your lists overlap? If so what does that tell us about the
    meanings of these two terms?

3. List 10 towns which elect M.P.'s. Do they all have railway
    stations? Suggest reasons why the denotation of 'towns having
    BR stations' should include the denotation of 'towns with their
    own M.P.'s (or <u>vice versa</u>).

4. (i) You ask an ironmonger for 'some bathroom scales', but when
    you get home you find the box contains kitchen scales weighing
    up to 2 lbs. Can you make him take them back?

    (ii) At an auction you bid for an item described as 'Ming vase'
    but when you clean it up at home, more letters appear: (BIR)
    MING (HAM). Can you get your money back?

    (iii) You are so convinced by the house-agent's glowing
    'particulars' that you pay a deposit on the house, but find
    out later that it is next to a tannery and the lounge is
    smaller than he said. Can you back out?

5. You are an officer of an exclusive club. The committee is
    anxious to exclude from membership a further class of persons,
    without saying so. Devise membership rules having this
    effect. (Pick your own class!)

6. Take 5 names from the local paper and for each construct a
    'definite description' which picks out that one person without
    naming any names ('tallest grocer in town' is O.K., 'Jane
    Smith's uncle' is not).

Chapter Thirty Four: <u>Tidies and Bottom Drawers</u>

Instead of looking for the items which a term denotes, we might first form a group of items and then start thinking of a word for it. But how does one 'form a group'? How do we decide on subdivisions which will sort everything away neatly and finally, like those decorated plastic tidies we give people to revolutionize their dressing-tables with?

Anyone can make a box with compartments. The problem is, knowing how to label them. Should studs go with cuff-links? Shall we put safety-pins with hairpins (as varieties of pins), or keep them with buttons, tapes, and other fasteners? We could put them in both, but then we won't know where to look.

A school is divided into 'classes': sometimes by age, sometimes by progress in the work. Each pupil is a member of one class, and only one; for he can't be in two rooms at once, and if he were left out altogether he would not get taught at all. For effective schooling, then, the division must be exhaustive (each pupil in some class) and exclusive (nobody in two). It is also essential that each pupil can find out easily which class he should be in: the division must be definite and evident.

Most classifications have the same requirements. If you have to sort out the books in your class-library, do not divide into poetry, children's, cloth-bound, exciting and big-print, for that would leave some out in the cold (a paperback dictionary), and have others clamouring for a place on several shelves at once: e.g. <u>Now We are Six</u> and <u>Robinson Crusoe</u> (library edition). First decide on a basis for

division, on what to sort them by: by binding, by size, by literary type
or by intended audience ... A division into children's, teenage and adult
may be handy in a public library, there will be less mutual disturbance if
they are in different rooms, but there will also be lots of borderline
disputes: is Thurber for teenagers? Aren't Alice and Gulliver for adults
too? It may suit the borrower if we sort into poems, plays, biographies,
history, mystery, travel and romance: that is, if he knows what sort of
book he wants to read. But Shakespeare will still claim a place on
several shelves. And every library ends up having a large lower shelf for
folios, atlases and other outsize books.

One way to make sure that nothing gets left out is to add a final
catch-all class marked 'miscellaneous'. Club treasurers always need some
such heading for minor odd expenditures: bunting for royal visit, chalk
for billiard cues, secretary's rubber stamp, replacement of ashtrays found
missing after Boat Race Night ... These items have to go together because
each has nowhere else where it could go. If bored at an A.G.M., try
asking what the 'miscellaneous outgoings' are.

To make sure as well that nothing gets in twice we could resort
to 'dichotomy', which just means dividing into two: e.g. those who
play football and those who don't, or those who take school lunch
versus 'the rest'. The second, negative half is a catch-all class:
non-footballers come in all sorts and sizes and shapes, non-lunch-takers
are much more varied, more of a rag-bag then their positive and chewsome
counterparts. A division into A and non-A is guaranteed to be exhaustive
and exclusive -- so long as you have strict and clear rules on what
counts as A ('Are you a footballer?' --'Well I do play sometimes').
Classification by dichotomy does not get you very far: you can't tidy

a dressing-table just by picking up the pins. But we can always re-divide, by a second and independent dichotomy: chop one way and then chop across: footballers taking school lunch, footballers not-taking, non-footballers taking ... Each cut doubles the number of compartments overall. This repeated cross-chopping is different from sub-division, where each division is divided up again, perhaps quite differently: the classes of mammals do not correspond at all to the classes of birds.

A division may be exclusive, exhaustive and definite and still not be much use; for that depends so much on the items classified, and on our purpose in classifying them, factors too various for any textbook to specify. But there is one general feature which very many useful classifications have: they are predictive. Consider a school in which the pupils are classified by age. As schooling is compulsory, all the pupils in a class will have had the same amount of it. They may not all have learnt the same amount, but at least what they've forgotten should be familiar to all of them. And though some will be bigger than others, the members of each class should all be near enough the same size, to play class games. With age there comes experience, so a grouping by age will mean that some subjects can be usefully discussed in Form Four, and others in the Sixth. Now we could classify the children much more precisely, for each one of these purposes; but a class selected for sporting purposes might be so various otherwise that common work in calculus or dramatics became impossible: and a bunch of calculus buffs might be too ill-matched at athletics or ping-pong.

Age-groups are fairly good, for several different purposes. They are 'predictive', i.e. a group selected on one basis may be quite a good

grouping for <u>other</u> purposes as well. In this case, the reason is obvious:
children are all growing and developing as they get older, admittedly at
slightly varying pace, but still an age-bracket should bracket together
pupils still within sight of each other in various areas, whether
geography or golf.

It used to be said that classification should follow the 'nature'
of the items classified, and bring out their 'essences'. That is
true, unhelpful and mysterious: no-one quite knows what an 'essence'
is supposed to be, and we may want to divide things up while still
finding out what their 'natures' are. But clearly a division based
on 'natures' should be predictive; so it may be enough for now,
here below, if we aim just for that.

Examples

1.   'Its no good making laws against this and that, for those who
       want to do it will, and the others do not need the rule'.
       Consider how far this applies to rules against (i) embezzling,
       (ii) overtaking on the left, (iii) running in the corridor,
       (iv) listening in to police radio messages, (v) leaving phone
       off the hook.

2.   Political parties are usually spoken of as arranged in a line,
       right-left or blue-red. Take 5 local parties and suggest
       (i) the area of policy by which they are conventionally so
       arranged, (ii) two other areas, by which they would be ranked
       in a different order. Do you regard the linear/spectrum
       classification as an over-simplification, or as satisfactory
       for practical purposes? (see also SWIFT's Bigendians,
       Gullivers Travels iv).

3.   Write down the first 12 items on your mantelpiece, starting
       on the left. Construct three different classifications for
       them, each dividing them into at least four groups (solo and
       empty groups allowed). Check that your divisions are exclusive
       and exhaustive. Consider which of your classifications would
       be most useful for purposes of (i) insurance (ii) sale
       (iii) decorative arrangement.

4.   Landing on Mars, you find that buildings grow 'naturally', as
       weeds do here. Hacking your way through this concrete jungle,
       evolve a fourfold division of these growths which will be
       fairly useful for (i) taxation AND (ii) housing allocation
       AND (iii) specification of selective 'weed' killers.

5.   What is a 'white-collar job'? Can we lump the rest together
       as 'blue-collar'? Suggest three other rough-and-ready
       divisions of labour, e.g. by footwear, hairstyle, mode of
       payment, times of work ... Is there some basic cleavage
       in society, 'predictive' of these various dichotomies?

Chapter Thirty-Five: <u>Classes Within Classes</u>

A class is sent out to classify the contents of the car-park. One lists cars by the maker's name, written on the boot: Austin, Bentley, Citroen ... One goes by the 'model': Cortina, Fiesta, Metro, Golf ... One collects estates, hatchbacks and saloons; another studies engine size; one counts doors, one considers gears; colour; upholstery; registration year.

These are all valid ways of sorting out the cars, depending on your interests. But some of them are thought more 'basic' or 'natural'; surely engineering matters more than paintwork or trim, when considering a vehicle? And several of these 'natural' features select classes which 'nest', one set in another and then those in another; this gives us an overall classification system into which all the cars will fit, and generates the standardized trade rigmarole for picking out an individual motor-car (as found in the small-ads): 'Austin Allegro 1300 Estate 1978, hardly used, must be seen to be believed ...'

A system of classes nesting one in another is called 'hierarchical' (as the same pattern is found in organizations where orders pass from superior to subordinate: office, army, church). Once such a system is set up we can devise a simple and standardized way to locate any individual in it. The address on a letter works like this, directing the sorters at each stage (reading from the bottom up): post-town first, then street, then house-number and name.

In a hierarchical system of classes-within-classes-within-classes we can think of each class as a 'family' of those classes which nest

in it; and the Latin word for family, genus, is used in just this sense.
The member-classes which make up the family are then called 'species'.
Thus a stamp album might have one section devoted to British stamps
(genus), with separate pages for the different reigns (species). But
a specialist could take 'British stamps of George VI' as genus, with
a page for each denomination: then 'George VI twopenny' would be one
species, and 'threepenny' another. Which group you regard as genus
and which as species depends on you: any level of the hierarchy can
be taken as 'family', with regard to those subordinate classes which
make it up. A species is a class within another class; a genus is a
class consisting of other classes, the species which come into it.

The terms species and genus were first used in classifying animals
and plants, and this was the first elaborate hierarchical classification
to be worked out and analysed. Now in biology a species is a basic
type of animal or plant -- just as a 'model' is a basic type of car.
A species is now taken to be a population of animals (or plants) which
can interbreed, thus producing more of the same sort of animal. As
'species' is in biology kept just for this basic level of the hierarchy,
genus is used for the next level up, and then other words are used for
higher and higher levels: tribe, order, class, sub-kingdom and
kingdom.

Working down this line, a lion may be specified as of the animal
kingdom, vertebrate sub-kingdom, class of mammals, order carnivore,
digitigrade tribe, genus felidae. And within the species lion there
are varieties: African, Indian etc. For someone familiar with the
system as a whole, a short but sufficient 'address' for the species
consists of the genus, felidae, plus the distinctive feature or

'difference' which marks lions off from tigers, panthers and domestic cats: tawny colour and distinctive mane. Indeed, this arrangement seemed so neat and compelling that people for a long time thought such 'placing' of animals or of other things and even of ideas had to be by 'genus et differentia'.

Until the last century it was supposed that each living species was 'fixed': as cats could only have kittens and dogs only puppies, each sort would go on reproducing 'after its kind', unchanging, while the earth endures, and must have done so, since the start of time. But Darwin suggested that the slight variations which do take place in reproduction would, if beneficial, spread through the population until a new and separately-breeding species had been formed. Given enough time, all present and known extinct species might thus have 'evolved' from a single common original. This theory is now widely accepted, and found most convenient; but owing to the time-scale involved it is difficult to collect experimental evidence for or against it as a whole.

Examples

1. Read Macbeth's speech to murderers 'Aye in the catalogue ...' (III 1).
    Draw out his list of canine species, with their 'differences'.
    Sketch the implied catalogue of human variety. What sort of
    'difference' is relevant, for his analogy?

2. Produce a fourfold cross-classification for (i) school members
    (ii) soldiers (iii) groceries (iv) diseases (v) TV programmes.
    (Cross-classification, e.g. students into graduate, women,
    living at home.)

3. Distinguish 6 features by which cars might be classified,
    and arrange these in order of importance for (i) driver
    (ii) elderly female passenger (iii) pedestrian (iv) car
    repair firm (v) Transport Ministry.

4. Why should a genetic classification be predictive? (Assume
    that like begets like.)

5. Consider the suggestion that, as the classification of living
    forms into species, genera, etc., is a human achievement, the
    question whether such species have evolved, or not, is a matter
    for our choice.

Chapter Thirty-Six: Rational Animals But Naked Apes

Man, said Aristotle, is a 'rational animal'; that is, humans are living-beings-able-to-move-about (animals), and unlike all other animals they engage in argument and reckoning (rational); they think. This brief statement puts man precisely in his place; he and she are just exactly that, in the whole scheme of things; no more, no less, no different.

Other systematic accounts can be given, of the same class of specimens: man is the only featherless bi-ped, the solitary naked ape. These descriptions are true, and they do pick out that particular species from all the rest; but we may feel they are less satisfactory as an account of 'what man is'.

A precise account of 'what man is' will also define or explain just what we mean (or ought to mean) by the word 'man'; for of course that word or 'term' is meant to stand always and precisely for that very thing, which our account described. Saying what a thing really is, and saying just what we mean by a word standing for that thing, seem very much the same.

Someone familiar with lots of examples of the species Man, can learn quite a lot more about them from the systematic definition, rational animal: for this tells him their precise place in the whole scheme and descent of living things. But someone who knows the system but does not know the thing can learn from the definition only where that thing fits in: thus a visiting botanist will certainly learn something from the botanical name Urtica dioica, and still have a lot to learn in practice when he meets the common nettle in a ditch: knowledge by description, however systematic, is no substitute for direct acquaintance with the thing! In general, book-knowledge is useful for organizing and connecting what we already and personally know, but you cannot learn all about life from a textbook or a dictionary.

Still, dictionaries and encyclopaedias do help, explaining complex and unfamiliar ideas or things in terms of those that are familiar: e.g. a thermostat is 'a device for switching something on or off when it reaches a certain temperature' and car-drivers and coffee-makers are better off for knowing this much, even if it does not qualify them to tinker with the thing.

People often quote 'the dictionary' as if it were Holy Writ, but outside the game of Scrabble this is a mistake. Dictionaries do err, just now and then. Each dictionary offers only a selection from the language current at that time: so you can't safely argue 'It's not in this dictionary so it's not a proper word'. Each dictionary is addressed to a certain audience; for the writer must decide which words his readers will already know; otherwise the reader will soon feel he needs a dictionary to help him understand what the dictionary is trying to explain.

Can we define definition? Here is one attempt: 'making another understand by words what idea the term defined stands for' (John Locke). This makes it clear that only terms or words can be defined: things have to be explained. Which is where a dictionary differs from an encyclopaedia. It also suggests that the definition given should correspond precisely to the term defined, not take in more or less;

and that the definition needs to be understood by the receiver, it is to make things easier and clearer for him, not more difficult.

These requirements may be more easily grasped from examples of how definitions can go wrong:

BICYCLE   'a mode of personal transport'. This is <u>too wide</u>, lets in horse, camel, donkey, and elephant. Even with 'wheeled' inserted, it would still cover skateboards and wheelchairs.

CAR   'four-wheeled vehicle driven by petrol engine'. This is too narrow: what about diesels, and three-wheelers? Too wide too, covers lorries.

NET   'a reticulated fabric', decussated at regular intervals, with interstices between the decussations' (Dr. Johnson). That may well be correct, but is <u>more obscure</u>; it will hardly be understood by anyone not familiar with 'net'.

CHURCH   'a building used for ecclesiastical purposes'. This is <u>circular</u>, as 'ecclesiastical' means 'to do with church'. That does not make the definition incorrect, just useless. If you don't know what a church is you can't tell which ones are ecclesiastical.

In sum, the definition should mean just the same as the term defined (have the same connotation); but must be put in different terms, which are more familiar.

Examples

1. Suggest minor changes which improve these definitions, and say
   why you think your version is better:

   (i)   A tube train is an electric train running underneath
         London in a tube.
   (ii) Soap is stuff to help you wash your hands.
   (iii) A politician is someone who makes his living out of politics.
   (iv) Physics is the study of physical phenomena, empirically and
         objectively.
   (v)   A garden fork is a metal tool for digging the garden with.

2. Write out correct definitions of any three of these musical
   terms, and suggest minor alterations which would make them
   (c) too wide, (b) too narrow (c) more obscure:

   symphony,   organ,   semi-tone,   juke-box,   conductor.

3. For the following terms propound definitions which are effectively
   circular:

   racing cycle,   marriage,   orthodoxy,   a magnet,   cleverness.

4. Comment on these definitions:

   (i)   A concert is a lot of people being paid to make a noise.
   (ii) Life is the co-ordinated sum of all the vital functions.
   (iii) An acute-angled triangle is one with one angle less than 90°.
   (iv) An ambassador is a man sent abroad to lie for his country.
   (v)   A school is an educational institution paid for out of
         public funds.

5. Suggest five things which cannot be known adequately by description
   alone, and three for which such knowledge would be quite adequate,
   indeed preferable.

Chapter Thirty-Seven: Please Define your Terms

Can we define everything? If definition is always into terms simpler and more familiar, then surely we must reach bottom sometime, and come to items so simple they cannot be explained; basic colours, for example, or tastes. And we find that in very ordered systems of thought, like geometry, where every theorem has to be proved from other theorems, until at last you get back to axioms which just have to be taken for granted as a start, in such systems there are also very rigorous definitions of all the terms, like circle and triangle, but these chains of definitions also lead back to certain basic original ideas which cannot be explained but are just taken for granted as 'primitive'. For if all the terms were explained and defined -- in terms of each other -- then the whole fabric of explanation would be circular.

Does this mean that some things are basic by nature, intrinsically primitive? Not quite. Perhaps the system-builder has to choose which terms to treat as primitive. Thus we might start with ADD and define SUBTRACT and MULTIPLY in terms of it; but if we were feeling negative we might start off with SUBTRACT instead. Such choice may however be available only in artificial systems created by human thought, such as drama, geometry and chess. In the real world which we live in but did not make, perhaps some things just are basic and unexplainable, 'brute facts'. It is certainly not easy to explain scarlet to a blind man, or toothache to someone inexperienced in that respect. And some have held that good and bad are just basic facts of life which we may or may not recognize but can never explain in any other terms.

Some say it is essential to a good definition that it be not negative (as this one is!); that the definition must say what the thing is, not what it is not. In most cases, saying what the thing is not is an endless undertaking, which we shall give up much too soon, leaving our definition too wide: thus if we say a pedestrian is 'someone using public roads but not in a bus or a car' this may well represent the Ministry's attitude but it will mistakenly make cyclists and horse-riders into pedestrians -- not to mention tobogganers and tiny tots in prams.

Definition by opposites is usually unsatisfactory because it so rapidly becomes circular: sleep is the opposite of being awake -- but what is it to be awake? But this caution applies to all definitions: do not use terms which themselves need to be explained, unless you know you can explain them without coming back to the term you were trying to explain! (circularity). It is alright to say that 'Death is the End of Life' if you think we know what life is, or that you could explain what it is without bringing Death into it.

Some things are meant to be negative or opposites, and are best explained as such: a bachelor is an unmarried man, an alien is someone not belonging to this country, a man of leisure is someone who need not work for his living, a spiritual being is non-material.

An item which comes into the definition of a thing is said to be essential to it (or part of its essence). It is essential to a 'car' that it can carry people; one with no wheels could hardly be called a car, nor could one in which all the seats were taken up by gas-tanks, navigation equipment, super-duper suspension ancillaries and general quadrophonic rocketry. Naturally enough, all cars (all real ones) have all those items which are essential to being-a-car. Things which a car may or may not have, without it affecting what it is (a car) are called 'accidental': colour, wing-mirrors, licence disk (this does not mean they were acquired 'by accident').

In between essentials and accidents there come those things which, although not mentioned in the definition, do belong to all examples of that thing; e.g. all cars have engines, as no-one has yet found out how to get along just by whistling. Such universal accompaniments are called properties. In some cases they can be deduced from the definition (e.g. 'the properties of the triangle').

Very many of our statements 'attribute' some quality to some thing: that car is red, triangles are flat, Mercy is not-strained. Attributing an accidental quality is always informative, for, being an accident, that quality might have not-belonged to that thing, e.g. the car might have been green instead. Attributing a property is a more scientific business; if you are learning all about triangles, then you will want to know whether they are flat or curved. Any property you discover will be true of all triangles, even if you discovered it in a particular one. Your announcement of your discovery will be informative -- at least to those who know less about triangles. Thus your neighbour may well not have realised that, for each triangle, some point can be found which is the same distance from all three corners; so it may be worth your telling him that 'A (or, Every) triangle has a mid-point'.

Attributing an essential item to the thing it is essential to is absolutely safe, shockproof, copperbottom-guaranteed; but it isn't useful and it isn't news. 'All carnivorous animals are non-vegetarian' can be verified by anyone, without inspecting Nature or Biology, but just by glancing in the dictionary. 'Every bachelor is an unmarried man'. 'All men are animals'. 'All pentagons have five sides'. Truths come thick and fast on this system, truths-by-definition, empty repetitions, verbal truisms. They don't advance discussion, but they do sound grand and can be used to fog debate.

Examples

1. Suggest covertly circular definitions for: Trade Union, psychology, chemical property, musical melody, illegal act.

2. Define the following correctly but in more obscure terms: spiral staircase, dream, disability, common chord, clutch.

3. Decide which of these are too wide or too narrow as definitions, and propose amendments:

    (i)   A music teacher is someone who helps children play the piano.
    (ii) Happiness is a mint with no middle.
    (iii) A moped is a small motor-cycle.
    (iv) Propaganda means bullying people with words.
    (v)   Poetry is writing which wastes most of the paper.

4. Decide which of these are needlessly negative, and suggest replacements:

    (i)   An escalator is a staircase which won't stand still.
    (ii) Peace is the absence of war.
    (iii) A spinster is a lady who could get married but doesn't.
    (iv) A living being is one which is not dead yet.
    (v)   A vacuum is a space with all the air sucked out of it.

5. Which of these statements do you regard as informative? To whom?

    (i)   Every triangle has three corners.
    (ii) All cows are mammals.
    (iii) Tomorrow and tomorrow and tomorrow creeps on this petty pace from day to day.
    (iv) Taxes are payments by individuals for the expenses of government.
    (v)   A plumber is a man who is usually assisted by a plumber's mate.

Chapter Thirty Eight : <u>Move the Goalposts, Win the Game</u>

Are definitions free? Humpty-Dumpty thought they were:

'there are three hundred and sixty-four days when you might
get un-birthday presents ... and only one for birthday
presents, you know. There's glory for you!'

'I don't know what you mean by "glory"', Alice said. Humpty
Dumpty smiled contemptuously. 'Of course you don't -- till I
tell you. I meant "there's a nice knock-down argument for
you!"'

'But "glory" doesn't mean "a nice knock-down argument"'
Alice objected. 'When <u>I</u> use a word, Humpty Dumpty said
in rather a scornful tone, 'it means just what I choose
it to mean -- neither more nor less'.

'The question is', said Alice, 'whether you <u>can</u> make words
mean different things'.

'The question is', said Humpty Dumpty, 'which is to be
master -- that's all'.

(<u>Through the Looking Glass</u>, Chapter VI)

The question is, which is right? We are all on Alice's side,
partly because H-D sounds so rude and dogmatic. But there is <u>something</u>
in what he says.

First, <u>red</u> didn't have to mean red, and <u>blue</u> blue. The French use
different words, for most things, and get along quite happily. There's
nothing 'right' or 'natural' about our words, or theirs; they are just
the words we always use. We're used to them. Of course we could get
along with the word <u>glory</u> meaning 'a nice knock-down argument', provided

we all got used to the new sense and dropped the old; just as we could all get along driving on the right, after a day or two, provided everyone else stopped driving on the left. Its when there are people following both conventions that they get a bit embrangulated.

As the words we use are 'arbitrary' or conventional in this way, anyone who has something new to name can give it any name he likes: well, any new name. Some new things get called after their inventors or discoverers: volt, ampere, ohm, sandwich, malapropism; others acquire invented names: gas, tram, roundabout. It does not matter what name the new thing gets, if only it is generally understood, and not also used for something else.

Second, for most ordinary (non-scientific) words the precise boundaries of usage have never been laid down. Each speaker or writer is thus free to decide in detail what items he will count into the denotation of each term. Is a whale a fish? Are tomatoes fruits or vegetables? For most everyday purposes nothing hangs on our reply. So the general attitude is 'Have it your own way', i.e. define it any way you like, and then get on with the job! For the definer can speak only for himself. He can say 'In this book the term parallelogram will be used to mean ...'; but if he is free to lay down his definition (to state how he intends to use the term) others also must be free to adopt or reject that definition for themselves. Every now and then this 'free-for-all' leads to considerable confusion in this or that science; and those scientists then solemnly hold an International Conference on Terminology.

Definition is free, then, in two ways: first, it does not matter what word society picks on to mean a certain thing; second, each of us

is free to suggest more precise lines of demarcation round these usages.
It does not mean (as H-D suggests) that anyone can make any word mean
anything he likes, any time, just by choosing to. That way madness
lies.

One reason for wanting to improve our definition of a term is
just to make things clearer: e.g. keep <u>fish</u> for cold-blooded animals
with gills and fins, and open a class of 'aquatic mammals' to cater
for whales. The main aim here is to reduce on-the-spot decisions,
and eliminate overlap.

Sometimes we 'improve' a definition so that the term will (on
the new account) do more to prove a point we wish to make. All know
that democracy is about 'people's rule' -- but in just what way?
Along comes our ready reckoner and says '<u>Democracy</u> means ruling the
people for the people's benefit'. Once this is allowed he can
rapidly conclude that various dictatorial, non-elective or one-party
regimes are 'really' democracies -- making us feel we must approve
of them!

How do these 'persuasive re-definitions' operate? The trick
is this: take the point-at-issue, which you would like to establish
by means of argument; re-define one of its terms so as to include
that point in the new definition. You can then assert your point
with all the force of a truism; and your hearer may be so bewitched
by the certainty of this last step (where the point-at-issue follows
from the new definition) that he may not realise how you salted the
mine -- by bringing in that new definition for his point to follow
from.

Because of this underhand character, persuasive definitions are called 'tendentious' and even 'question-begging'. The main thing to remember is that you don't have to agree to it. When someone defines a term in the middle of an argument, no matter how learned and precise it sounds, you can refuse to grant it, and just wait and see what rabbit he intends extracting from that hat. You may even discover, if you watch carefully, that he can't stick to his own definition, later in the book.

EXAMPLES

1. The word 'buzz' sounds like what it means. Find five more such onomatopoeic words. Make up two more. Find a short piece of poetry or prose which makes its effect partly in this way.

2. Find out how five of these got their names:
   Big Ben, Bikini, Braille, blimey, cartesian geometry, Derby (race), Jerusalem artichoke, bus, penknife, September, talent.

3. How does an alphabetic script differ from an ideographic one? Apply the distinction to the following:

   a. Morse code b. shorthand c. numerals d. weather map
   e. traffic signs f. semaphore g. logical symbols

4. Collect ten words from the Bible (Authorized Version) or Shakespeare which no longer bear the same sense. Also five too new to appear in the dictionary. Suggest two reasons why word-meanings change.

5. Sketch out debates in which these definitions could be used to help one side; and consider whether a more objective definition can be given, in each case:

   a. A cup of tea is too hot if it is hotter than I like to drink it.

   b. An action is liable to cause a Breach of the Peace if it could lead someone else to do something violent, if present at the time.

   c. Democracy means governing in a manner beneficial to the people at large.

   d. A guarantee is a promise by a manufacturer to replace admittedly faulty goods.

   e. An obstruction is something, e.g. a parked car, which a policeman when on duty and on due consideration thinks is in the way.

6. With the help (or hindrance) of one of these passages consider whether all dispute over terms could be avoided if only people would stick to the proper original meaning of the words:

   'No man hereafter shall print or preach to draw the Article aside any way, but shall submit to it in the plain and full meaning thereof: and shall not put his own sense or comment to be the meaning of the Article, but shall take it in the literal and grammatical sense' (Preface to 39 Articles).

   'So long as I confine my thoughts to my own ideas divested of words, I do not see how I can be easily mistaken. I cannot be deceived in(to) thinking I have an idea which I have not. It is not possible for me to imagine, that any of my ideas are like or unlike, that are not truly so' (Berkeley).

SOME FAMOUS
BAD ARGUMENTS:

A Nest of Fallacies

Chapter Thirty Nine : <u>How Not To Do It</u>

For everything which can be done right there is also a way of
doing it wrong -- if not several. 'Truth is one, but error infinite',
saith the sage; a depressing thought, for it seems to make our chance
of getting it right so very slim, and also suggests that error is too
manifold to classify. But in most areas there are certain obvious
and well-recognized and much-frequented ways of going wrong, worth
naming and warning ourselves against.   Thus in cricket there are
plenty of ways to not defend your wicket and not hit the ball; but
it still seems worth advising novices to keep the bat parallel with
the stumps and with the flat side in front. Those who go down to
the sea are told to 'trim the boat', i.e. not sit all on one side.
Learner-drivers are instructed when not to overtake.

In all these cases 'doing it wrong' means doing it less
efficiently: thus the batsman's aim is to stop the ball hitting his
wicket, and his chance of doing so is less if he holds the bat
sideways-on. Argument, however, is a form of persuasion, of A getting
B to share A's view; B may need warning that A is doing this wrongly,
but too <u>well</u>; for a trick of persuasion is 'better', the worse we
are deceived.

Conjurors also are in the business of persuasion, but they
do not credit the tricks they fool us with. A debater, however, who
uses a faulty argument, may himself be taken in by it. A fallacy is
an argument which <u>seems</u> reliable (but only 'seems'), like a sum done
wrong: you were not trying to make a mistake, you were trying (and
failing) to get it right.

We may spot our own and others' mistakes in reasoning more easily, if we have names for some recognized ways of going wrong; and if we study and even practise-for-fun these ways not-to-do-it, we may come to appreciate better the right ways of arguing.

The best way to explain something, usually, is to give some example that seems familiar; for a theoretical explanation can be understood better if we already have something concrete and definite to think about and apply it to. New and difficult 'technical' words should be saved up for later on, when we have got quite used to the things which they stand for. So the ideal order is: instance first, then explanation, technical term a long time afterwards. Unfortunately, if we stick to this ideal in explaining fallacies, the examples will often strike an alert reader as ridiculous.

For centuries, logic-books have given this example of Ambiguity: 'People are not made of paper, but all pages are, so no pages are people'. The premisses are true (about pages in books). The conclusion is false (about pages in castles or hotels). So we can't have it both ways, but must decide which ones we mean. Now the example seems silly, because it is so obvious; 'only a philosopher could confuse a hotel page with the page of a book!' Maybe so. But then, the example is meant to illustrate a mistake, and so to illustrate it that every reader sees just what mistake is being made. So do not be insulted, dear reader. Surely you will agree that there are some other readers, not quite so bright as you, who need a v-e-r-y s-i-m-p-l-e example, to make quite sure they get the point.

Once you have got the point, keep looking out for real-life examples. Your teachers will provide a few, though you may decide not to tell them so. So will conversation, on buses or in shops. Almost all advertisements (except small-ads) contain or imply some fallacy. In newspapers you can sometimes strike it rich, especially columns like 'Yesterday in Parliament'. You need never lack for amusement, once you start this game.

There have been many attempts at classifying fallacies, none wholly satisfactory. We divide them into non-reasons, verbal muddles, jumping ahead, deceptive inference and debating tricks.

EXAMPLES

1. List five things-not-to-do (a) when cooking, (b) when entertaining, (c) when cycling, (d) when visiting Grandma, (e) when drawing maps. Suggest reasons for the DON'Ts on any one of your lists, and classify these (e.g. reasons of safety, tact, efficiency ...).

2. Explain any two conjuror's or card-tricks, and say what sort of illusion or deception is involved (e.g. sleight-of-hand, spare cards, optical illusion, faulty reasoning ...).

3. Take two ideas special to your subjects of study (e.g. romanticism, osmosis, cube root ...) and construct explanations for them in technical, abstract jargon without referring to any particular

   examples. Test these (a) for correctness, on someone who already understands those things, and (b) for helpfulness, on someone who doesn't. Report progress.

4. Collect three advertisements (from papers, hoardings, TV) which seem to you to involve trickery or mistaken reasoning; and explain in your own words the mistake or trick involved.

5. Consider any two political parties, in any country, and think up bad reasons why people should vote for their candidates. Try to cast your reasons into snappy, slogan form likely to appeal to particular groups. Explain why you think your slogans are bad, as reasons.

Chapter Forty : <u>Reasons Which Are No Reasons</u>

Arguing is giving reasons; showing that B must be so, <u>because</u>
of A. We would not bother saying 'A, so B', if we could make sure of
B on its own, without appeal to A. Hence all the fuss about 'validity',
i.e. reliability; for when we do need reasoning, we need to be able to
reply on it. You don't need a rope, to walk up steps. When you do need
a rope, e.g. in climbing rocks, you want one that will really take your
weight. If A is our reason for B, that means we accept B <u>just because</u>
of A. So we must make sure that A really is a 'reason' for B.

'Two and three make six, and you'd better believe that 'cos
I'll mash your face in otherwise'. What the bully might do is no reason
at all for any answer in arithmetic: not even for 2 plus 3 makes 5.
And his threats cannot make me believe what I see to be false. But they
might be a reason of sorts (if he's much bigger ...) for going round
the corner before saying so. This is called the Appeal to Force, or
the Big Stick Argument, 'Or Else'. We have all met it, and I guess
we have all committed it.

'Yes, your worship, she was drunk and disorderly, but she has
five children and a disabled husband to support'. Her domestic difficulties do not of course change the facts on which she was brought before
the court (though they might go some way towards explaining it). It
would be silly to argue ' she has these problems at home, therefore
she was not drunk'. A wise lawyer will not put it as baldly as that.
He will work on the problems side, painting as harrowing a picture as
he can, hoping that the judge's natural and proper feelings of pity

will blind him to their irrelevance. This is the Appeal to Pity, the Sobstory line of (irrelevant) defence.

Sobstories have their place, of course. It may be quite right for the lawyer to plead domestic difficulties 'in mitigation', i.e. to show that although guilty she deserves less than the usual punishment. But saying that Jane can be partly pardoned or excused for what she did is quite different from claiming that she did not do it at all.

An appeal to pity is made in the belief that most human beings will react predictably, with 'normal' human feelings of sympathy. Most, but not all. Sobstories would have been wasted on Judge Jeffries or on Genghiz Khan. The arguer propounding non-reasons should first study his audience!

An arguer (or persuader, anyway) who has studied his audience may find several emotional matters that will work his way as well as pity does. Perhaps they all dislike long hair, or pot bellies, or false teeth; if so, he can somehow work in a reference to them, and get the audience's prejudices working on his side. This Appeal to Prejudice works just like the Appeal to Pity, but it needs more work, for you have to pick your prejudice to suit your audience. We all do it, sometimes: advertisers do it all the time, politicians feel they can safely let themselves go at Party Conference; family know how to get their way by remembering what Aunty does not like.

People may notice, if you appeal to their prejudices in a separate argument: its irrelevance becomes more obvious, and it is easier to throw away. Better work the likes and dislikes right into the matter of your case, so that they seem part of the facts you are describing and appealing to. All good propagandists rely on these sly, emotive, question-begging terms:

> Alcohol is a disgusting paralysing drug

> Why should our village streets be blocked by
> stinking juggernauts?

Anyone can see this is 'laying it on a bit'. The trick is, to lay it on while describing facts. Who can deny that alcohol, taken in certain quantities, may render people motionless? But 'paralysing drug' makes the stuff sound really poisonous.

The only defence against such propaganda is to re-describe the same highly-coloured facts in plain and even quantitative terms, e.g.

> two thirty-foot lorries cannot pass in the High
> Street without mounting the pavement.

An emotive label offers a value wrapped up with the fact; it offers to save you deciding whether the fact is good or bad. Thus a change in the system of milk delivery will surely be put to customers as 'an improvement'; and when cricket-bats are at last made of plastic we shall be told it is more scientific and more up-to-date.

We are all prejudiced against liars, thieves, swindlers and perhaps adulterers: people who have been caught doing something we have not been caught at yet. So if Brown persuades us of something (e.g. that the earth goes round the sun) and if Smith wants to persuade us that Brown is wrong, Smith may just mention that Brown is a liar, thief, swindler, etc. Now it could well be that Brown IS a liar, thief, swindler, etc., AND that the earth DOES go round the sun, for these are two unconnected points; either could be true (or false) while the other one is false (or true), so neither can be a good reason, or indeed any reason at all, for the other one. But the tactic does work, as that old lawyer knew who wrote on a brief 'No case: abuse plaintiff's attorney'.

Now suppose Brown gave evidence that he had seen Jones prowling near the scene of the murder carrying an axe. Jones denies this, of course, but then, if it was true, he would. So Jones' lawyer is very pleased to learn that Brown has an earlier conviction for perjury. For the fact that Brown had lied on oath before will <u>discredit</u> his testimony in the instant case; and rightly so. The jury cannot convict Jones <u>on Brown's evidence</u> if Brown stands convicted of dishonesty.

The Appeal to Abuse is like the Appeal to Prejudice, simply irrelevant to the point at issue (Brown's views on astronomy). But the 'abuse', if shown true, may rightly be used to discredit a <u>witness</u>: to show that 'Brown says X' is no good reason for believing X.

Just as Brown's previous (alleged) misdeeds may prejudice us against his views or arguments, so also Robinson's long research, world-famous scholarship, influential books, public position, academic degrees, convincing manner, white coat or gadgetry may well influence us towards accepting what he says. It is usual, and better, not to formulate this as an argument:

Aristotle said so: so it must be right

for that argument is so obviously wrong. But if Robinson's 'qualifications'
are just paraded, without saying why, then we shall be influenced. It
would be so nice to have an expert, who <u>knows</u> all these difficult and
puzzling things. If someone offers us Robinson, why should we turn him
down?

Are we wrong to be influenced like this? No, if Robinson really
is an expert on the topic -- not a know-all, but someone really well
informed, as far as anyone can be, cautious and judicious too -- then
clearly his opinion is very well worth having. Just how far it will
take us, can usually be reckoned by getting two 'experts' and waiting
till they disagree.

The problem is, how to tell which 'experts' are experts and which
are mere quacks. Of course, an expert (in that subject) could tell you
right away, and often does; but then the quack will be just as rude
about <u>him</u>, and we are left guessing at the ringside. However, we can
rightly be guided by experts (known to us) on bordering subjects; and
to some extent by the manner of the candidates: as quacks are in the
business of claiming to be what they are not, they are more likely to
make brazen, immodest or plainly false claims, so the one who is
always modest and judicious will win our confidence. (Please do not
show this statement to prospective quacks.)

The Appeal to Authority may properly be heeded by those who know
or have good reason to think it <u>is</u> an authority; but is improperly used
to influence those who cannot tell the difference. Name-dropping is
an amusing variant of this.

Note: Some examples may come under more than one official fallacy, some under none. Always say first what seems to you wrong with an argument, then try to put a name to it.

Examples

1. What flaws, if any, do you see in these reasonings:

   (a) I signed the H.P. agreement under pressure, I didn't really want the set, I can't afford it with six children and no wages coming in.

   (b) Australia is an island. It shows that in the atlas.

   (c) Parties which favour totalitarian ideas should not be allowed to take part in democratic elections, for, if they won, that would be the end of democracy.

   (d) 'I must have a religion, and it must be different from father's' (Mill).

   (c) Parties should not be allowed to take part in democratic elections. They are set up to get voters to vote differently than they would have done.

2. Devise advertisements for any two of the following products: (a) 15-speed lightweight plastic bicycles, (b) waterproof shirts, (c) coloured milk, (d) crease-resistant handkerchieves, (e) non-stick shoes. Describe the audience to whose prejudices, fears, preferences or sound good sense your advertisements are intended to appeal.

3. Choose some public figure and write a short speech attacking his views on Capital Punishment/Common Market/Compulsory R.E./Transport Subsidies/Pornography, making effective use of any five of:

   > atheist, blimp, chauvinist, deviationist, elitist,
   > fascist, gringo, occidental, permissive, Quixotic,
   > racist, sexist, Trot.

4. Complete the alphabet of abuse begun in 3. (omit X and vowels: abuse must refer to opinions). Estimate relative importance, when slinging mud, of (a) finding relevant mud, (b) finding mud which will stick, (c) finding real mud.

5. Read Socrates' 'Apology' (Last Day's of Socrates, Penguin). Set out

   (a) the appeals to prejudice he said his accusers made,

   (b) the appeals to pity he said he would not make,

   (c) Do you think Socrates' proposal for sentence reasonable, appropriate, sensible in the circumstances?

Chapter Forty One : Fiddle and Muddle

In many cases the same word may mean several different things: bank is (i) the side of a river, (ii) any heap of earth, or (iii) a place to keep your money in;   point means (i) a sharp end, (ii) a spot or sharply defined place, (iii) an item in scoring, and, for Shakespeare, (iv) what your braces hitch on to. These various meanings are often numbered, in dictionaries, and are referred to as the different 'senses' of the words. We can often see how one sense might have grown from another: a bank of earth is heaped up and running along just like a river-bank. In a few cases, words originally quite different have 'grown together' in our tongue: thus 'red' and 'read' may sound just the same, while neat (= tidy, from Latin for shiny, spick and span) had originally nothing to do with the neat's-foot-oil some people put on cricket-bats, neat being a Saxon word for ox or cow.

We can usually tell from the rest of the sentence which sense we are to 'take': it would not be easy to think of a sentence in which 'neat' could be taken either way (you try!). But in some cases the word, and therefore the sentence, can be understood two different ways:

He took cover behind the bank and reloaded his gun.

'I take your point' he said, grabbing the compasses.

Where a word not only has two senses in the dictionary, but is used in a sentence compatible with both of them, it can be called 'ambiguous' (going two ways).

Ambiguity can also arise from uncertainty about grouping the words and phrases within the sentence:

> For sale, an umbrella, by a lady, with whalebone ribs.
> Wanted, a plumber, to put in cold water tank.

In some cases the uncertainty could be cleared up by punctuation; or a particular interpretation may be favoured by emphasis:

> Thou shalt not bear false witness against thy <u>neighbour</u> .
> Thou shalt not bow down to <u>them</u> nor worship <u>them</u> (the graven images you must not make).
> Acting is not <u>thought</u> to make people much more deceitful.

Puns depend on ambiguity; the intended meaning is usually obvious, but a second meaning is possible, which is either ludicrous in itself, or amusing by its sudden contrast with the general tone of the passage or conversation:

> The three sisters who lived in a treacle-well were learning to draw -- treacle (<u>Alice</u>)

Ambiguity is also employed when the second meaning cannot be stated directly but only hinted at, for some reason, political or conventional: this technique of saying one thing but conveying another comes in very handy on the stage ('<u>double entendre</u>').

In these instances the two meanings are so different they could not be confused: the second meaning forms a violent contrast, out of step with the first.

The Delphic oracle was supposed to specialize in ambiguous predictions, Thus King Croesus was told 'attack the Persians, and you will destroy an empire' which he did, not thinking that the empire he destroyed might just be his own (Herodotus I). Here the meaning was indefinite, flexible enough for adjustment 'after the event'. Deliberate ambiguity of this sort is a favourite trick in political speeches and manifestoes: if you gain the support of all who agree with meaning 1 plus those who agree with meaning 2, you are doing well (now). In Diplomacy a double meaning leaves room for manoevre later on: get them to agree to A now, then later on if it suits us we can always say they really agreed to B. In advertisements and in public dispute we may find ambiguous claims, one meant to be swallowed whole, while the other, lesser version is kept for last-ditch defence when challenged to substantiate the claim:

> Shall's cigarettes are most enjoyable and do no known
> damage to the body.

People also resort to partial quotation, 'out of context',which can be as good as re-writing the quote, since the original context determines the precise meaning intended by the speaker. It is unfair for Brown to cite some of Smith's words if this makes them mean something different: 'The Good Caff Guide said Bert's Caff serves the best Nescafe' (Guide went on "among those 5-blob establishments marked 'truly horrible'"). That is not to say that Smith may not quote anything Brown says unless he repeats everything else Brown said as well: for then quoting would be just impossible. But it does mean that the words as quoted should carry the meaning they had in the remark or passage they are quoted from.

The same principle applies to arguments. The terms used must keep precisely the same sense throughout, otherwise we cannot safely rely upon the argument, i.e. it will not be safe to accept the conclusion just because we have found the premisses acceptable. Thus a syllogism is meant to link two terms together, by a third; but if one of them has two meanings that undoes the link, making a 'Fallacy of Four Terms', e.g.

> Man is the only animal which talks
> No woman is a man
> So no woman is an animal which talks.

Here man means 'human being' to begin with, but then quickly shifts to its narrower sense of 'male human being'. (If we stuck to either meaning throughout then the inference would be valid but one of the premisses would turn out false).

No argument containing a pun is likely to impose on us (e.g. boy-pages and paper-pages). To deceive, the ambiguity must be a fairly narrow one, which can be shown up only by careful and precise definition, a defence sure to attract the charge of 'hair-splitting', in a debate. In fact, we are less at risk from dishonestly engineered inference-fiddles put forward by others, than from unnoticed shades of meaning in arguments we ourselves rely on and propound. Consider

> Scientists study laws of nature so there must
> have been a lawgiver, namely God.

That seems attractive at first, but then discomfort follows -- it seems too slick, such a nice knock-down argument! And then we may for the first time realize that a 'law' need not be a rule of conduct laid

down for someone else <u>by somebody</u>, but may mean just a regular relationship.

Serious ambiguity can sometimes be found in such important little
words as <u>or</u>, <u>not</u>, <u>all</u>. The question 'Will you have tea or coffee?'
presumably intends Either-Or (not both!); but the rule 'The meeting
shall be attended by the Chairman or Vice-Chairman' hardly requires one
of them to stay away, if the other should attend; here <u>or</u> means 'and/or'.

<u>All</u> may mean all-together, or sometimes each-and-every-one; and
fallacy can follow if we move from the first 'collective' sense to the
other 'distributive' one. The angles of a triangle all come to two
right angles, but woe betide the pupil who infers that each one does.
And the opposite move is just as dangerous: each and every angle of
a triangle is less than two right angles, but we cannot transfer that
property to the sum of them. What they all have individually may not
be what they all together have (see Ch. 32).

EXAMPLES

1. Distinguish five of these, giving examples: antonym, autograph, antinomy, homonym, homograph, homophone, gramophone, isomorph, isobar, synod, synonym.

2. Explain the various meanings of the following, and say how the ambiguity arises:

   (a) Alsation for sale, eats anything, very fond of children.

   (b) The poor wren, the most diminutive of birds, will fight
       Her young ones in the nest (Macbeth IV 2).

   (c) The Astronomer Royal, after appearing to give evidence on
       behalf of the Flat Earth Society, affirmed his continuing
       faith in terrestrial motion.

   (d) Did Socrates advance knowledge by pretending to be ignorant?

   (e) Children of both sexes admitted free.

   (f) Everyone wants to be happy so we all want everyone to be (Mill).

   (g) Male and female created he them (Genesis 1).

   (h) College creche -- places available for the children of both
       staff and students.

3. Describe Socrates' discovery of the second meaning of the oracle 'No one is wiser than Socrates' (Apology, in Last Days of Socrates, Penguin).

4. What contribution did ambiguity make to the gulling of Malvolio (Twelfth Night II 3,4, III 4)? What other factors were involved?

5. Construct a question which some politician of today might wish to put to the Delphic oracle, and a suitably 'oracular' response.

Chapter Forty Two : Leaping in the Dark

        Much of our reasoning life is spent on argument from instances to
a rule. Such an argument can achieve certainty only if all the instances
are examined, and are known to be all the instances. There is a gate in
Oxford which is to be opened for the next Tudor monarch to pass through;
but we may think there won't be any more, and that we already know all
of them. In that case we can practise induction safely, in their case;
and conclude, perhaps, that they all wore ruffs. Now clearly most of
our inductions are not of this simple, safe-and-sealed 'enumerative'
sort. But even 'risky' inductions, in an open class, with an incomplete
set of instances, may be sound and strong enough to assure you, for
everyday purposes, that the sun will rise tomorrow or that all dogs
have tails (see Chs. 26-29).

        Some arguments from instances are so feeble and yet so likely
to mislead that they have been given special names, as fallacies; NOT
for failing deductive standards of validity, but for not even making
their conclusions probable. You would not criticize a push-bike for
being slower than a bus, but only by comparison with better bikes:
e.g. for being a ramshackle heap of old iron with oval wheels and
elastic chain, and likely to go quicker when pushed.

        A full moon has been thought to cause a change in the weather,
which came just after it, and comets have been held responsible for
famine and pestilence. We call it 'superstitious' when other people --
-especially those of past ages or other countries -- make connections
of this sort. But can we be sure that the recent severe winters have

not been due, in some way yet unexplained, to the exploding of atomic bombs? No, we can't be sure, indeed we need hardly bother either way, until someone puts up a definite causal connection for proper testing against all the instances.

If a full moon did cause a change in the weather, that change would come just after it; and whatever did cause the weather-change was presumably something that happened not very long before. So if we notice something unusual or out-of-the-way or even merely different which happened just before, we may rightly ask ourselves whether that was the cause. But just asking is not good enough. We must at least go on to consider the weather after other full moons, and the state of the moon before other weather-changes. Without taking that much trouble we have no right even to suggest a connection. In arguing from instances, one can never be enough. "It's dangerous going underground. I once went on the Tube in London and I was laid up in bed for a week afterwards with flu". Lazy 'jumping to conclusions' about 'what happened next', is called Post Hoc ergo Propter Hoc (It came after X so X was the cause of it), or simply False Cause.

It is possible to argue from many instances and still go badly wrong. In 1936 an opinion poll backed the wrong (i.e. unsuccessful) presidential candidate, in America. The poll was big enough (10 million papers sent out, 1 in 4 returned). But the addresses had been taken from the phone books and car dealers' lists of customers. Less trouble, but also less representative. Any argument from an obviously biassed or insufficient sample can be dismissed as Hasty Generalization. Not

that anyone knows how to ensure that your sample is sufficient and
(blessed word) representative. If they knew that they could get
their inductions right every time. But we do know that some are too
small, and some are otherwise unsuitable, so we can rule some inducations
out as lazy -- as not trying hard enough to get it right. A fresh visitor
to France might leave Dieppe station convinced that all Frenchmen wear
a beret and blue blouse - not realizing that there is such a thing as
railway uniform.

The move from rule to instances is easier: all policemen carry
radios therefore this one does. Fair enough, provided 'this one' really
is a policeman, and that rule applies to all of them. Maybe CID men are
not all required to carry radios? Sometimes we must ask: Is this rule
meant for the case in hand? For example, we do not prosecute surgeons
for sticking knives into people, though no-one else can do it with
impunity. Why make them a special case above the law? Because knife-
sticking, as they practise it, is not an instance of the sort prohibited
by law. There is, we may say, an accidental similarity between what
surgeons do and what muggers and rapists do: so the argument from
these to those is called the Fallacy of Accident. We could call it
the move from a real rule to some non-instances. A famous law prohibited
betting 'in a public place' and led to many lucrative law-suits about
whether a phone booth, a railway carriage, a public-house, etc., were
'places within the meaning of the Act': i.e. were they instances to
which the rule applied, or non-instances?

An opposite error consists of affirming the rule but making
certain (perhaps silent) exceptions without good reason, usually in

favour of oneself. The motorist returns from a spin in the country
and complains of all those motor-bikes and trucks blocking the country
lanes and fouling up the country air. The headmaster, perhaps, silences
Assembly by shouting louder than the rest that shouting is not to be
allowed. We are quick to spot it when people's actions 'belie their
words', i.e. form an exception to the rule that they announce. When
the exception is made explicitly, in words, it is called Special
Pleading -- 'please leave little me out of this'. Such pleas, very
nicely wrapped up, form a large part of public debates about planning,
trade restrictions and import duties, and tax. But there are plenty
of instances in other fields. It really is very difficult to maintain
the conviction that other people also count for one. And after all,
why should 'they' put a motorway across _my_ front lawn?

EXAMPLES

1.	Suggest five closed classes, which you could hope to review in their entirety (e.g. days of this week); five which you couldn't (e.g. leaves on that tree this year); and five open classes (e.g. dogs).

2.	You are conducting a Public Opinion Poll to establish what people at your school think about

	(a) whether games should be compulsory, (b) whether the changing rooms are warm enough, (c) whether Russian should be available in the VIth, (d) whether cheaper but less nourishing dishes should be available at lunch, (e) whether monitors should have to wear school uniform. Say how many people you would question, and how you would choose them, in each case.

3.	Think of pairs of events, A, B, where B happened just after A and (i) you reckon A caused B, or (ii) you reckon it didn't. Find five of each, and give some reasons for the causal connections you suspect in (i), and for not suspecting them in (ii).

4.	Which of these inferences strike you as unsafe, and why:

	(a) That penny has come down heads six times running, there must be something wrong with it.

	(b) Bishops always wear clerical collars -- I've never seen one without.

	(c)	It has rained all week so it's sure to be wet on Sunday.

	(d)	The longer you serve at the front, the less your chance of being killed.

	(e)	I won't eat that for it always gives me tummyache.

5.   Comment on:

(a) Policemen can't pursue speeding motorists without
    speeding themselves.

(b) Yes, it is a non-smoker, but I asked all the others
    and it helps me relax.

(c) Now Johnny, what would it be like if we <u>all</u> stood on
    the table?

(d) This monkey of yours is a father -- so Darwin was right
    after all!

(e) Have you cooked that frozen pork you bought last week?
    But I <u>told</u> you it's unsafe to cook pork without first
    unfreezing it.

Chapter Forty Three : <u>Non-arguments</u>

In the chapters on the syllogism and on symbolic inference
various rules were laid down, to which a good argument should conform
(Ch.17). Any contravention of those rules, and any inference not
allowed by them, can be counted as a fallacy. Here we shall briefly
recount those that are committed frequently, and can be seen to have
something wrong with them. This may also help to show what makes the
good ones work.

A syllogism works by establishing a link between two terms,
by the aid of a third ('middle') term which comes in both the
premisses. This cannot be done if both the premises actually separate
their terms (are negative). Thus the information that no dogs are
cats and no cats are two-legged is no help in settling the number of
legs per dog. Knowing what dogs aren't, and what two-legged things
aren't, cannot show what dogs <u>are</u>. (A Venn diagram shows this well.)
So it is a fallacy to start out from two negative premises. Though
this can sometimes be cured by turning one of them inside out: given
that some monks are not musical and none of them are married we can
(after some cookery) infer that some unmusical folk are bachelors.

The conclusion to a valid argument can at most repeat the
information contained in its premises. This information may be
re-arranged in the process, but cannot yield items <u>extra</u> to those
the premises supply. From a pint pot, regrettably, only a pint of
liquid can be drunk. So the conclusion can't be about 'all policemen'
if the premises only mentioned 'some'. Terms 'distributed' in the

conclusion must have been distributed in the premises, otherwise the fallacy of Illicit Process will result.

We must also make sure that the two premises do link up. For this, the middle term has to be distributed exactly once: otherwise the premises can slip apart without engaging, like those remote-control cranes in amusement arcades which always pass over gold watches and just occasionally disturb a tiddlywink. All Hollywood actors speak English, as do all U.S. Presidents, yet the link between the two classes was established quite recently, and not by argument.

Finally, we may encounter fairy-trouble with a syllogistic argument. Some moods are valid only on the assumption that their terms do all have instances to be about. These moods should perhaps carry a logical health warning LEPRECHAUNS PROHIBITED; for if such a reasoning were accepted with regard to what turned out to be an empty class, then the terrible Existential Fallacy results. There are more empty classes about than you may have supposed, with this light-hearted talk of leprechauns. What about 'unselfish financier', or 'disinterested adviser', or 'honest politician' or even 'government committed to a stable currency'? Empty classes are well worth watching for, even if fairies are not.

One very common connection between statements is if ... then. Starting with some such connection, as premiss, we can work our way onwards, from the fact of the if-bit to the then-bit being a fact, or we can work back, from the then-bit not being so to the if-bit not being either.

Thus: (given)   If it rains then we get wet

    (forwards) it is raining   (backwards) we're not wet
           so we're getting wet   so it can't be raining

The forward argument is called Modus Ponens, or Affirming the Antecedent:
the backward version is called Modus Tollens, or Denying the Consequent.
Note that the forward argument is positive, and the backward negative.
Because of this slight complexity we may quite easily imagine we can
work back positively, or forward negatively. But a moment's quiet
thought will show that these moods are unreliable:

    (forwards) Its not raining   (backwards) we're wet so
           so we aren't wet   it must be raining

(These moods would be valid, if we started with 'If we get wet, its
raining'. But we were not given that. There is quite a difference
between 'if I sleep I breathe' and 'if I breathe I sleep'.)   The
bad forward argument is called Denying the Antecedent, and the bad
backward argument is called Affirming the Consequent. And both are
fallacies, totally ineffective 'reasonings' masquerading as real
powerful arguments, and sometimes deceiving even the elect.

    These are all called 'formal fallacies' because they are bad
as arguments, i.e. something in the arrangement ensures that they are
invalid and without force. This could be compared to a radio set which
is 'dead' because a wire has come adrift inside: with a break in the
circuit, the signal cannot pass, so you don't hear anything. It
doesn't work.

There is one other formal fallacy, in which the argument does work (is valid) but cannot achieve anything. If someone argues from A to B to C and back from there to A, his inference may be quite reliable, but it will be useless. There is no point in proving A by an argument which includes A among its premisses, for you can't make anything more certain by relying on it, any more than you can pull yourself up by your shoelaces. Circular Reasoning could also be compared to a radio fitted with a microphone; if both this and the speaker are switched on, a very nasty squeaking can result, the set picking up its own hum and amplifying it.

Arguing in a Circle is so obviously fallacious that there are few obvious examples of this fallacy, except for the old favourite about the Bible being true because it says so in 2 Timothy 3.xvi. But there are quite a few unobvious instances to be seen, if you watch out for them.

EXAMPLES

1.   Construct three arguments, each of which commits two of the fallacies studied in this chapter. (True conclusions preferred, as more plausible.)

2.   Comment on these statements, and suggest circumstances in which they should be regarded as (i) true (ii) false

(a) In his hand are all the corners of the earth (Psalm 95).

(b) No toothpaste is a better safeguard than Coldoor in fighting decay.

(c) 'I see nobody on the road'. 'I only wish I had such eyes' (Alice).

(d) The author is to receive 10% of royalties on the published
price for the first 5,000 copies sold, and 12½% thereafter
... all matters concerning format, jacket design and size of
edition remain the exclusive concern of the publisher'
(standard contract with publisher).

(c) 'I will wear no clothes to distinguish me from my
Christian brethren' (clergyman).

3. Say what, if anything, is wrong with these arguments, and suggest
slight amendments with a view to proving something:

(a) He said he'd marry me if I changed my hairstyle but I
haven't so he can't.

(b) The murderer was without his third left toenail, just like
Jones, so Jones must be the murderer.

(c) Some people of artistic temperament are financially
incompetent, as you can see from the fact that bankers
are all experts on finance, naturally, and none of them
are of an artistic bent.

4. Comment on these reasonings:

(a) Real things are better than merely imaginary ones, so the
best possible being would simply have to be real.

(b) In science, all proof rests on assumptions which cannot
be proved, though they are justified by our finding their
consequences satisfactory.

(c) The biggest number must be a multiple of seven, otherwise
you could make a bigger one which was, just by adding some
number between one and six.

Chapter Forty Four : <u>Dirty Tricks of Debate</u>

Debaters down the centuries have developed many twists and tricks
of camouflage, by which to win the argument even though the other fellow
has the better case: a sort of logical Gamesmanship ('the art of
winning games without being better at them'). In many cases it is
enough just to <u>persuade the audience</u> that you have won.

One device is to present only one side of the case -- our side.
Such one-sided advocacy is quite proper in court, where another lawyer
is being paid to do the best he can for the other side. Is it all right
in a newspaper editorial? Well, each reader is free to buy another
newspaper, and anyone is free to start one, if he feels a view is not
being fully, fairly put (AND if he has several million pounds to throw
away). Perhaps this situation does impose some obligation on leader-
writers to be fair - well, what they see as 'fair'. In the case of
the BBC, which has a semi-monopoly, we demand high standards of
even-handedness -- and can promise that no balancing act however
skilful will earn everyone's applause.

What about lobbies? A lobby is a sort of club of like-minded
citizens who have come together to press on the public and on ministries
a certain point of view. No Abortion, No Exams, No Caged Birds, No
Motorways. These citizens put money and effort into making their case,
which the public get quite free of charge. Are such public-spirited
souls to be told that they must also put the other side? Well, yes,
they can be <u>told</u>.

The Emperor Claudius had the motto 'audi alteram partem' --
'listen to the other side' (as well). There always _is_ another side,
and sometimes we, the audience, will have to seek it out or even work
it out or make it up.   If someone makes an impassioned speech in
favour of your doing X, ask yourself 'What are the reasons against
doing X, or for doing Y instead, which this orator is trying to
conceal and to combat?

Advertisements, which are always one-sided advocates, can
thus sometimes be made to disclose what they were hoping to conceal.
Those marketing the Friedegg Unstick Swedish Twenty-first Century
Frying-pan may claim that 'its sophisticated ultra-scientific Piflon
coating is guaranteed not to wear off for fifteen long months, longer
than any comparable brand'. Good. That tells us that non-stick
frypans have a detachable coating which comes off after some time --
perhaps in the middle of an unsophisticated twentieth-century fried
egg. Now this is just the sort of thing that frypan buyers need to
know, and frypan sellers would not dream of telling them.

Except in judges, one-sided advocacy is not criminal, not
even illogical. But we are illogical, or at least not very sensible,
if we consent to hear the pro. without the con., or are conned into
swallowing the con. alone without even looking for the pro.

When we have heard both sides, and the debate is fairly joined,
one party may try to undo their opponents' case by disproving something
slightly different. For example: some wish to restrict the occasions
when abortion is legal, while others favour widening 'the woman's right
to choose'. The first party may retort that we don't favour her right

to murder other people, not even relatives. But of course their
opponents do not regard the foetus as a 'person', at that stage.
So those opponents, at least, will not accept the argument, and the
audience might be misled if they took it as a refutation of their case.

This 'Straw Man' fallacy of 'proving the wrong point' is of
course open to the first speaker as well. Prosecuting counsel may
dilate at length on the mean and contemptible nature of embezzlement:
the creditors' families deprived of their summer holidays, the widows
in garrets, the children starving in the cold. But his job is not,
to persuade the jury that embezzlement should be punished, but to show
them that this defendant is guilty of embezzlement. There is a tale
of a judge who thanked counsel for his excellent reasoning, and hoped
he would one day find a case to which it did apply. That mild irony
can be ours, in reading many books, if we keep awake to 'what the
author was offering to prove'.

Proving the wrong point is effective in debate only before an
audience which chan't tell one from the other, or has gone to sleep.
Several other debating moves depend on the audience' ignorance of
logic and the rules of reasoning; or even on the unreasoning respect
for it. One such is to argue that 'you can't prove it isn't', which
may well be so, but does nothing to establish the contrary. No-one
can _prove_ that the earth is not filled with cream cheese, or that
Juluis Caesar did not compose all his commentaries in Welsh, or that
Joe Stalin was not a secret member of the John Birch Society, and
distantly related to the Royal Family. But the fact that you can't
prove he wasn't is no evidence that he really was.   This trick is

fairly called 'the appeal to ignorance'; for, come to think of it, what you don't know can't prove anything!

If you can't prove he was, would that help show he wasn't? That depends how provable the thing in question is. Those who don't want fluoride put in their water-supply try hard to find people who have been harmed by it; and if it does do any harm then that should become evident in time -- too late perhaps, as with the thalidomide tragedy -- but the longer the search for harm goes on without success the stronger will be our conviction that it will not come. There is a theory of science which says that scientific laws are never proved but that those which resist disproof more vigorously are the more acceptable.

Any statement needs its own positive evidence. If you have some reasons for believing X, then the repeated failure of attempts to find contrary evidence or arguments leaves us with (i) our original reasons for believing X, plus (ii) an inductive hunch that they will not be countered or undermined or explained away. How sensible it is to rely on that hunch depends on how likely we reckon it is that counter-evidence would show up if we looked for it. So the man with a theory to commend should really go round looking for evidence the other way (see Ch. 28).

One way to win a debate is to discredit your opponent, thus persuading the audience to disbelieve his evidence and disregard his reasonings (see Ch. 40). Another way is to suggest a special motive he may have in his side of the debate: just as shopkeepers who shout 'bargain' should not be heard, so we may think a politician 'is only saying that to get my vote', or that arguments for the existence of a Deity should not be attended to when advanced by clergymen. Now

certainly the fact that a clergyman says it and has an interest in its
being true is no reason for treating it as false; but it may be a reason
for treating it with due caution, and looking round for alternative views
and arguments. If however, the arguments he propounds are sound (valid,
with true premises) then if we reject them because their conclusion
fits in with his interests, the only loser is ourselves. It would be
rather foolish to deny that three and four make seven just because you
heard this advanced by a teacher of arithmetic, who presumably had a
vested interest in it being so. Idiocy of that sort is called 'the
genetic fallacy'.

In the heat of debate the retort is sometimes made 'you're
another!' This is dangerous. If Smith is accused of bank-robbery,
and Brown, another member of the gang, who has turned King's evidence,
is producing damaging details about Smith's movements, motives and
accomplices, Smith may well be tempted to cry out 'You were in it
too' -- and surely the jury should give less credit to a robber's
evidence? The trouble is that this counts as a confession too:
if Brown was also 'in it', what was the 'it' that Brown was 'in',
and what was Smith doing at the time?   People tempted to say 'Tu
quoque' (you too) should therefore think carefully first.   Third
parties can more safely make a remark to the same effect: 'it's
the pot calling the kettle black'. Of course Brown's evidence of
Smith's robbery may still be evidence: but we shall treat it with
more caution when we know that Brown was also in the game: just as
we may attend less to a lecture on the evils of smoking, from a
doctor, over a friendly cigarette.

EXAMPLES

1.   What can you properly infer from no-one being able to prove that

      (a) Brutus killed Caesar;

      (b) Smoking causes cancer;

      (c) the murder victim did not die of a heart attack;

      (d) the stars have no influence upon our lives;

      (e) jogging is good for you.

2.   Try to undermine these statements by suggesting reasons the speaker might have for making them:

      (a) the seats in here are all taken;

      (b) this car's a lovely runner;

      (c) Gladstone was a very great man;

      (d) taxes will not be raised this year;

      (e) everyone who goes in for this competition will receive a prize, by post.

3.   Study the story of the Man Cured at Dinner (Luke 14.1 - 6), and explain the type of reasoning involved.

4.   What is meant by the 'presumption of innocence', in court? Consider the objections (i) that it means taking sides before the case even starts, (ii) that then people can get away with whatever can't be proved.

5.   Explain what this author is trying to prove, and comment on his argument:
'We cannot argue from the reason of the thing, that death is the destruction of living agents, because we know not at all what death is in itself; but only some of its effects, such as the dissolution of flesh, skin and bones ... Nor can we find anything throughout the whole analogy of nature, to afford us even the slightest presumption, that animals ever lose their

living powers; much less if it were possible that they should
lose them by death; for we have no faculties wherewith to trace
any beyond or through it, so as to see what becomes of them.
This event removes them from our view. It destroys the sensible
proof, which we had before their death, of their being possessed
of living powers, but does not appear to afford the least reason
to believe that they are, then, or by that event, deprived of
them'. (Butler, Analogy I).

Chapter Forty Five : <u>Questions for the Unwary</u>

Besides bamboozling the jury or the audience, an advocate may also think it his duty to play tricks on witnesses, to get them to produce the evidence he wants. One trick is to put a question which assumes or indicates the answer to another question, not then being asked, e.g. 'What time did you pass the cemetery on your way home from the pub?' The witness may think it better not to admit passing the cemetery at all, and if asked directly might say he came home another way, so the lawyer wraps the question up a bit. The classic instance takes the form 'Have you stopped nagging your husband?' -- please answer Yes or No', where either reply involves an admission the witness does not wish to make. Of course the lawyer cannot insist on Yes or No, he can only ask: the witness, but not the lawyer, is on oath; so 'I never started' is a proper reply -- to an improper question.

It is not possible always to ask questions in which nothing is assumed. But it is possible not to ask questions which assume one of the points at issue: questions which do need asking should be asked directly, not wrapped up. There is no actual fallacy in a 'Complex Question'; but asking several questions rolled into one, in a serious matter, is either a muddle or a dirty trick.

Finally, a debater may try to trick his opponent into giving away the main point of the debate. Thus if Jones favours capital punishment and Robinson is an abolitionist, Robinson may rightly ask Jones if he agrees on certain points from which he, Robinson, can then

build his case. So far, so good: for if the parties do not agree
on anything, their debate can never start. Now suppose Robinson asks
Jones to agree that no man has the right to take another's life. If
Jones consents, it will clearly be 'checkmate in one', for it follows
at once that capital punishment cannot be rightly carried out (except
by lady executioners?). Jones would agree to such a request only if
unable to foresee that single and simple killing move. So we say it
is indecent for Robinson to 'beg the question' in that way; it is a
low trick to play on Jones, and an insult to the audience, who came to
hear fair debate.

There is a puzzle here. Robinson has to 'beg' something, or
he cannot get started on his argument. Its no good his begging
premisses from which his conclusion is not to be derived. But if
it does follow from the points he asked Jones to concede, we call
it 'begging the question' and disallow it as a dirty trick! The
answer seems to be that it is alright to ask for several premises
and then try to prove your point from all of them, but all wrong to
ask for one in which it is concealed, and then decorate the derivation
with irrelevancies to distract the audience. So 'begging the question'
is alright if you beg it bit by bit!

    *   *   *   *   *   *   *

Two further and quite proper debating moves may be mentioned
here. If Smith objects to private education as offering to some
people benefits that the rest cannot afford, Brown may reply that
this argument would 'prove too much'; for the same test would also
prohibit yachting, whisky and holidays abroad, and even hi-fi and
fashion clothes. Brown does not mean, that these things also ought

to go, but that Smith's argument must be at fault, as it would rule them out as well (see Modus Tollens, Ch. 4). Sometimes this line of refutation is applied to _further_ consequences: when Robinson declares that no man has the right to take another's life, Jones may suggest 'taking that to its logical conclusion', viz., that we disband the Armed Forces and rely on the goodwill of our enemies. Not that Jones agrees with Robinson: just the opposite. Jones thinks we must keep the army, for defence, and that everyone who agrees to this must reject Robinson's original statement, as leading to something unacceptable. Of course Jones must choose his audience; his vision of disbanding the Forces of the Crown will bring no tears to an audience of pacifists.

Sometimes we argue that Smith's views conflict with the consequences of other things he is known to hold: i.e. that he is inconsistent. Thus the hunting fraternity might be reminded that they usually _favour_ landowners deciding what is to happen on their tenants' land, and object only when public bodies start banning foxhunting on publicly held land. Such an argument is 'ad hominem', i.e. personal, based on views held by Brown and without force against others, including the man who puts the argument to Brown.

EXAMPLES

1.   Construct Complex Questions designed to extort admissions that Smith

(a) has done no piano practice this week,
(b) holds no M O T certificate for his elderly vehicle,
(c) was inside the Dog and Duck last night.

2.   Suggest ways to 'beg' the following disputed points:

(a) the evolution of species
(b) undesirability of adding fluoride to water-supply
(c) creation of the world

3.   Propose arguments which 'prove too much', against

(a) wearing nylon vests
(b) drinking instant coffee
(c) going to Art College.

4.   Devise _ad hominem_ arguments against:

(a) general proposing an armistice,
(b) brewer advocating heavier penalties for drunken driving,
(c) egalitarian demanding a hearing.

5.   Construct syllogisms in these moods

(a) Barbara, (b) Celarent, (c) Darii,

and consider whether your syllogisms may fairly be said to 'beg the question'.

Chapter Forty Six : Logical Fault-Finder

Table giving: name of fallacy, example(s), description, what's-wrong-with-it.

REASONS WHICH ARE NO REASONS, i.e. non-supporting premisses,

appeals-to-X presented as arguments against Smith's saying S:

BIG STICK	'You'ld better agree, or else ...' (Galileo)
Unpleasant results of Smith asserting S	irrelevant to truth of S (maybe relevant to wisdom of saying it)
PITY	'Wife and 6 children to support'
Unpleasant results for Brown of Smith asserting S	irrelevant to truth of S (maybe relevant to consequences, e.g. punishment)
AUTHORITY	'Prof. Snorkel says -- and I need hardly draw attention to his European reputation -'
Invites submission to opinion of alleged expert	Allegation unsupported. If true, would provide reason for attending to what he says
ABUSE (attack on arguer)	'Why listen to a bankrupt adulterous goalbird?'
Alleges qualities in Smith which we dislike	Smith's qualities are irrelevant to truth of S (but may be relevant to reliability of Smith as witness)
STRANGE BEDFELLOWS	'That's what Hitler thought'
Point to qualities we dislike in someone sharing Smith's view	Personal qualities of other holders of opinion S are, so to speak, even more irrelevant
PREJUDICE	'To support this view is disloyal, indecent and cowardly, and will bring us all into disrepute'.
Associate S with things we already dislike without reason	Association not shown relevant to truth of S. Arguer not concerned with soundness of dislikes, if only they be vigorous.

PREJUDICE seems to include ABUSE and STRANGE BEDFELLOWS as special cases. STRANGE BEDFELLOWS is the converse of AUTHORITY.

FIDDLE AND MUDDLE

AMBIGUITY
Term has to be taken two
different ways, to make
both premisses true.

'Only man talks. So women must be silent, then'.
You can have two true premisses,
OR a valid argument. Not both.

DIVISION
Term used collectively
in premiss but distri-
butively in conclusion.

'The electors voted this government in so
they must favour all its policies'
Depends how we decide what is 'true
of group as whole'. Majority?

COMPOSITION
Collective statement
not justified by
particular given facts.

'Every individual wants to be happy, so
they must all want everyone to be' (Mill)
Depends what counts as being 'true
of group': common aim, direction,
organization?

LEAPING IN THE DARK

POST HOC ERGO PROPTER HOC
= FALSE CAUSE
Assumes what happens
next must be the result.

'I put the washing out. That made it rain'.
What is the result must happen next,
but so may several other things. So
one 'next' is poor evidence.

HASTY GENERALIZATION
Seeing several AB's
infers all A's are B.

'All Russians wear fur hats'
Coincidence? Or maybe some
responsible for those AB's (cold
day). Not looked for non-B A's, etc.

ACCIDENT

Applies to A what is true
of B, just because this
happens to be B.

'The judge has a right to his political
opinions, like everybody else'.
May be true qua B, but not if
excluded by nature of A (no
politics in court)

SPECIAL PLEADING

Making excuse for one's
own case, finding
reasons for being an
exception

'In a time of general unemployment the
country needs all its' teachers' skills'
A skill all may need! Works if excuse
is good and applies only to oneself
and others cant'think of any near as
good'

NON-ARGUMENTS

TWO NEGATIVES	'No cats are dogs or are two-legged, so all dogs have four'
Distinguishes one class from two others without relating them	No connection shown
ILLICIT PROCESS statement about entire class inferred from information on part of it	'Lawyers are all cautious and wordy, which shows that cautious people talk too much' Goes beyond the evidence
UNDISTRIBUTED MIDDLE middle term applies partially in both premises	'Footballers are sportsmen just like cricketers so some footballers play cricket too' maybe subject linked to one part of middle class, predicate to another
EXISTENTIAL FALLACY inference which is reliable only if the subject-term has instances	'Some investments are inflation-proof, for all safe investments keep their value, and anything which does that is inflation-proof' if premise made true by empty subject-term, can't infer conclusion which made false thereby

(which arguments commit this fallacy depends on conventions adopted, see Chs. 10, 19).

DENYING ANTECEDENT given an if - then, says NO to if-bit and infers No to then-bit	'We can't be wet -- it's not raining' inference works only with an only-if
AFFIRMING CONSEQUENT given an if - then, says YES to then-bit, infers YES to if-bit	'It must be raining -- look, we're wet' back to front, needs only-if
CIRCULAR ARGUMENT valid but ineffective argument whose conclusion is also found among its premises	'George says he's telling the truth so we'll have to believe him' relies on A, to make A reliable

DIRTY TRICKS OF DEBATE

ONE-SIDED ADVOCACY

   Selective presentation of
   arguments, one way

'This is the best car on the market --
ask any of our salesmen here'
    gives misleading impression of
    overwhelming case

PROVING WRONG POINT = STRAW MAN

   Apparent refutation, but
   point established does not
   contradict point opposed

'How can you condemn militarism while
relying on the police?'
    appears damaging though actually
    irrelevant

APPEAL TO IGNORANCE

   Support case by claiming the
   contrary is unprovable

'No single case of fatal bronchitis has
been shown due to nicotine poisoning'
    What's unprovable may still be true

GENETIC FALLACY

   Suggest personal reasons
   for asserting X, to discredit the assertion

'The bank manager says we're overdrawn
do you think that's because he's wanting
to charge interest?'
    What it would suit him to say may
    still be true

YOU'RE ANOTHER

   Jones suggests Smith has
   no right to criticize, as
   he was in it too

'Why shouldn't I use bad arguments?
You often do'
    Offence Jones thus admits is not
    reduced by (bad) company.
    (Expensive way to shut up Smith)

QUESTIONS FOR THE UNWARY

MANY QUESTIONS

   Two questions wrapped as
   one, using complexity to
   extort unintended admission

'Whom did you meet when you went out
with her?'
    Not fair: disputed questions must
    be answered one by one

BEGGING THE QUESTION
   Invite opponent to concede
   something from which the
   point in dispute follows
   without further argument

'You will surely agree that natural
foods are best. So only organic
fertilizers should be used'
    Insulting; concessions are worth
    accepting only if fully understood.

(Many instances of this also involve Ambiguity-to sugar the pill)

---

1.   Did the promises and prophecies made by the witches to Macbeth
      ruin him by their ambiguity? (notice V.8 'accursed be that
      tongue', etc.)

2.   Collect three ambiguous oracles and describe briefly the
      consequences for their recipients (see Herodotus, Histories I,
      Penguin).

3.   Correct the following, and say what sort of ambiguity is involved:
      (a) You are all Welcome to The Good Old Days (compère)
      (b) The wicked flea, whom no man pursueth but the righteous (Psalm)
      (c) My God, I love thee not, because I hope for heaven thereby (Hymn

4.   Which of these views should be rejected on the ground that Hitler
      held it too?
      (a) Wagner is the best composer,
      (b) Mechanized attack deep into enemy territory is a good
      strategy,
      (c) 2 + 3 = 5,
      (d) the Aryans are a master race.

5.   'You must never tell a lie, not even to a murderer waving a
      carving knife'. Does that count?

6.   'Although Planck's constant has dominated the computations of
      atomic physics for half a century, its magnitude cannot be
      explained ... Sir Arthur Eddington once observed that any true
      law of nature is likely to seem irrational to rational man;
      hence Planck's quantum principle, he thought, is one of the
      few real natural laws science has revealed' (Barnett, The
      Universe and Dr. Einstein, 1952). What premiss would Sir
      Arthur need, to make this conclusion rational?

7.   'Do you know the accused? No. But you know Mr. Smith, the
      butcher? Yes. And Mr. Smith the butcher is accused before
      this court?'   Can the witness get out of this?

8.   'Supernal meditation re-civilizes city life, for in cities
      where one per cent practise supernal meditation, the crime
      rate goes down not up'. Is this argument sufficient as it
      stands? What further steps could be taken to check on the
      supposed connection?

9. Is there any evidence that lightning causes thunder?

10. Suggest prior questions to settle first, to avoid these traps:
    (a) Why was Esau wrong to sell his birthright?
    (b) What punishment is appropriate for such spivs and twisters as tax avoiders?
    (c) Why is it that adding a live fish to a full goldfishbowl does not make it overflow, but adding a dead fish does? (James II, to Royal Society).

Chapter Forty Seven : The Field of Reasoning

Logic is the critical study and assessment of arguments. Arguments come in many different varieties. We have studied several logical systems devised to deal with them. We have not studied all the types of logic that there are -- much less, those that are yet to be invented, to cater for still-unevaluated types of arguments. Though old and well-known, this subject is still an open, growing one.

Deduction is mainly used to make sure of the implications of what we have already said. It will not discover anything new, i.e. extra to the premisses; but may well reveal an aspect of their content that is news to us. That sounds odd, at first; surely we must know what we ourselves have said, so how can deduction teach us anything more unless it _says_ something more, something additional to the premisses? Direct answers to this question rarely satisfy, but an example may: - take a first book of geometry, and read the axioms several times, until you are sure you have understood fully all they have to say. Now look at a theorem part-way through the book: e.g. that every triangle has a mid-point, or that its corners when put together make two right angles. Surely these are _extra_ points? But no, the proofs show that they are all there in the axioms. So it takes quite a geometer, a Euclid or Pythagoras, just to realize what he was saying, in those axioms. And we also may need the help of deductions, to work out just what we have said.

The system of deductive logic presented here has been developed much further, in mathematical logic; in particular, the attempt is made to construct a fully satisfactory proof-structure for arithmetic. These logical systems have also found application in building computers, and in working out foolproof strategies for winning games. Recently much work has been done in 'modal' logic, to bring operators like <u>can</u> and <u>must</u> into the system of formal reasoning.

Induction governs the business of finding a rule for a given set of items to exemplify; or (to look at it the other way) of finding further features which a given group may share -- questions like Can all mammals swim? Coming up with some rule or other is not difficult; the problem is to say <u>which</u> rule is best supported by given or discoverable instances. Such reasonings never achieve proof, but they can increase probability, or at least indicate which hypotheses deserve a check, and where to look for further evidence. Further study of such arguments would lead us into statistical theories of probability, a still unconquered realm. Study of the knotty points and problematical ideas involved occupies much of the philosophy of science and of 'epistemology' (theory of knowledge).

How far do these strict rules for reasoning apply in other subjects or in real life? Mathematics is mostly deductive in character; and if you want to know what really follows from X, even at the fish-mongers, then you are asking a deductive question and only a deductive answer can give you what you want. In the matter of implication -- what <u>guarantees</u> the truth of what -- there is no room for 'everyday' half-measures, no scope for 'flexibility'. And if you are engaged in trying to spot the cause of something important and obscure -- Why are some marriages unhappy?, What causes lemmings to migrate? -- then

you will find matters too puzzling and life too short to waste any of
it in sloppy reasoning. You expect your dentist to have a sharp drill
and strong tweezers, made in top-grade steel; in scientific enquiry
also, only the sharpest tools are good enough.

Can we also apply logical principles to everyday affairs, or to
history, or poetry? Many will say that nit-picking and logic-chopping
is here out of place. It is indeed true that the best thing to do,
in some crisis, can rarely be deduced from agreed laws of ethics or
of etiquette; that history does not quite 'repeat itself' nor offer
much hope of our discovering its 'laws' by studying the instances;
that it would be wrong to write off 'my heart's an arbutus' or 'Beauty
is Truth, Truth Beauty' as simple fallacies. It is unwise to be
doctrinaire, or Procrustean. Yet it may be that knowing what can and
cannot be deduced, or induced, and acquiring the precision which is
sensitive to ambiguity, does enable one to manage rather better life's
problems and history's puzzles and that bewitching nonsense which is
poetry. Maybe. Anyway, you've got the bug by now, if you're going
to get it at all. You'll have to see.

INDEX AND GLOSSARY

with thumbnail 'reminders',
for a stricter account, see
the chapters referred to

CONDITIONAL PROOF 7	of if-then conclusion, by combining the if with the premises to show the then
CONJUNCTION 2	joining by AND ($\cdot$); argument from two things being true separately to their being true together
CONNOTATION 33	what a term means
CONSEQUENT 1	then-bit of if-then statement
CONSTRUCTIVE DILEMMA 4	modus ponens argument applied to one or other of two given 'if's.
CONTINGENT 4	proposition which is not a tautology and not a contradiction
CONTRADICTION 11,22;4	see-saw relation of propositions, one must be true and the other false; complex proposition which always turns out false
CONTRARY 22	two propositions which cannot both be true
CONVENTION 10,19	agreement about how to do things, e.g. hold one's fork
CONVERT 20	derive back-to-front version of same statement
COUNTER-EXAMPLE 29	Exception, which disproves a suggested rule
DE MORGAN'S THEOREM 5	(replacement rule) a conjunction denied is two denials, disjoined
DEDUCTION 1,23	argument to show C must be true if A and B are so
DEFINITE DESCRIPTION 33	phrase of type 'the so-and-so' yielding a singular term
DEFINITION 36	attempt to say more clearly just what a word should mean
DENYING ANTECEDENT 1,43	If A then B, but not A, so not B (invalid)
DESTRUCTIVE DILEMMA 4	modus tollens argument applied to one or other of two given 'if's

DICHOTOMY
8,34
dividing items into A and non-A

DIFFERENCE, METHOD
OF
27
selecting as cause that one factor which 'makes
all the difference'

DILEMMA
4
Either-or argument, presenting unpalatable
consequences of two given alternatives

DISANALOGY
27
aspect in which two rather similar things differ

DISJUNCTION
joining by OR (v)

DISJUNCTIVE
SYLLOGISM
4
argues by excluding one alternative

DISTRIBUTED
17
term referring to all its subject class

DISTRIBUTION
5
(replacement rule) spells out AND combined
with OR

DISTRIBUTIVELY
32
applying to the items taken one by one

DIVISION
8
process of sorting things (on paper) into groups

DIVISION
32,41
Fallacy of transferring quality of collective
to its members, e.g. calling eyes symmetrical

DOUBLE NEGATION
5
(replacement rule) two NOTs cancel out

EMPTY CLASS
10,19
set aside for a certain sort of so-and-so,
but there aren't any, e.g. mermaid

EQUIVALENT
2,20
two propositions which never take different
truth-values ($\equiv$)

EVALUATE
1,23
Check an argument to see if it is valid or sound

EXCLUSIVE DIVISION
34
with no overlaps, not reckoning anything twice

EXHAUSTIVE DIVISION
8,34
which leaves nothing out

EXISTENTIAL FALLACY
10,19,43
move from premiss whose subject-class might be
empty to conclusion whose isn't

EXISTENTIAL GENERALISATION 24	rule saying if someone is a so-and-so then 'some people' are
EXISTENTIAL IMPORT 10,19,25	whether given statement, e.g. 'fairies dance' actually says that there are some
EXISTENTIAL INSTANTIATION 24	rule that there must be <u>somebody</u> whom what is true of 'some people' is <u>true of</u>
EXISTENTIAL QUANTIFIER 24	says the statement does have something to be about
EXPORTATION 5	rule equating two IFs in tandem with two side by side
FALLACY 17,39	particular named variety of bad argument
FALSE CAUSE 42	thinking X caused Y, when Z really did, e.g. because Y happened near and after X
FIGURE 18	sub-group of syllogisms, all having their middle terms arranged the same way
FORM OF ARGUMENT 1,23	pattern or structure, what two similar arguments have in common
GENERAL TERM 32	applying to any member of a given class, e.g. man, dog
GENERALIZE 26	suggest a general rule of which certain given items would be instances
GENUS 35	group of similar and, we think, related animal species
HASTY GENERALIZATION 42	suggesting rule before considering enough instances
HIERARCHY 35	exhaustive and exclusive set-up in which everyone comes under somebody, e.g. army
HYPOTHETICAL SYLLOGISM 4	argument from two if's to another one
IFF	if and only if
ILLICIT PROCESS 17,43	syllogism invalid because conclusion refers to a wider class

IMMEDIATE INFERENCE 11,23	with only one premiss, needing no 'working' in between
IMPLICATION 2,22	tag-along relation; if A is true then B has to be so too
INDEPENDENT 22	(statements) not affecting each other, standing (or falling) quite separately
INDIRECT PROOF 20	show not-A to be false, thus proving A
INDUCTION 1,23,26	non-compulsive diagnosis of rule governing given instances
INDUCTION, PROBLEM OF 27	worry whether sun has any reason to rise tomorrow, etc
INFERENCE	Argument
INFORMAL FALLACY 1,40	improper or spoof argument, consideration lacking logical relevance
INSTANCE 26	item coming under general rule, actual example
JUSTIFY 14	show some conclusion true, by a separate argument
LOGIC	study of reliability in arguments
LOGICAL CONSTANT	logical operator
LOGICAL EQUIVALENCE 5	two statements having to have the same truth-values
LOGICAL OPERATOR 2	connecting word used to build complex proposition, e.g. AND, OR
LOGICAL RELATION 22	way in which one proposition may stand to another and influence its truth or falsity
MAIN OPERATOR 2	one taken first, in taking a complex proposition
MAJOR PREMISS	Premiss in syllogism, supplying predicate to conclusion
MATERIALLY EQUIVALENT 5	having the same truth-value as

MATERIAL EQUIVALENCE   allow trading an equivalence for any IFF or
RULES   an alternative

MATERIAL   rule replacing if-then by alternative
IMPLICATION
5

MEDIATE INFERENCE   needing some reasoning to extract that conclusion
23   from those premises

MIDDLE TERM   which comes in both premises of a syllogism
12   are not in its conclusion

MILL'S METHODS   checklist for describing and improving proposed
28   inductive generalizations

MINOR PREMISS   in syllogism, premiss supplying subject to
18   conclusion

MODUS PONENS   argument going on from an 'if'; b if a, a,so b
4

MODUS TOLLENS   argument going back from a 'then'; b if a,
4   not-b, so not-a

MOOD   classification of syllogism by whether its
18   propositions are A,E,I or O

NECESSARY CONDITION   'it won't happen unless ...'
27

NEGATION   joining by NOT- ($\sim$)

NEGATIVE PREMISSES   syllogism held invalid because two exclusions
17   get nowhere

NEGATIVE   saying X <u>isn't</u> so-and-so
PROPOSITION
11,18

PARITY OF   principle that similar arguments must be of
REASONING   equal strength
23

PARTICULAR   statement about only some items in its
9,22,33   subject class

PLACE-MINDER   symbol standing for one of several things
24   (or symbols)

PREDICATE   what a proposition   <u>says</u> about its subject
17

RESIDUES, METHOD OF 27	seeking cause for what the other known factors fail to explain
RULES OF SYLLOGISM 17	set of simple tests which picks out just the valid ones
SHORTER TRUTH-TABLE 6	indirect validity test, seeking circumstances in which premises could be true but conclusion false
SIMPLE PROPOSITION 2	non-complex
SIMPLIFICATION 4	argument from two things being true to just one of them
SINGULAR TERM 32	referring to just one thing, e.g. my house, the government
SPECIAL PLEADING 42	arguing that an exception should be made, in your own case
SPECIES 35	distinct set of animals able to breed together, so producing more
STANDARD FORM 2,12	conventional way of stating an argument, to make checking easier
STATEMENT 1	remark which says something, unlike question or command. Same statement may be made in different ways - Man bit dog, dog bitten by man
STIPULATION 38	statement by author of what he will use a certain word to mean
STRAW MAN 44	bogus refutation of A by really disproving something slightly different
SUB-CONTRARY 22	two propositions which cannot both be true
SUBDIVISION 34	dividing up a class into several smaller ones which do not overlap
SUBJECT 17	what a proposition is about
SUBSTANCE 22	Thing or Stuff that could be there, all on its own
SUFFICIENT CONDITION 27	'it definitely will happen if...'

SYLLOGISM 12	inference from two premisses linked by a middle term
SYMBOL 2	written sign with agreed meaning, e.g. → = 'implies' (unlike letters, which indicate sounds)
TAUTOLOGY 3,5	complex proposition which always turns out true; rule allowing repetition, as conjunction or alternative
TERM 12,30	part of proposition, i.e. subject or predicate; clearly-defined word or phrase
THEOREM 13	item in a system, proved from first principles
TRANSPOSITION 5	(replacement rule) applying Modus Tollens
TRUISM 38	obvious truth which turns out trivial, e.g. I don't like my tea too hot
TRUTH-FUNCTION 3	complex proposition whose truth depends only on that of its constituents
TRUTH-POSSIBILITIES 3	possible combinations of truth-values
TRUTH TABLE 3	to show values of a complex proposition, depending on truth-values taken by its component parts
TRUTH-VALUE 3	According to circumstance a proposition may take the values True, False
UNDISTRIBUTED MIDDLE 17,43	Syllogism invalid because premisses could refer to quite distinct classes
UNIVERSAL GENERALISATION 24	rule that what is true of any so-and-so is true of all of them
UNIVERSAL INSTANTIATION 24	rule saying what is true of all so-and-so's is true of each such individual
UNIVERSAL QUANTIFIER 24	says the statement is about all the subject- class
UNIVERSAL PROPOSITION 9,33	about all the members of its subject-class

VALID 1	argument in which the conclusion <u>has to be</u> true if the premisses are so
VENN DIAGRAM 15	Three overlapping circles marked to represent an argument
WELL-FORMED FORMULA, WFF 2	string of symbols which obey the rules

GAMES

Rollasyllogism

Dice can be used to help make up syllogisms to practice on.

In each premiss, there are just six distinct types of proposition that could occur; in the conclusion, only four:

Premiss I: 1. PiM   2. PoM   3. MoP   4. PeM   5. PaM   6. MaP
Premiss II: 1. SiM   2. SoM   3. MoS   4. SeM   5. SaM   6. MaS
Conclusion: 1. SiP   2. SoP   4. SeP   5. SaP

Dice can be made by marking these symbols on wood or cardboard cubes.

Alternatively, use ordinary dice, and interpret the numbers as shown above.

First player declares terms for S and P, second player for M.

Game I   Throw dice in turn to settle form of premisses I and II;
          first to declare a conclusion following validly from
          them, wins.

Game II   Throw dice in turn to settle form of Premiss I and Conclusion
          (take another throw if 3 or 6 comes up). First to declare
          second premiss which would complete a valid argument, wins.

Game III Determine premisses as in I; continue throwing dice,
          first to throw a conclusion which does follow, wins.

Game IV   First player throws three times, second player wins if he
          can make up a valid argument from these throws, being free
          to decide which throw is 'conclusion' and which are premisses.
          If he can't, first wins.

Players may care to re-state the Rules of the Syllogism in this number-
code, e.g. one premiss must be more than 3, sum of both must be odd.
The conclusion is determined by the difference between the premisses.
The mnemonic jingles can also be put into numerical form, instructively.

LOGICON

The play-as-you-learn method of mastering formal logic

GAME ONE WFF (Well formed formula)

Each pack consists of fifty three cards; four each of p, q, r, s, ·, v, ⊃ , ∼ , ≡ ; sixteen (, one M.

Dealer   Each player draws a card from the pack. The highest numbered card denotes the dealer.

The Deal   Eight cards are dealt to each player. The remainder are placed in a pile face down on the table and the top card exposed and placed alongside. For three or more players it is necessary to use two packs.

The Play   The player on the left of the dealer commences. Then the next player to the left and so on. Each player can at each turn choose one and only one of the three alternatives:

(a)   Form one well formed formula (WFF) and place it face up on the table.

(b)   Discard one of his cards, if he so wishes, and take either the exposed card or the blind one from the pile. If he wishes he may retain all his cards and add to his hand by picking up in either of these two ways. When he chooses to discard then he must discard before picking up. The discarded card is placed on the top of, or in place of, the exposed card and becomes the exposed card on the table.

(c)   When a WFF is exposed on the table a player can insert a card, or cards, in any such WFF. In doing this the order of the letters or symbols must not be disturbed or the WFF reversed. The other letters or symbols must be added at either end, or inserted. Only one WFF can be attacked in the same turn.

e.g.   p ⊃ q can become p   ⊃   (q v r)

p ⊃ q can become (p ⊃ q)   v r

p ⊃ q can become   r ·   (p ⊃ q)

No player is allowed to pass his turn without taking one of the three alternatives a, b or c. He is only allowed to take one at each turn.

End Game   The object of the game is to get rid of your cards as quickly as possible. The first player to do this ends the round and the other players count their scores from the numbers on the cards left in their hands. As the rounds proceed players reach the total of

100 and in so doing drop out of the game, until eventually only the winner is left.

All formulae placed on the table have to be formed according to the accepted rules of formation laid down in the propositional logic.

Challenges   A WFF proposed by one player may be challenged by another. If it turns out to be well formed the challenger suffers a penalty of ten points and forfeits his next turn. If the challenge is upheld then the challenger has ten points deducted from his score and the WFF is withdrawn, the proposer having to play his turn again.

Master Card   The card marked M may be used in place of any other card in the pack. The player using it must declare its role in that particular hand.

If the pack runs out the cards on the table in the discarded pile may be reshuffled and put face down on the table. The top card is exposed and laid alongside etc.

SOLO WFF

For play by one person. Deal twelve cards. Play according to the rules of WFF. (The player of course makes all the moves in Solo).

End Game. The object of the game is to empty one's hand in the least possible number of turns.

One may compete with oneself - aiming always to lower one's score of turns required. (Theoretically it is possible to go out in one turn though the odds against this occurring are considerable.)

GAME TWO   TRUE AND FALSE (T & F)

This game is played as wff with one difference.

The dealer calls for either true, false, or (either true or false) wff's at the beginning of each hand. Always presume in this game that p and q are TRUE and that r and s are FALSE. If, for example, the dealer calls for true wff's then p·q would be acceptable whereas ~(p·q) would be unacceptable.

SOLO TRUE AND FALSE

This is playable by means of the arrangements made in Solo WFF.

GAME THREE MUST AND CAN'T

This game is played as game two with one difference. The dealer calls
either for tautologies, contradictions or (either tautologies or
contradictions) ...

There is no need to assume any particular truth values of p,q,r and s
in this game for tautologies are true for all possible values of their
constituents and contradictions are likewise false.

Thus p v ∼ p would be acceptable as a tautology as would the much more
complex (p·q·r) v ∼ (p·q·r).

SOLO MUST AND CAN'T

This is playable by means of the arrangements made in Solo WFF.

GAME FOUR LOGIC DOMINOES

This game may be played in groups or as a solo game by making the amendments
made in Solo WFF. [2 packs of card should be used].

16 cards (24 in Solo) are dealt to each player.

The first player has alternatives a and b of Wff open to him.

Once a Wff is placed on the table players are only allowed to place on
the table Wffs which follow from (by one or more rule inference) or are
equivalent to it or to the formula which is the immediate neighbour of
the one being placed.

The game may proceed in a horizontal or vertical direction as shown in
the diagram. (Numbers in the diagram refer to WFF's).

```
                2

      6     1     3     4   etc.

                5
```

End Game   Group games end when no more moves can be made. Penalties
on cards in hand are totalled. The person with the lowest penalty over
an agreed number of hands is declared the winner.

Solo games end when no more moves can be made. The number of cards
placed on the table are counted. This number becomes the target to
beat in succeeding hands.